Hijacking and Hostages

Hijacking and Hostages

Government Responses to Terrorism

J. PAUL DE B. TAILLON

Foreword by General Ulrich K. Wegener

Praeger Studies in Diplomacy and Strategic Thought
B.J.C. McKercher, Series Editor

Westport, Connecticut
London

Library of Congress Cataloging-in-Publication Data

Taillon, J. Paul de B., 1953–
    Hijacking and hostages: government responses to terrorism / J. Paul de B. Taillon :
foreword by Ulrich K. Wegener.
        p. cm.—(Praeger studies in diplomacy and strategic thought, ISSN 1076–1543)
    Includes bibliographical references and index.
    ISBN 0–275–97468–5 (alk. paper)
    1. Terrorism. 2. Terrorism—History—20th century. I. Title. II. Series.
HV6431.T377   2002
303.6′25—dc21   2002025206

British Library Cataloguing in Publication Data is available.

Library of Congress Catalog Card Number: 2002025206
ISBN: 0–275–97468–5
ISSN: 1076–1543

First published in 2002

Praeger Publishers, 88 Post Road West, Westport, CT 06881
An imprint of Greenwood Publishing Group, Inc.
www.praeger.com

Printed in the United States of America

(∞)™

The paper used in this book complies with the
Permanent Paper Standard issued by the National
Information Standards Organization (Z39.48–1984).

10 9 8 7 6 5 4 3 2 1

Contents

Foreword

It is a real honor for me to write the foreword for this excellent book. During the last twenty years, a number of books about counterterrorism units and also about the Operations "Thunderbolt" (Entebbe) and "Magic Fire" (Mogadishu) were written and published. Most of them were just good stories.

By presenting this new book, my friend, Professor Dr. J. Paul de B. Taillon, has provided an insightful and outstanding report of the two operations, but with the necessary historical and military background. With well-researched detail, he tells the fascinating story of the fight against terrorism in the last thirty years and the evolution of some of the world's best special operations forces. He describes the events of the Operations "Thunderbolt" and "Magic Fire" as if he was an insider and member of the commando forces.

I agree with his outlook on terrorism in the future: that terrorism has matured from random violence of the primitive type to that of a highly evolved military intelligence operation that poses a serious threat to peace and stability in the world and that terrorism, in another form than that of the 1970s, will remain a severe threat, especially to the Western countries. There is no doubt that in the wake of the dramatic attacks in New York City and Washington, there is a need for an international counterterrorist strategy and for tactical concepts and, of course, for special operations units.

Dr. Taillon has also emphasized the cooperation of intelligence agencies and special operation units, which in my view is essential for the creation and evolution of a successful counterterrorist strategy and their operations.

Finally, I'd like to thank Professor Dr. Taillon on behalf of GSG9 Mogadishu fighters for this brilliant book. I wish him the success he deserves.

Ulrich K. Wegener
General (Ret.)

Acknowledgments

I would like to thank all of those who assisted me in preparing the research for this material. This includes many people at the University of London, the Royal Military College, the Royal Canadian Military Institute, and the members of the special operations and intelligence community. In particular, I would like to thank both Dr. H. P. Klepak and Dr. James Finan for their support and advice.

A special thank you goes to General Ulrich K. Wegener for his vital insights and his generous contribution to this work.

I would also like to thank my editors, Heather Staines and Valerie Geary, whose patience, knowledge and keen eye have been invaluable.

Introduction

Throughout our evolution and history, man has employed the fear of pain of death to ward off foes. In fact, fear or terror has been an inextricable element of human existence. Terror has been employed by individuals and groups, and in some cases by entire social structures, to impose an individual or collective will upon those who were helpless, powerless or irresolute. The reigns of Communism, Nazism, and, more recently, religious extremists such as the Taliban in Afghanistan are notable examples of the utilization of fear.

In a sense, the development of terrorism paralleled social change. Developments in social and political cohesion engendered the seeming requirement to impose fear not just on one's fellows, but also on other groups. Terrorism has thus evolved as mankind has progressed.

Although contemporary observers tend to see the post-1967 period as an "age of terrorism," close scrutiny reveals that this is a parochial view of the phenomenon, for historical study is filled with examples of terrorist acts. As society has changed, terror has been used in different ways and at different levels. The development of nationalism, the modern state system, and particularly the vulnerable economic and social structures common to the late twentieth century, have permitted the organized imposition of terror in ways which differ radically from those available to early man in his relations with his neighbors and his predatory animal opponents.

The nature and complexity of this issue are reflected in the many definitions for terror and terrorism; moreover terrorism is difficult to define in a nominalist way. Therefore, a totally acceptable, all-encompassing definition evades us still. Terrorism is always intended, often well-planned, and coldly executed. It has been said that "modern terrorism is a form of contemporary warfare."[1] Despite this, it is also a very old form of psychological warfare. One expert, Paul Wilkinson, suggests:

> Terror, to state a truism, is a subjective experience: we all have different "thresholds" of extreme fear and tend to be more easily terrified by certain experiences, images and threats than by others. It is the interplay of these subjective factors and individual irrational, and often unconscious responses that makes the state of terror, extreme fear or dread a peculiarly difficult concept for empirical social scientists to handle. It has been the tendency recently in the social sciences to shy away from the study of phenomena that are extremely difficult to define and almost impossible to measure. Furthermore the concepts of terror and terrorism have obviously very strong evaluative and emotive connotations.[2]

Violence today encompasses a broad panorama of real and potential threats emanating from many areas of the globe and linked to a variety of causes.

This study is concerned with that aspect of terror that is politically motivated. Such systematic terrorism, orchestrated by cells, groups, or states, employs death and destruction—or the threat of them—to achieve political aims. In contemporary terms, it is considered a mode of psychological or low-intensity warfare. This type of terrorism was clearly demonstrated, both in psychological and destructive terms, in the 11 September 2001 attacks on New York City and Washington by suicide terrorists utilizing fully fueled commercial aircraft as flying bombs.[3]

The simplicity and low cost of terrorism is both attractive and frightening. As Paul Wilkinson puts it:

> A primary target for terrorization is selected; the objective, or message to be conveyed, is determined; and credibility is established by convincing the target that the threat can actually be carried out. The victim or victims of the actual act of terrorist violence may or may not be the primary target, and the effects of relatively small amounts of violence will tend to be quite disproportionate in terms of the number of people terrorized: in the words of an ancient Chinese proverb, "Kill one, frighten ten thousand."[4]

In accomplishing their mission, the terrorists hope that the national and international media will exaggerate the terrorist threat or act and multiply the effect of a solitary outrage, while at the same time publicizing the terrorist cause.[5] Terrorists prefer to have many people witness their activities on behalf of the cause rather than have many people dead or suffering due to it.[6]

ROLE OF THE MEDIA

To comprehend fully the nature of modern terrorism, one must be cognizant of the role of the mass media (i.e., television, radio, movies, newspapers and magazines), and the ensuing amplification effect. As underlined by Hilde L. Mosse in her paper "The Media and Terrorism," "Violence has entered their homes, glorified and in profusion, via the mass media. This has contributed mightily to the implicit acceptance of violence as a means of getting things done."[7]

Television is probably the single most powerful medium. It makes communication between people almost instantaneous, and allows individuals from diverse nationalities to partake of the world's cultural and intellectual life. Television has thus been said to be "potentially the single most important antiviolence device."[8] Consciousness of violence through the media, particularly television, has been pervasive in the social development of young people growing up during the brutal and turbulent decades of the 1960s to the 1990s. The Middle East Wars, Vietnam, Afghanistan, Northern Ireland, Rwanda and the conflicts in the former Yugoslavia, insurrection, invasions, revolution and street crime became a part of the daily diet for these generations. For this audience:

> Violence is very effective in fact and in fiction. It attracts attention and therefore viewers faster and more predictably than any other theme. Fast, gory, brutal action is much easier to write about and to portray than the complicated subtleties of genuine and humane human relationships. To kill someone settles a conflict quickly. It takes time, careful reasoning, and emotional restraint to solve it nonviolently.[9]

By definition terrorism uses violence, either expressed or implied. However, in doing so, it finds an unwitting ally in the press, which while carrying out its task of reporting the news, publicizes the deeds of terrorists and propagates their cause. Because terrorist activities make news in an age of mass communication, the agents of the media serve the needs of the terrorists while they answer the demands of the citizens to be informed. In short, terrorists take advantage of the "amplification effect" of the media so as to ensure that their initiatives or deeds are given the widest possible audience. Therefore, terrorism today is in many ways violent theatre, dramatic, emotional, deadly and attractive. Similar to the writers and producers of television entertainment shows with their eye on television ratings, the terrorists of today choreograph their actions with the aim of achieving maximum publicity and the widest audience. At the same time, it also gives the terrorists the upper hand in employing fear as *the* psychological warfare weapon. However, the media could deny, or at least lessen, the impact of terrorist violence by how they report the incident and, in doing so, decrease the prospects and impact of this type of warfare.

The impact of terrorism and the media was summarized in an editorial regarding the 1996 Olympic bombing and the mysterious crash of TWA Flight 800.

> Contrary to what you might conclude by watching CNN, we are not living in an age of rising terrorism. By the U.S. State Department's count, international terrorism is less frequent in the 1990s than in the 1980s.
>
> What has increased is the power of terrorists (and those who are presumed to be terrorists) to command live television coverage.
>
> In the new era of media television, CNN becomes the agent of terrorists and murderous nuts indiscriminately. Along with other networks, CNN has covered the pipe bombing at the Olympics as exhaustively and zealously as it has reported on the deaths of 230 people aboard the TWA Flight 800—reporting both from the start as terrorism.
>
> Neither case has yet been demonstrated to be a terrorist act. Both have been treated in the news media as terrorists acts of enormous political significance.
>
> Through TV, terrorists and criminals alike can order up their own celebrity. They become a kind of occupying force, occupying our minds and so influencing the acts of governments.[10]

Notwithstanding the exploitation of media by terrorists, there are counterbalance issues relating to censorship. In late October 2001, there were reports that American national security advisor Condoleezza Rice suggested that major U.S. network executives meet with her on a regular basis to discuss media coverage of stories relating to terrorism. It was also reported that the BBC and Sky News had similar requests made of them by the British government, but these were rejected.[11]

THE FUTURE

It is probably safe to assume that terrorism as a form of conflict will persist, particularly as societies become more vulnerable to this type of violence. Yonah Alexander has expressed the following problem:

> What is particularly disturbing is the fact that the advances of science and technology are slowly turning the entire modern society into a potential victim of terrorism, with no immunity for the noncombatant segment of the world population or for those nations and peoples who have no direct connection to particular conflicts or to specific grievances that motivate acts of violence. Clearly, the globalization of the brutalization of modern violence makes it abundantly clear that we have entered a new Age of Terrorism with all its frightening ramifications.[12]

In general terms, terrorism can thrive wherever there exist grievances stemming from apparent injustice. This can include the complete lack of, or simply inadequate, participation in the political process, poverty, prejudice, or other forms of oppression, be they perceived or real. Where these grievances are not addressed, popular dissatisfaction will almost certainly spawn disorder and, eventually, even terrorism. This *center of gravity,* in Clausewitzian terms, for terrorism would be more easily addressed if such grievances were resolved rather than simply dealt with through heavy-handed oppression, which can itself engender terrorist activities. This is, of course, extremely difficult because of differing views on the grievances and their legitimacy, entrenched interests, and issues outside of, but related to, the problems which result in a particular terrorist manifestation.

Societies with minimal political activities and the most injustice are often the most free from contemporary terrorism; perhaps this is because repressive regimes can be highly effective. Although in democratic nations, citizens may voice ideas across the spectrum and bring grievances to the surface, we must also be aware that we, as humans, are not perfect and in turn neither are our institutions. Therefore, the problems of a whole society may be reduced but never totally erased. In that light, it is well to accept that "However democratic a society, however near to perfection the social institutions, there will always be disaffected and alienated people claiming that the present state of affairs is intolerable and there will be aggressive people more interested in violence than in liberty and justice."[13]

TYPOLOGY OF TERRORISM

Wilkinson has divided political terrorism into three types: revolutionary, sub-revolutionary and repressive. He defines revolutionary terrorism as the employment of systematic tactics of terrorist violence with the aim of bringing about political revolution. He characterizes revolutionary terrorism as having several distinct traits: that it is always a group phenomenon no matter how small that group may be; that the revolution and the employment of terror in its promotion are incorporated within some sort of ideology; that the organization has leaders who motivate the members to pursue a revolutionary ideology; and that it develops "alternative institutional structures."[14]

Further, a more accurate assessment of politically motivated terrorism should incorporate the following features: that it is integral to a revolutionary strategy; that it employs socially and politically unacceptable violence in pursuit of its aims; that there is a pattern of symbolic or representative selection of targets; and that lastly the orchestrators of these activities aspire to achieve a psychological effect, thereby forcing an adjustment in political behavior on the target audience.[15]

Wilkinson has further classified his definition of revolutionary terrorism into the following seven subtypes:

1. Organizations of pure terror (in which terrorism is the exclusive weapon);
2. Revolutionary and national/liberationist parties and movements in which terror is employed as an auxiliary weapon;
3. Guerilla terrorism: rural and urban;
4. Insurrectionary terrorism: normally short-term terror in the course of a revolutionary rising;
5. The revolutionary Reign of Terror: often directed at classes and racial and religious minorities;
6. Propaganda of the deed, when this form of terror is motivated by long-term revolutionary objectives, and;
7. International terrorism (that is terrorism committed outside the borders of one or all of the parties to the political conflict), where it is motivated by revolutionary objectives.[16]

Wilkinson defines his second type, sub-revolutionary terrorism, as violence employed for motives that are political in nature but do not include either revolution or governmental repression.[17] He differentiates revolutionary from sub-revolutionary terrorism by suggesting that the former demands total change, while the latter aspires to achieve more limited or selected aims, as for example, making the government change its stated policy.

The third type, repressive terrorism, is the systematic use of acts of terroristic violence to suppress groups, individuals and forms of behavior that are perceived to be unacceptable or undesirable by the authorities.[18] This form of terrorism requires the services of an effective secret police force and an efficient intelligence service, both of which may be perceived by outsiders and themselves as elite. These organizations are directed against any opposition, as was the Shah of Iran's infamous SAVAK.[19]

Wilkinson finally defines, for himself, that terrorism is the threat of, or the systematic use of murder and destruction to terrorize individuals or other organizations such as groups, communities or governments into submitting to the political demands of terrorists.[20]

Terrorism is separated from other types of violence by the political context of the act and its shock value. It is this psychological aspect that is often most disconcerting, rather than the act. While there are other typologies developed by other commentators on terrorism and despite the ambiguities and inadequacies noted above, the Wilkinson framework is frequently used because of its clear definitions.

There are nonetheless some shortcomings in these definitions. Assuming that a series of individual acts can only be considered to be terrorist tactics if they are systematic, and acknowledging that terrorism can be employed by both guerrillas as well as regimes in power,[21] Grant Wardlaw defines political terrorism as:

the use, or threat of use, of violence by an individual or a group, whether acting for or in opposition to established authority, when such action is designed to create extreme anxiety and/or fear-inducing effects in a target group larger than the immediate victims with the purpose of coercing that group into acceding to the political demands of the perpetrators.[22]

In conclusion, terrorism is seldom mindless or irrational. To those who employ this tactic, it remains a logical means to an end. Unfortunately, for many regions of the world terrorism has become, and remains, an integral part of the world's ever-evolving political system. To the uninformed, terrorist acts may seem random, harming persons and interests that may seem of little importance to the cause. However, the aim of instilling fear in the collective psyche for coercive purposes is achieved. This was seen dramatically in the cancellation of Seattle, Washington's planned Millennium celebrations. In capitulation to fears of a terrorist attack, Seattle's elected officials decided to scrap the planned celebrations at the city's well-known landmark, the Space Needle.[23] The well-planned and coordinated suicide attack on the destroyer USS Cole in Aden Harbor on 12 October 2000, which killed seventeen American sailors and wounded another thirty-nine, underlines the serious threat posed by dedicated suicide terrorists. The blast reportedly consisted of 225 kilograms of plastic explosive, which tore a twelve-meter hole into the hull of the ship. Just before the explosion, some of the USS Cole's crew waved to the two suicide bombers who approached the destroyer. The terrorists stood up and waved back, and while standing at attention, were vaporized in the blast. [24] This attack was only surpassed by the self-sacrifice demonstrated by the suicide operators who flew three commercial aircraft into New York's World Trade Center towers and the Pentagon in Washington, with a fourth aircraft crashing in rural Pennsylvania, killing all aboard.

NOTES

1. Interview with senior British Parachute Regiment officer, London, England (4 October 1998).
2. Wilkinson, *Terrorism and the Liberal State,* 47–48.
3. Delacourt, "Terror Is, after All, Psychological."
4. Ibid., 49. This is actually a saying of Sun Tzu.
5. See Slone, "Responses to Media Coverage of Terrorism," 508–522. It is noted that the media can produce an "anxiety-inducing effect," supporting the view that the media has a powerful effect on an audience, and argues for further exploration of links between the broadcasting of political violence and its impact upon the psychological processes of the audience.
6. Wilkinson, *Terrorism and the Liberal State,* 47–48.
7. Hilde L. Mosse, "The Media and Terrorism," in Livingston (ed.) et al., *International Terrorism in the Contemporary World,* 282. See also, Combs, *Terrorism in the Twenty-First Century,* 143–145.

8. Ibid., 283. For an interesting counterview see Grossman, "Television's virus of violence."

9. Ibid., 284.

10. "Media Terrorism." For an excellent overview see Perl, "Terrorism, the Media, and the Twenty-first Century: Perspectives, Trends, and Options for Policy Makers," 93–102.

11. Vincent, "Fighting Censorship in the 'New War.'"

12. Livingstone, *The War Against Terrorism,* xi.

13. Ibid., 266.

14. Wilkinson, *Terrorism and the Liberal State,* 56.

15. Hutchinson, "The Concept of Revolutionary Terrorism," 385.

16. Wilkinson, *Political Terrorism,* 38. It should also be underlined that acts orchestrated by two terrorist parties against each other would also be considered terrorism.

17. Ibid.

18. Ibid., 40.

19. Dobson and Payne, *The Dictionary of Espionage,* 195.

20. Wilkinson, *Political Terrorism,* 49.

21. Ibid.

22. Ibid.

23. The cancellations occurred after the Algerian Ahmed Ressam was arrested on 14 December 1999 and charged with bringing bomb-making materials into Port Angeles, Washington from British Columbia. Mr. Ressam, formerly residing in Montreal, was traveling under an assumed name and had a reservation for one night at a motel near the Space Needle. Koring, "Terrorism Jitters Lead Seattle to Cancel New Year's Plan: 'We Did Not Want to Take Chances with Public Safety,' Says Mayor as City Scrubs Celebration at Space Needle Landmark." Also, Saunders, "Bin Laden at Heart of Ressam Trial," and Saunders, "Witness Implicates Ressam." For an overview of potential threats to America, see Perry, "Preparing for the Next Attack."

24. See Brodie, "U.S. Navy Changes its Story on Cole: Terrorists Not Part of Mooring Operation"; Koring, "17 Feared Dead in Warship Blast." See also Nordland, et al., "A Sneak Attack"; Ratnessar, "Sneak Attack: a Terrorist Bombing in Yemen 17 U.S. Sailors and Raises Questions about American's Vulnerability"; and "U.S. Navy Revises Story of Ship's Bombing: New Version of Events Contradicts Report That Bombs Struck While Vessel Mooring." A more interesting and notable issue relating to the attack on the USS Cole was that, according to court documents, a suspect in the 1998 bombing of the American Embassy in Nairobi, Kenya, had warned of another attack in Yemen. The suspected terrorist, Mohamed Rashed Daoud al-'Owhali—who was arrested and questioned for the bomb attack in Nairobi—advised his interrogators that another attack was planned for Aden. In return, American investigators offered him limited immunity. American officials noted that Islamic militants had botched a January 2000 attack against the American warship USS Sullivans. At the time of writing, little is known about the investigation follow-up. Weiser, "Embassy Suspect Warned U.S. of Yemen Attack, Papers Show." See also Hirschkorn, "Convictions Mark First Step in Breaking up

Al-Qaeda Network." The counterterrorist campaign in the fall and winter of 2001–2002 in Afghanistan has reportedly derailed or delayed other al-Qaeda initiatives because American and allied forces have been successful in destroying or disrupting al-Qaeda's communication system as well as capturing or killing key terrorist operatives. See Koring, "Al-Qaeda Plots Foiled, U.S. Claims."

1

An Overview of Terrorism

A HISTORICAL PERSPECTIVE ON TERRORISM

To fully appreciate the implications of terrorism today, it is appropriate to review and assess terrorism within the context of history. Grant Wardlaw argues that "Part of the solution to the question of whether or not contemporary terrorism poses a unique threat to social order lies in an appraisal of its degree of continuity with previous manifestations of political terrorism."[1]

It is not possible in this study to produce a complete history of terrorism. However, in order to place contemporary terrorist activities in a proper perspective, it is germane to identify some of the major historical benchmarks of terrorism.

Walter Laqueur wrote that the term terrorism was defined in the 1798 supplement of the *Dictionnaire de l'Académie Française* as a "système, régime de la terreur."[2] From that moment on this word has been, and continues to be, employed to describe a spectrum of violent activities, many of which are not encompassed within the dictionary definition. Although the word terrorism is, in historical terms, relatively new, Laqueur argues that this form of political violence can be seen much earlier in history in the activities of a movement known as the Sicarii, operating at the time of the Zealot movement in Palestine in the period 66–73 A.D.[3]

Probably the most notable "terrorist group" of early times was the Assassins, who surfaced in Persia in the eleventh century, only to be smashed by the Mongols two centuries later. Contemporary political analysts have compared recent terrorist groups to the Assassins. The group's first leader, Hassan Sibai, appreciated that his small group could not take on his enemy in open warfare; however, a planned, protracted campaign of terror executed by a small, highly disciplined and dedicated force was to prove to be a highly effective political weapon.[4]

An historical study would reveal the existence of other isolated organizations that employed terrorism. However, some observers believe that the usefulness of the systematic deployment of political violence was not fully appreciated until the French Revolution[5] and the rise of nationalism in Europe. Laqueur writes of this phenomenon:

> Systematic terrorism begins in the second half of the nineteenth century and there were several quite distinct categories of it from the very beginning. The Russian revolutionaries. . . . Radical nationalist groups such as the Irish, Macedonians, Serbs or Armenians used terrorist methods in their struggle for autonomy or national independence. Lastly, there was the anarchist 'propaganda by the deed,' mainly during the 1890s in France, Italy, Spain and the United States.[6]

His view suggests that terrorism, in all its manifestations, has a common and quite recent origin associated with the twin movements of democracy and nationalism. Adherents to both increasingly found political or national subordination unacceptable. They insisted that these conditions be improved and were not reluctant to employ violence if there seemed to be little prospect that their demands would be met.[7]

Although it was active only from 1878 to 1881, the Russian Narodnaya Volya was one of the most important of the formative terrorist groups. This organization was responsible for the evolution of a sophisticated terrorist campaign against the Czarist authorities. According to one of Narodnaya Volya's foremost thinkers:

> Terrorism . . . was an altogether new fighting method, far more 'cost effective' than an old-fashioned revolutionary mass struggle. Despite insignificant forces, it would still be possible to concentrate every effort upon the overthrow of tyranny. Since there was no limit to human inventiveness, it was virtually impossible for the tyrants to provide safeguards against attacks.[8]

Already, one can see the emergence of organized terrorists employing violence as a psychological weapon. However, for many, terrorism was simply a better ethical choice than initiatives that aimed at a mass insurrectional movement. Romanenko, a Russian proponent of the terrorist approach, perceived terrorism as a moral alternative. He argued that terrorism was both effective and humanitarian considering that it took fewer victims than the casualties that would accrue via a major uprising. Furthermore, in a popular revolution it was thought that the best that a country had to offer were killed off, while the real villains were safe looking on from the sidelines. Therefore, the terrorist attacks were aimed against the real culprits; unfortunately a few innocents might suffer, but this was the inevitable cost of war.[9]

The terrorism orchestrated by the Narodnaya Volya was markedly different from the activities of their contemporaries, the Anarchists, as their terror campaign was seen to be an individual act while Russian terrorism was in reality a well-directed and planned campaign.[10] In short, the Narodnaya Volya sponsored discriminate acts of terrorism.

Russian terrorism fell with the early demise of the Narodnaya Volya. It was another twenty years before major violence began again, with the assassination in 1902 of the Minister of the Interior, Dmitrii Sergevich Sipyagin, by the political offspring of the Narodnaya Volya—the Social Revolutionary Party.

Laqueur states that terrorism, in Russian revolutionary thinking, was not aimed at replacing the mass struggle; rather its purpose was to aid and strengthen the revolutionization of the people.[11] It is from this idea of the role of terrorism, as an adjunct or a stage of the revolutionary process, where contemporary analysts have noted strong comparisons with the modern practitioners of terrorism. It should be underlined, however, that once terrorist acts become a part of a revolutionary process all discrimination is lost.

Russian terrorism in the early 1900s was more favorably received by the masses than had been the activities of the Narodnaya Volya, which had only succeeded in acquiring supporters from the middle- and upper-class intelligentsia. Revolutionary parties continued to be at odds regarding the various ethical, operational and utilitarian aspects of terrorism for some time.[12]

Several noteworthy political trends appeared in the late nineteenth and early twentieth centuries in Russia. The two most prominent, the related theories of anarchism and nihilism were elaborated perhaps most completely in the writings of Mikhail Bakunin and Sergei Nechaev. With the publication of the former's *Revolutionary Catechism* in 1871, the characteristics of an anarchist revolution and an anarchist revolutionary were defined. This document begins with a list of rules for organization and defines the revolutionary as a nameless soldier absorbed by a single all-consuming aim— that of revolution. He is void of any human feelings, hard on himself and others, and revolution becomes his only "pleasure, gratification and reward."[13] To achieve his aim, this true revolutionary was to penetrate all aspects of society, even the bureaucracy, secret police and the Church. In the end the Catechism argued for total revolution; all "institutions, social structures, civilisation and morality were to be destroyed, root and branch."[14] In short this publication called for the complete annihilation of the existing order.

Bakunin is probably best known for the concept of "propaganda of the deed" which insists that revolutionaries must plan and execute violent acts as "individual revolutionary statements." These would be essentially practical demonstrations, which once executed could not be ignored and would ideally stir the minds of the masses.[15]

Anarchist attacks, particularly in the last decades of the nineteenth century, received extraordinary notoriety, thereby allowing their perpetrators to proclaim the positive virtues of violence. A perception of an international anarchist conspiracy was generated. While this movement was, initially, nonexistent internationally, anarchist methods and thinking frequently influenced future foreign terrorists.[16] The acts of these pre-1914 anarchists and terrorists and the resulting publicity foreshadow today's controversy regarding the ends and means of terrorism, particularly in discussions of the differences between politically motivated violence and ordinary criminal activities. In fact, examples exist throughout recent history where terrorism has become synonymous, at least in the general public's mind, with criminal acts.[17]

The modern world is dominated by trends and influences that had their birth in the massive revolutionary changes of the period from 1914 to 1945. In this period, the political structure of the world was completely changed. The continental great powers saw their power positions decline while two peripheral powers, the United States and the Soviet Union, emerged as superpowers.

The destruction of the strength of, and the confidence in, the great imperial powers created a political vacuum in the Third World, and spawned frequent and sometimes ferocious conflict amongst those vying to succeed the imperial powers. Economic dislocation and rapid change accompanying these political revolutions brought about a new political order which arose during the initial four decades of European decline, and the subsequent four decades of restructuring of the international system. This loose bipolar and now unipolar world has set the stage for the development of modern terrorism.

The nineteenth-century phenomena of democracy and nationalism, mentioned earlier as essential elements of the emergence of modern terrorism, have been exported *mutatis mutandis* to the Third World. Nationalism, in particular, has been accepted wholeheartedly by at least the governments, if not by all the segments of the successor regimes to the European empires. Questions of religion, frontiers, status, recognition of separate existence, irredentism, ethnic tribal religions or related differences, all have contributed to the vast difficulties in creating viable states in the Third World. Incorporating these states into an international system that is itself far from stable creates further difficulties. Many individuals and groups committed to a nationalist or separatist objective, such as the Israeli independence movement or the Palestine Liberation Organization or the Serbo-Croatian situation, see that the employment of limited force or low-level revolutionary violence is required to achieve their aim.[18]

The strength of anti-colonialist sentiment has increased. Since 1945, a much more sympathetic attitude has developed toward "liberation" forces. As Kupperman and Trent argue, this trend connected easily with "the writings of Mao, Guevara, Frantz [*sic*] Fanon, and Carlos Marighella [which] illustrate strategy, foster a quasi-religious faith that history is on the side of the oppressed."[19] This situation has emerged during a period of a growing awareness of the interdependence of nations and the promotion of a wide spectrum of international organizations that are predicated upon this ideal.

A striking example of nationalist objectives and serious political grievances which were not being addressed by the international community, and the employment of a concerted terrorist campaign aimed at resolving these problems is that of the Palestine Liberation Organization. Without discussing the legitimacy of the movement or its aims, it is clear that the employment of terrorist methods, widely decried and denounced by much of the world community, has been effective. Certainly the acceptance of Yasser Arafat as the spokesman of the Palestinian people[20] by the UN General Assembly meeting in 1974 indicated that the use of terrorist tactics did not itself detract from widespread acceptance of the legitimacy of a cause. In particular, the tactics of terrorism employed by the PLO forced international attention to the Palestinian issue; attention that this cause may otherwise have not received on an international scale and, in fact, garnered the necessary political legitimacy to be recognized as an evolving nation.

THE PRE-1972 RESPONSE TO TERRORISM

The late 1960s witnessed a most dramatic evolution in terrorism. For the most part, governments experiencing the effects of terrorism did not know how to deal effectively with this type of violence. Furthermore, government leaders and their bureaucracies viewed this activity as just a passing phenomenon. They hoped, somewhat naively, that it would go away quickly. The following section will show how governments attempted to address this problem and how effective their measures were.

This violent trend had been spurred on, according to some analysts, by three major developments.[21] The dramatic Israeli victory during the 1967 Six-Day War brought home to many Palestinians that their Arab allies either would not or could not assist them in achieving Palestinian political goals. This initiated the 1968 wave of 35 Palestinian orchestrated hijackings of commercial airlines, the terrorists seeking either the release of prisoners or ransom.[22] The second notable occurrence was the killing of the Latin

American guerrilla leader Ernesto Ché Guevera.[23] The last and probably the most memorable event was the Vietnam War and, in particular, the unleashing of American domestic anti-war elements that manifested themselves in numerous student groups that "began to probe the cracks in American society with some well-aimed terrorist blows at the system."[24]

Air Hijackings

The late 1960s also experienced a growing number of airline "sky-jackings" to Cuba particularly among aircraft crossing the southern United States. The problem by 1968 had become "so epidemic that one airline servicing Miami and other Southern cities in the U.S. has decided to equip pilots with approach charts for Havana's José Marti Airport and written instructions on dealing with hijackers ('Do as they say')."[25]

A typical skyjacking of the day was the incident involving National Airlines Flight 1064 from Los Angeles to Miami. After a stopover in Houston, a Cuban identifying himself as R. Hernandez seized a stewardess, using a gun and an object wrapped in a handkerchief which was believed to be a grenade. "Fidel ordered me back to Havana, dead or alive,"[26] Hernandez reportedly said in Spanish. The pilot convinced the hijacker that the aircraft required a fuel stop at New Orleans before attempting the flight to Cuba. The New Orleans police believed that they could not attempt the recovery of the aircraft without risking the lives of the crew and passengers. The flight continued to Havana, where Hernandez revealed that his hand grenade was in reality a bottle of Old Spice aftershave lotion. Cuban authorities apprehended Hernandez and released the crew to return the DC-8 to Miami. A DC-6 chartered by the U.S. government returned the passengers to the U.S. On reflection, it was apparent to all observers that "nothing has been done thus far to try to thwart skyjackers."[27]

An earlier outbreak of similar skyjackings in 1961 had seen the Federal Aviation Administration (FAA) permitting airline crews to be armed. This action was generally opposed by both the airlines and the pilots themselves. It was argued that a side trip to Cuba was "preferable to a mid-air gun battle."[28] The simple solution of locking the cockpit cabin during flight operations was also considered but it was not effective as the terrorist (or hijacker) could still take a stewardess hostage and thereby give orders to the crew over the aircraft's intercom system.[29]

By the late 1960s the suggestion of searching each passenger was rejected as both "time-consuming and unsettling."[30] However, a detection device was being readied for demonstration by an aerospace manufacturer. This device, which used sensitive magnetic film, would alert security personnel to the presence of metal objects. The aviation industry had for many years sought such a device "capable of detecting metal objects as passengers pass through terminals and also distinguishing, for example, between an alarm clock and a revolver."[31] While this endeavor continued, the airlines, in conjunction with the U.S. State Department, began to advertise the fact that anyone who wanted to travel to Cuba could purchase a ticket on one of the regular DC-7 flights that fly from Miami to Havana to bring back refugees.[32] These special government flights are discussed later.

Hijackers at this time were simply viewed "as 'nuts and bolters,' but in addition to the borderline psychopaths there have been fugitives from justice, exhibitionist hippies, and several Cubans who may have been Castro agents hitching a ride home."[33] Cuba, although granting asylum to those responsible for hijackings, reportedly "never let on whether they regard the hijackings as a welcome embarrassment for the U.S. or a simple nuisance for Cuba."[34] Today, terrorist profiles fall into a number of disparate categories from highly professional and hardened individuals with familial links to the cause stretching back to their parents, criminals, to innocent youth who succumb to pressure, religious zealots and mercenaries. Some are young, bitter and out of touch, while others are recruited through bribery. Some are sociopaths with little education or scant training in terrorist operations.[35]

The character of the hijacking phenomenon took a dramatic and qualitative change in 1968, when El Al Flight 426, from London via Rome to Tel Aviv, was seized just after leaving Rome by three well-dressed Arab passengers. Brandishing pistols and hand grenades, they entered the cockpit, assaulted the co-pilot and ordered Captain Oded Abarbanell to change course for Algiers. This time the political aims of the hijackers were obvious as "this was no ordinary case of skyjacking and . . . the Palestinians who commandeered the plane were interested not in a free ride to Algeria but in humiliating the Israeli Government."[36]

It was reported that one of the hijackers moved up and down the airline's aisle speaking of his dedication to the cause. "'I have no father or mother—they were killed in the six-day war,' he shouted. 'I don't care if I'm blown into small pieces with the rest of you.'"[37]

The Boeing 707 was impounded upon reaching Algiers' Dar-el-Beida Airport and the next day all non-Israeli passengers were released by the hijackers and flown on to Paris. However, twelve Israeli passengers and the crew of ten were held on board. The hijackers were identified as members of the Popular Front for the Liberation of Palestine (PFLP). The PFLP had been competing with other Arab terrorist groups for political power, support and money, and this was an occasion "to score a publicity coup. More important yet, the PFLP wanted to exchange the Israeli passengers for some of its guerrillas who had been captured by Israel."[38] The Israeli government immediately appealed to the United Nations and international air organizations to obtain the release of its plane, passengers and crew. It was reported, "It may take a while. Algeria formally declared war on Israel a year ago and rejected the cease-fire that ended the six day Arab-Israeli conflict.

Because El Al carried military cargo in the war, Algeria considers it a para-military organization."[39]

At this juncture it was safe to assume that if Israeli diplomacy failed, Tel Aviv would likely retaliate directly against Algeria. This action might have taken the form of "punitive raids to redress alleged Arab wrongdoing."[40] It was further noted that "Air Algérie flights call regularly at Cairo, which is not far from Israeli airspace. It would be a relatively simple matter for Israeli fighter-interceptors to force one to land at Tel Aviv for use as a bargaining weapon."[41]

Now that hijacking as a means for trips to Cuba and monetary gain gave way to politically motivated hostage-taking on air carriers, several nations sought ways to establish an air crimes convention. One of the more important international agreements was the Tokyo Convention, formulated with the aim of establishing a continuity of jurisdiction over crimes committed on air carriers in international services. Although this convention had been drawn up in Tokyo in 1963, by 1968 it had been signed by only twenty-nine nations, including the United States. Twelve ratifications were required before the treaty could be put into effect. Yet, even after a full five years had elapsed, only six nations had deposited their ratification, so the treaty was still not in force.[42] Nonetheless, it established an international agreement among those nations which had ratified it. It acknowledged that the country in which an aircraft is legally registered is "competent to exercise jurisdiction over offenses committed aboard it when in international or overseas flight."[43]

Although not establishing any single country's exclusive jurisdiction, the convention permits the exercise of concurrent jurisdiction by concerned nations. However, the acceptance of one's claim to shared jurisdiction is dependent upon the degree of national interest in the incident. The convention further noted that a contracting country, although not the state of registration, may attempt to foil a criminal act in flight when the:

- Offense has effect on the territory of such a state.
- Offense has been committed by or against a national or permanent resident of the state.
- Offense is against the security of the state.
- Offense consists of a breach of any rules relating to the flight of aircraft in force in the state.
- Exercise of jurisdiction is necessary to ensure the obligation of the state under other multilateral agreements.[44]

The convention further acknowledges the authority of the chief pilot or captain, and that he "may take 'reasonable' measures . . . to protect the safety of the aircraft, maintain discipline onboard or to deliver the offender to the proper authorities."[45] This convention enables the captain to turn over to the authorities of a signatory to the agreement anyone who he believes has perpetrated an offence as defined by the laws of his country. Further, any "Offenses committed in an aircraft will be treated as if they had occurred in the state of registration of the aircraft."[46] In short the Tokyo Convention on offences and certain other acts committed on board aircraft required contracting states:

1. To make every effort to restore control of the aircraft to its lawful commander, and;

2. To make every effort to ensure the prompt onward passage or return of the hijacked aircraft together with its crew, passengers and cargo.[47]

By late 1968 the Air Line Pilots Association (ALPA), concerned by the rash of airline hijackings to Cuba, began urging the U.S. government to take action to halt such offences. This forced the State Department to look for ways in which alleged hijackers could be returned for prosecution in the United States. ALPA, during its biennial meeting of November 1968, decided to send messages to both President Johnson and the Transportation Secretary, Alan S. Boyd, asking for governmental action to stop aerial hijackings.[48] However, a State Department spokesman said that they were "pursuing all possible angles to meet this hijacking problem, but we are not in a position to talk about what is being done."[49] Due to the strained political situation in the late 1960s between Cuba and the United States, all regular diplomatic contact was maintained through the Swiss legation in Havana. This complicated the use of diplomatic channels and made any attempts to extradite extremely difficult.[50] Indeed, according to some American sources, the climate of relations during this period between Cuba and the U.S. had actually worsened as a result of these aerial diversions, which the Cuban government appeared to have no particular desire to assist in stopping.[51]

A new approach was made by the State Department in July of 1968 when it offered free transportation to anyone wanting to go to Cuba from the United States.[52] This could be viewed as a pre-emptive move on behalf of the government to deal with this issue. However, this initiative did not address the problem as both the airline carriers and the U.S. government expressed "a general state of helplessness in devising any clear cut preventative for the forcible seizure of an airliner in flight that does not endanger everyone onboard."[53] Nevertheless the airline industry looked for an antidote. It was then concentrating its anti-hijacking effort upon detection equipment in the hope of apprehending potential hijackers before they boarded. However, the detection equipment available during this period was not fully developed and did not perform satisfactorily. The airlines were worried that these detection devices would jeopardize passenger relations.

In resignation, one airline representative said that "compliance with the hijacker is about the only thing we've been able to come up with."[54]

The FAA began a Sky Marshal program by hiring 1,500 customs security officers to provide security on the nation's aircraft and prevent, forcibly if necessary, hijackers from seizing aircraft. The airlines themselves were concerned about high-altitude shootouts and asked that the Sky Marshal program be abandoned. As with many other responses to aircraft hijackings the oft-held view of this initiative was that, "the number of FAA personnel available is so small in relation to the number of flights . . . that the program is relatively meaningless."[55]

By the end of 1968 it was apparent that both the U.S. government and the major airlines had no solution for the problem of aerial hijacking.[56] Most of the methods focused on dealing with the hijacker himself while the aircraft was airborne. Some of the proposals consisted of "shooting him, gassing him, isolating him, locking him off from the pilot, even dropping him through a trapdoor into the baggage compartment."[57] Inevitably it was felt that any attempt at disarming or neutralizing the air pirate would result in the use of a weapon, which could have disastrous results in midflight. One suggestion was the "squirting [of] a nerve gas at the hijacker in hopes of paralyzing him."[58] Experts noted, however, the risk to passengers and crew if the gas were to enter the aircraft's air circulating system.

The standing order of the day to airline personnel as quoted from United Air Line President George E. Keck was: "Do what the man with the gun says, fuel supplies permitting."[59] This order remained, even though the airlines still sought preventive measures. In particular, they concentrated on finding a way of detecting weapons being carried by the potential sky pirates. However, no satisfactory technical breakthrough was obtained at this time. Although airline crew members were permitted to carry weapons, few did. Thus, it appears that by the end of 1968, airline officials and those in government both hoped that hijacking would turn out to be just "a passing fad."[60] In addition, each continued to feel that responsibility for dealing with this "fad" belonged to the other.

The International Federation of Air Line Pilots Association (IFALPA) drafted a resolution to boycott those countries that failed to release seized aircraft within 48 hours. This resolution, if adopted, would have had little effect as the Cuban government had been punctilious in returning both the aircraft and their passengers with no more than an overnight delay.[61]

Again, the FAA regularly sent "Sky Marshals" along randomly selected flights heading to Miami. It soon became apparent that there was little a law enforcement officer "could do to prevent plane piracy without increasing the already considerable danger to all on board."[62] Further, it was readily recognized that the costs of assigning marshals on board the many hundreds of daily flights would have been exorbitant.[63]

Meanwhile, metal detectors, costing around $1,000 (1969) each, were viewed by air carriers as too expensive even though the cost of a hijacking to the airline was approximately $8,550.00. Moreover, the airlines were reluctant to spend the necessary sums to search properly every passenger boarding those aircraft that could possibly be skyjacked.[64] The air carriers were apparently sensitive to the possibility of lawsuits should a passenger be unjustifiably searched.[65] This view would only delay the institution of effective airport security procedures as we know them today.

The FAA were, by September 1969, cautiously optimistic that, with airline personnel tasked to observe passenger behavior, and the use of ferrous metal detectors to detect weapons, would be hijackers could be foiled.[66] The U.S. government's Justice Department informed FAA officials that the employment of both techniques would "provide adequate legal grounds for asking to search a suspicious passenger who is carrying sufficient ferrous metal to trigger the magnetic detection equipment."[67]

The procedure was to have airline-passenger boarding-agents check for individuals whose general appearance and overall behavior resembled that of the profile of a hijacker.[68] Those people would then undergo a metal detector test. If the test proved positive, the passenger would undergo a more thorough search. An FAA spokesman stated that this was not an infallible method. Nonetheless, it was somewhat of a positive move and did not seem to greatly trouble the public. A well-publicized experiment, conducted in nine cities, using this combination of observation and detector devices, was benignly received.[69]

At the same time, the U.S. State Department was formulating a presentation to the United Nations calling for the strengthening of the procedures for extradition of hijackers. Although the Tokyo Convention dealt with hijacking, it did not call for extradition. Moreover neither the United States nor Cuba had ratified this agreement.[70] In mid-January 1969, a federal court in Brooklyn issued an arrest order for the hijackers of an Eastern Airlines DC-8 seized earlier that month. Although there was little hope of prosecution, the federal judicial system signaled that action would be taken against hijackers.[71] This was predicated on a 1961 U.S. law that imposed prison sentences of up to twenty years, and in some cases the death sentence, for aircraft seizure. As one airline attorney argued, "one arrest followed by full conviction might solve the whole problem."[72] The reality was that the majority of hijackers, at this time, did find political asylum.

Although Knut Hammarskjold, the International Air Transport Association Director-General, contacted the Cuban authorities regarding the issue of airline hijacks, it was reported that, because so few states had experienced this potentially disastrous phenomenon, chances were slim that the U.N. could assist in resolving the problem at that time.[73]

By February 1969, "frustration over high-flying hijackers had risen well past the fever point."[74] Further there was a real feeling of desperation which permeated the meeting of the International Air Transport Association.[75] As one very concerned IATA official reportedly announced, "Anything that can be done to deter hijacking without inconvenience or risk will be a good thing."[76] This sentiment carried through to special hearings organized on behalf of the U.S. House Interstate and Foreign Commerce Committee. There, James G. Brown, a once-hijacked pilot employed by National Airlines, noted that the aircraft-seizure phenomenon "is a tragedy waiting for some place to happen."[77] Concurrently, the FAA confirmed that "no new methods of detecting concealed weapons were currently feasible on a day-to-day basis."[78] A spokesman for the U.S. State Department could "offer little more than veiled reports of diplomatic efforts aimed at seeing if Fidel Castro might eventually accede to proposed international agreements requiring the extradition of skyjackers—be they political refugees or psychopaths acting out some inscrutable fantasy."[79]

The pirating of a Trans World Airlines aircraft, Flight 840, by members of the Che Guevara Commando unit of the Popular Front for the Liberation of Palestine (PFLP) led by Lelia Ali Khaled in August 1969 was an ominous change in the tone of hijacking. Hitherto it had been the preserve of homesick exiles or deranged psychopaths. Now, it appeared that skyjacking had become a tool to help attain political, rather than personal, aims. It presented the "serious possibility that a major international political crisis could be triggered by the hijacking of aircraft . . . underscoring the vulnerability of commercial transports in global air operations."[80]

This action was described as follows:

> Shortly after takeoff, a woman and a man forced their way into the cockpit brandishing a knife and hand grenade and told the pilot, Capt. Dean Carter, to divert to Tel Aviv. The two hijackers were later identified as Arabs, Lelia Ali Khaled, 23, and Salim Issawi, 30. They had flown from Beirut to Rome the day before the hijacking.
>
> Miss Khaled appeared to be familiar with cockpit procedures, according to the TWA crew, and had even calculated the fuel consumption of the 707. When the aircraft reached Tel Aviv, she ordered Carter to an altitude of 12,000 ft. and radioed propaganda messages to the Tel Aviv tower. As she was moving around the cockpit, the crew noticed that she had a map and a typewritten operations plan. The map showed a line drawn from Tel Aviv to Damascus.[81]

The saga of TWA Flight 840 revealed the growing sophistication of some terrorists and demonstrated their efficiency and technical competence. (This efficiency and competence were taken to even higher levels in September 2001, when terrorists were shown to have been trained sufficiently well to competently fly sophisticated passenger aircraft into the World Trade Center towers and the Pentagon.) In the wake of the TWA hijacking, IATA continued to argue that it was the responsibility of governments to stop aircraft hijacking and, more importantly, that tough laws were necessary to deter future aircraft hijackings.[82] Unfortunately there appeared to be, at this time, a definite lack of international will to undertake the required action.

The fall of 1969 saw the voluntary return of six Americans to stand trial for diverting aircraft to Cuba. This act was hailed in an editorial as the "first glimmers of hope on the otherwise dark horizon of air piracy."[83] These individuals, who had been in Cuba for six months or more, preferred to undergo trial in the United States than continue to live in Cuba.[84] It was hoped that the publicity regarding the trials would deter those who might consider hijacking an aircraft as an easy means of leaving their personal troubles.[85]

Meanwhile, other countries soon developed sterner measures to combat hijacking than did the Americans. After two Ethiopian airliners were hijacked, plainclothes security personnel were assigned to scheduled flights. Ignoring the basic rule put in place by most other airlines, "do not attempt to argue with a hijacker,"[86] the Ethiopians employed a rapid counter-violence response to foil a hijack attempt. On an Ethiopian airliner flying from Madrid to Addis Ababa, two armed men ordered the pilot to head for Aden. The three Ethiopian security officers on board quickly intervened. One hijacker, a 19-year-old Yemeni student, was tackled by a security officer and killed by his own gun in the ensuing struggle. His Senegalese companion was dispatched with a knife. Both terrorists, identified as members of an Ethiopian separatist group, were pronounced to be "the first would-be hijackers to be slain in mid-air."[87]

In September 1970, a crisis of a new kind captured the world's attention when PFLP commandos declared a terrorist war on the West. They orchestrated a triple-hijack operation. The capture of a Swissair DC-8, a Trans World Airline (TWA) 707 and a Pan-American 747, their passengers and crew, was described as "political extortion on a grand and unprecedented scale—a gross, new horror in a century already horrified by the enormity of its atrocities."[88] On 12 September, the three aircraft were blown up where they had landed at Dawson Field in Jordan. Although the terrorists sought vengeance against Israel, the "war" affected the hostages—unarmed men, women and children. The action was condemned in the U.N. by U. Thant as "savage and inhuman,"[89] while in Washington, President Nixon denounced the seizure and announced that security personnel would be on board a majority of American overseas flights. The President further recommended that all nations "take joint action to suspend airline services with those countries which refuse to punish or extradite hijackers involved in international blackmail."[90]

On 11 September, President Nixon demanded that the problem of air piracy must be addressed rapidly and described the implementation of a series of measures to counter this threat.[91]

1. The employment of armed guards on both domestic and international flights assessed as susceptible to hijacking.
2. Wider usage by U.S. airlines of electronic and other surveillance devices at international airports.
3. Emphasis on research into new methods of detecting weapons and explosives. The installation of x-ray machines and metal detectors in airports.[92]
4. Urge other countries to boycott nations that refuse to punish or extradite hijackers.

The President emphasized that countries are responsible for American lives and property, if hijacked aircraft land in their territory.[93]

At the same time President Nixon was considering other proposals such as:

1. A quarantine area to search outgoing passengers.
2. Prohibiting all carry-on luggage, thereby removing a means of taking onboard weapons and explosive devices.
3. The employment of 'project managers' to review passenger lists and inspect passengers.
4. The placing of a delay on all airline ticket sales several days after the reservations are made to check the background of the passengers.[94]

These steps resulted from a sober assessment of the new direction of terrorism inherent in the PFLP hijackings. The assessment was that this "latest round of air piracy involved far more than 'crackpot' individual hijackings such as marked [the previous] diversion of plans to Castro's Cuba. This was a form of international warfare that, unless halted, threatened to hit civilians of all lands."[95]

Historically, the seizure of a country's nationals and their property had often brought about armed intervention by great, and even not-so-great, powers. Now, however, the international community was paralyzed by the threat that any retaliatory action could witness the murder of the hostages.[96] The PFLP thus demonstrated the potential use of classic terror tactics vis-à-vis the U.S. and other nations through this triple-hijack operation.

The spate of anti-hijack measures was shown to be a knee-jerk reaction of dubious value, "halfhearted, hobbled by fears of inconveniencing passengers and the high cost of protective forces."[97] Yet, more importantly, there was little co-ordinated international co-operation.

One aspect of the PFLP hijack operation in particular caused grave concern for American intelligence, as it was reported that "secret NATO documents" were on board the Pan American 747 which was hijacked and later blown up. The CIA subsequently issued a directive that all their couriers carrying classified documents must travel on U.S. Armed Forces aircraft.[98]

By September 1970, the profile of a hijacker[99] had broadened to include Arab commandos who were described as "highly trained, disciplined people, armed with the best weapons for the job."[100] What the world was seeing now was the evolution of a virtually professional terrorist. This situation has since evolved to the extent that a senior British Army officer imparted that the IRA maintain a highly professional and competent core of dedicated terrorists and openly admitted to respecting their professional capabilities.[101] Recent Israeli experience, in particular the losses within their elite units which were attributed to pro-Iranian Hezbollah, Shiites and Amal militias, strongly suggests a growing professional capability.[102] Lastly, no one would doubt the professional cold-blooded dedication of the suicide hijackers whose successful high-concept, low-tech approach brought about the destruction of the World Trade Center while severely damaging the Pentagon, taking thousands of lives in both operations.

In January 1971, representatives of seventy-four nations and eight international organizations met in Washington to "exchange information on ways to eliminate aerial hijacking and piracy."[103] This forum, organized under the auspices of the FAA, drew representatives from major air carrier nations including those of the Warsaw Pact, who attended as observers.[104] Discussion covered many topics, including both ground and in-flight security, intelligence exchanges on likely hijackers, and recent developments in metal detectors, as well as more technical prevention systems.[105] The conference provided the following conclusions:

1. That the employment of sky marshals will likely decrease as metal detectors and other screening devices become more effective.

2. There was no indication of concern by the representatives regarding passenger disapproval of the screening systems.

3. Officials noted that the arrangements for the passage of intelligence should continue under the auspices of Interpol and IATA rather than constructing new organizations for this task.

4. Carl Maisch, the air transport security director of the FAA, noted that 259 arrests were made since September 1971 and mostly through the use of the screening system in place.

5. One representative from the United Kingdom revealed that progress has been made in the training of dogs to uncover explosives.[106]

Meanwhile, by mid-January, IFALPA began to pressure governments to ratify The Hague[107] and Tokyo Conventions. By April, those initiatives, called "T-Plus," incorporated a large number of pressure tactics involving pilot action and raising passenger awareness of the risks involved.[108]

Although the machinery of national and international law responded very slowly to skyjacking, airlines acknowledged the complexities of dealing with hijackers and began to deal with them. For example on 2 July 1971, a Braniff flight was commandeered just after departing from Mexico City. Although this was the first pirating of one of that company's aircraft, it was noted that such an eventuality had been anticipated by the management and, therefore, had been included in its emergency planning.[109]

In support of this operation, Braniff management set up command posts with the appropriate communication links including satellite relay. This command set-up was parallelled by emergency operations centres (EOC) in the State Department, FAA and the Federal Bureau of Investigation. Throughout this situation, the FAA monitored all air-ground communications and received situation reports from the Braniff EOC. The flight ended after forty-three hours in Buenos Aires, with no casualties. The hijacker, Robert Lee Jackson, a U.S. Navy deserter, wanted the flight to continue to Algeria, however, Argentine authorities would not allow the aircraft to be refueled, and they surrounded it with police.

What is surely important about this incident is that an airline, which had never experienced an act of aerial piracy, reacted efficiently and effectively in co-ordination with United States federal agencies. Just after the Braniff flight was hijacked, the chairman of the airline, Harding Lawrence, and the airline president, Edward Acker,

> had set up a command post in Braniff's administrative headquarters, in direct communication with the airline's operations and control center at its Love Field maintenance base here, which was headed by vice president–flight operations Herman Rumsey. The two posts were connected with open lines to Washington and, as the flight progressed from San Antonio to Monterrey, Mexico, Lima, Peru, Rio de Janeiro and Buenos Aires, to these cities. Braniff personnel in the airport control towers relayed running accounts of the scene to Dallas.[110]

Nor did this communications net cease there. The ability of Braniff Airlines to respond to Jackson's requirement was most impressive, particularly when he demanded that $100,000 in cash be delivered to Monterrey. The chairman, Harding Lawrence, reportedly approved the transaction and arranged to have a Monterrey bank provide the money to the airline's local manager. The money subsequently arrived at the airport just fifteen minutes after the aircraft's landing and was given to Jackson.[111]

From this incident one could conclude that airlines, from necessity, were rapidly preparing to confront, nationally or internationally, any skyjacking situation, to ensure the safety of the aircraft crew and passengers by use of the most effective means available. Governmental response, with few exceptions, seemed ponderous in comparison. This situation may be perceived today, as the world read in late December 1999 about the seizure of an Indian Airlines aircraft, carrying 160 passengers and crew. The Islamic hijackers requested the release of Kashmir separatists and a ransom of 200 million dollars U.S. from the Indian government.[112] On 14 October 2000, two Saudi hijackers took over a Saudi 777 bound for London, England, and redirected it to Baghdad, Iraq. The objective of the two hijackers was to garner attention to the issue of human rights in Saudi Arabia. The 103 passengers and crew spent the night in Baghdad and then continued on to London on the following day. It was not known if the hijackers were armed.[113]

Counterviolence: The First American Hijacker Dies

Although governments were slow to react to the hijacking menace, by 1971 the FBI began employing counterviolence techniques. On 23 July of that year, Richard Allen Obergfell of New York City boarded TWA Flight 335 at New York's La Guardia Airport. Just after departure, Obergfell grabbed flight attendant Idie Concepcion. Drawing a pistol, he forced her to the cockpit and ordered Captain Albert Hawes to fly to Milan, Italy. Hawes responded that the 727 jetliner did not have the range to fly to Milan, however, an arrangement was made to land in La Guardia, where Obergfell would board another aircraft that would carry him to Italy. At La Guardia, the passengers were released and Obergfell demanded a car to take his flight-attendant hostage and himself to Kennedy International Airport. He commandeered a maintenance truck and was escorted to the international airport. A fully fueled Boeing 707 was prepared, as were two FBI snipers armed with .308 Norma Magnum rifles with telescopic sights.

The marksmen were ordered: "If you get an opportunity for a clean shot, take it."[114] As Obergfell was moving towards the boarding ladder, holding his hostage so close that she accidentally stepped on his foot, he momentarily moved back from her. One of the snipers, FBI agent Kenneth Lovin, fired immediately. He had been tracking his target from behind a blast shield just seventy-five yards away. Obergfell dropped but was attempting to reach his pistol when a second round was fired, killing him. Some observers wondered about the acceptability of such actions, particularly as the hostage might have been killed had the agent missed his man. An FBI spokesman argued that it was "a calculated risk, but we felt it had to be taken."[115] Obergfell was the first hijacker to die attempting to seize an American aircraft.[116]

Despite this success, the Americans continued to search for other technology as a means of pre-empting aerial hijacking. Reports indicated growing interest in controlling the skyjacking dilemma. Major U.S. airports were reported to be "protected by electronic 'magnetometers,' and 1,200 specially trained 'sky marshals' were riding shotgun aboard the nation's airliners—with the number scheduled to rise to 1,500 by year's end."[117]

The Assistant Secretary of Transportation for Safety and Consumer Affairs, Lieutenant General (retired) Benjamin O. Davis, stated, "There has been a distinct turnabout in the hijacking situation. We have stopped being 'patsies.' The Government and the airlines have adopted an attitude of resistance—not recklessness, but a willingness to act when the opportunity arises."[118]

Sky Marshals, during this period, were under instructions to overpower a hijacker whenever possible, and, if necessary, shoot to kill.[119] In concert with the Sky Marshal program, refined computer-assisted weapons-detection devices were being tested and were reported to be addressing a major concern in America's anti-hijack effort.[120]

This new American policy of firm resistance to hijackers was intended to reduce the number of aircraft seizures. At the same time, Israel's El Al Airlines was tightening its anti-hijack procedures, which became known as being "the most stringent security procedures in the history of commercial air transport."[121] Furthermore, El Al was known to be providing security assistance and advice to other airlines flying into Tel Aviv.[122] It was in the wake of two sabotage attempts where explosives were discovered hidden in baggage and reports from Israeli intelligence that El Al enhanced its security procedures. These measures included the searching of *all* baggage, a regulation requiring that passengers sign a statement acknowledging the contents of their baggage, and the addition of more ground agents and Sky Marshals.[123] Such stringent measures did result in some delays in schedule.[124] Similar measures, however, are still in existence today, notwithstanding the high cost and delay.

The U.S., the U.K. and the USSR finally ratified the Tokyo Convention in the autumn of 1971,[125] indicating the growing momentum, particularly in U.S. government circles, to find a legal means to deal effectively with sky piracy. As governments attempted to maneuver national and international anti-hijack policies into place, it was reported that "Skyjacking poses a painful dilemma for lawmen: should they give in to the skyjacker's demands and allow him to escape unchallenged, or should they try to stop him, thereby endangering the lives of all on board."[126]

This dilemma was illustrated in the October 1971 seizure of a charter flight bound for the Bahamas from Nashville, Tennessee. When the aircraft landed in Jacksonville, Florida, an FBI agent ordered the pilot, Brent Downs, to cut his engines. He was also told that he would receive no fuel. After a desperate debate, the copilot, Randall Crump, climbed out of the aircraft to negotiate further with the agents. Moments later, the tires and one of the engines were peppered with bullets. The hijacker, George M. Giffe, responded by shooting Downs, then his own wife, and then himself.

One conclusion was that "it is by no means clear that the agents' actions constituted a blunder."[127] However, as one law official pointed out, "Suppose this guy had taken the plane off and crashed it, killing everybody? Then the FBI would have been roasted for doing nothing."[128] This moral dilemma for all security and law enforcement agencies, as well as governments, remains stubbornly with us to this day.

The effectiveness of maintaining onboard Sky Marshals was brought into question in November 1971, when an American Airlines 747 outbound from John F. Kennedy Airport for San Juan was hijacked by Angel Lugo and ordered to head for Cuba. Among the 221 passengers and sixteen crew members were three U.S. Sky Marshals and an FBI agent traveling on vacation. This flight became known as "the first successful snatching of a plane protected by the flying watchdogs."[129]

One of the Sky Marshals noticed a disturbed look on a stewardess's face and contacted the aircraft captain over the intercom asking if he should intervene. After conferring with both the captain and the other Sky Marshals it was determined that no one should do anything that would endanger those on board, as there was a distinct possibility of gunplay. The aircraft landed safely at José Marti Airport. This incident, not surprisingly, raised doubts as to the effectiveness of the 1,400-man Sky Marshal Program, which at this time expended about $37.7 million a year. On any given day, two-thirds of these officers were in the air, mostly on domestic flights on the East Coast and some select international routes.[130] Following this incident a controversy ensued as the marshals complained "that the airlines are generally lax in their security measures. (According to the Federal Aviation Administration, American Airlines had not bothered to turn on a metal detector which would have shown that hijacker Lugo was unarmed.) The airlines reply that screening procedures take too much time and irritate passengers."[131]

As far as the general utility of the Sky Marshal program was concerned, Captain O.R. Salmela said, on behalf of the aerial police force, "It didn't work this time, but I always like to have them with me."[132] Experience had shown that since the program began, "there have been no guerrilla-style hijackings and no airliner piracy has ended in a disaster."[133]

The frustrations with aerial piracy continued until the end of 1971 with probably the most notable action taken by Costa Rica's President, José Figueres Ferrer. After finishing a speech in the town of Puriscal, approximately twenty miles from San José, the President was informed that three gunmen had hijacked a Nicaraguan BAC 1-11 aircraft with forty-six passengers and crew on board. This airplane had just landed at the San José airport. The President was requested to authorize either the refueling of the aircraft so that it could continue its flight to Havana, or to provide another aircraft for the trip. The President immediately started for the airport and gave instructions over his car radio for "terrorizing the terrorists."[134] The aircraft was to be surrounded by armed guardsmen, the runway blocked and the aircraft's tires deflated. "Boys, this is war!," he reportedly shouted into his radio.[135]

By the time the President arrived, one of the passengers had been shot and the hijackers were identified as members of the Nicaraguan National Liberation Front. The three skyjackers released the passengers, but held the crew as hostages. One stewardess reportedly pleaded, "For the love of God, let us go to Cuba! Otherwise, they'll kill us."[136] The President's action was immediate. He directed that tear gas be forced into the aircraft's ventilating system. He then ordered an assault team to attack the aircraft. This action resulted in the death of one gunman. The other two members surrendered and the whole crew was evacuated without injury.[137]

It was noted that the President had, during this incident, fought "with his own guards, who were trying to wrestle a submachine gun away from him in order to keep him from getting hurt in any shootout."[138] In the end, although "Figueres did not get to fire a single shot, he was pleased with his performance."[139] Such examples of personal courage in the face of terrorist demands, although slightly comic-opera in style, continue to be rare.

In retrospect, the pre-1972 governmental response to terrorist hijackings was fraught with difficulties. Authorities responsible for dealing with such situations did so "without adequate information and with uncertain aid from their governments. In spite of public indignation that terrorists could strike with such impunity, the Western response was feeble and ad hoc."[140] The March 2001 hijacking of a Russian Airlines airplane by Chechen terrorists and the 11 September 2001 hijacking of four airplanes underline that the threat of aerial hijacking continues unabated.[141]

By the 1970s, centers of responsibility within Western governments and their national airlines were at odds. Each felt that the responsibility for dealing with this "passing fad" belonged to the other. Notwithstanding, airline pilots and their associations continued to press air carriers, governments and the U.N. to institute appropriate regulations, procedures, fines and penalties to preempt the hijack problem.

The early hopes of a purely technical solution through the use of profiles, metal detectors and the posting of ground and air security personnel had, and may continue to have, some deterrent effect.[142] However, it has not, to date, provided anything like a 100 percent solution to the hijacking problem. Israel appears to have led the way, and arguably continues to do so, by instituting probably the most stringent airline security procedures in existence. This is a direct result of the very great threat facing Israel and El Al, which makes rigorous security the most important aspect of its operations. El Al backs its security procedures with the latest information drawn from Israeli police and intelligence agencies. In this regard it is "accurate and timely all source intelligence provided to security and police authorities that remains the critical element in defeating terrorist initiatives."[143] For the most part this lesson appears to have often been ignored or not always appreciated and has sometimes been replaced with "a law enforcement knee-jerk reaction."[144]

The 1970s and '80s saw governments and their bureaucracies slowly turning to confront the terrorist dilemma and in some cases using this threat as a way of promoting national unity.[145] This was, for the most part, done in isolation by the various departments and agencies rather than through a concerted national and international effort. As national and international concern over the hijacking issue grew, this initial lethargic, piecemeal response would change.

CURRENT TERRORIST ACTIVITIES AND GOVERNMENTAL RESPONSE

Brian Jenkins, an authority on political violence, has said that terrorism has become "institutionalized."[146] In addition there is a "loose but global 'infrastructure'" that helps to sustain terrorism worldwide. This in turn has produced what has been described as "a semipermanent subculture of terrorism."[147] On that note, the purpose of this section is to explore the recent and more notable terrorist activities of the last five years and then review how governments could aim at further reducing the threat through a spectrum of initiatives.

By the end of the 1980s, the trend was toward large-scale indiscriminate violence so as to produce the maximum effect—particularly in casualties.[148] In short, "the bigger the better" has been for the most part the rule, as shown by the aerial destruction of the Air India flight in June 1985,[149] the Pan Am Flight 103 in December 1988,[150] the UTA Flight 772 over Niger in September 1989 and the bombing of the Israeli Embassy in Argentina in March 1992[151] which reportedly killed twenty and wounded 250.[152] The August 1998 bombing of the American embassies in Kenya and Tanzania, which killed more than 250 and wounded more than 5,000, the daring suicidal attack on the USS Cole, and the dramatic suicide attacks on New York City and Washington in September 2001, which killed over 3,000 people, further underline this trend. Jenkins notes that terrorists "may feel compelled to escalate their violence in order to keep public attention . . . or to recover coercive power lost as governments have become more resistant to their demands."[153] This appears to have occurred with bombings of the World Trade Center in New York in February 1993 killing six and wounding more than 1,000, and the U.S. Federal Building in Oklahoma City that killed 163 in 1995. Moreover, "Operation Bojinga," which was planned for January 1995, aimed at the midair destruction of twelve American passenger airliners and would have seen the destruction of thousands of air travelers if the perpetrators had been successful. The successful attacks on 11 September 2001 saw the slaughter of thousands and the total obliteration of the World Trade Center and a part of the Pentagon. Analysts estimate that the attacks against the World Trade Center and the Pentagon, also known by the military acronym PENTTBOM (Pentagon Twin Towers

Bombing) have cost between 30 to 50 billion dollars (U.S.); losses to the life insurance sector alone are estimated to be two to five billion dollars.[154] In contrast, it has been estimated that the price of this operation to those who executed it was approximately 13,000 dollars (U.S.) per person. Operating on "amazingly little money," Jack Blum, special counsel to the American Foreign Relations Committee, estimated that the entire operation for twenty people for one year would have cost between 200,000 to 250,000 dollars (U.S.).[155]

The nature of terrorist groups and their activities continues to change. One report noted that since 1993, there has been a steady decline in terrorism in both the Middle East and Western Europe. Although terrorist attacks are becoming less frequent, they are becoming more lethal.[156] Terrorists have "set out to distinguish themselves in the busy arena of international banditry, terrorist incidents seem to become more random, more arbitrary in their targets, less connected to any identifiable cause."[157] In the recent spate of suicide attacks by Palestinian extremists in the spring to fall of 2001, it was reported that this suicide offensive, which commenced 1 January 2000, had killed nearly fifty Israelis and injured fifty more by 17 August 2001.[158] The dramatic assault by suicide hijackers of four commercial airlines on 11 September 2001 in the United States underscores the impact that such operations have, as well as underlining the evolutionary terrorist philosophy that "bigger is better," particularly when the terrorists utilize high-concept low-technology against prestigious targets such as the Pentagon and World Trade Center.

As we, the audience, become accustomed to the frequency of violent action, terrorists will, in all likelihood, escalate their operations in the hopes of achieving their political aims. In that case, terrorism, as Jenkins has pointed out, "will become an accepted fact of contemporary life—commonplace, ordinary, banal, and therefore somehow 'tolerable.'"[159] Although this situation has evolved in certain countries, such as Britain and France, other countries, such as the United States, are still struggling to accept this new dimension to their everyday lives.

The late 1970s and the 1980s witnessed a series of notorious terrorist actions. The seizure of American hostages in Iran (1979), the Iranian Embassy siege in London (1980), the U.S. Marine bombing in Beirut (1983), a series of aerial hijackings including the bombing of the Air India 747,[160] the Achille Lauro incident, the brutal terrorist attacks in Vienna and Rome, and the bombing of the Pan Am flight over Scotland[161] are just some of the most notable examples. In this regard two approaches to modern terrorism have come into play: "Some experts see terrorism as the lower end of the warfare spectrum, a form of low-intensity, unconventional aggression. Others, however, believe that referring to it as war rather than criminal activity lends dignity to terrorists and places their acts in the context of accepted international behaviour."[162]

War or not, by the spring of 1986 the United States government was growing frustrated by its inability to cope with the violent actions orchestrated against its interests and those of its allies. This pent-up frustration was vented at one of the perceived orchestrators—Libya.

In April 1986, President Reagan ordered a series of aerial bombings against Libyan facilities believed to train and support terrorists. This action was, according to U.S. reports, executed only after numerous warnings went unheeded, and attempts to counter terrorism through economic and political sanctions were found to be unsuccessful.[163] It was only then that the U.S. Sixth Fleet was ordered into action with the purpose of striking a blow against Libya, which the Reagan Administration had threatened to execute many times before.[164]

As George Church suggested at that time, the "Libyan leader may not be the world's most effective governmental inciter of terrorist murder,"[165] particularly when one compares Libya to the other sponsors of terrorist violence such as Iran and Syria. It is common knowledge, however, that "Gaddafi has been the most open supplier of money, weapons, training and refuge to terrorist groups around the world."[166] This act was, for some, a strong signal underlining that the United States would act unilaterally and militarily under certain circumstances.

This initiative was embarked upon due to, in part, frustration. President Reagan had argued for, and had applied, economic sanctions on Libya. He attempted to persuade his European allies to do the same, with the hope of politically and economically isolating the "mad dog of the Middle East." Neither action brought about the desired effect on Libya.[167] Furthermore, the U.S. gleaned from electronic eavesdropping that Gaddafi had "ordered Libyan agents and their Palestinian supporters to 'cause maximum casualties to U.S. citizens and other Western people.'"[168] An American intelligence official reported, at this time, that one message, "which was sent from Tripoli and uses Gaddafi's authority, outlines operational plans for more than ten terror attacks."[169] In turn, the mood of the American people during this time was reflected in the words of George Schultz, who reportedly said, "We have taken enough punishment and beating. We have to act."[170]

The Libyan case touches on a significant lesson. In the attack on Libya, the United States demonstrated that when pushed it will employ military force in retaliation. But the retaliation must be taken in context. The reality is that Libya holds no place on the list of Middle East countries important to American political interests, nor is Libya involved in the Middle East peace process. The very fact that Libya was targeted proved to other terrorist-supporting countries, such as Iran and Syria, that nations important to American strategic or political interests would not likely be victims of military retaliation. In short, Libya simply did not matter as the country has no real allies in the Arab world. In contrast, the Syrians, who were accused of bombing the United States Marine Corps Headquarters in Beirut in 1983, killing 241 troops and wounding a hundred more,[171] suffered no such retaliation. Godfrey Hodgson noted this in a 1996 article in *The Independent* stating, "What about Syria, for one thing? Damascus, too, has supported terrorism in the past. Yet Washington does not include Syria in its anathema because the State Department hopes to involve Syrian government in the peace process with Israel."[172] It is notable that Libyan leader Muammar Gaddafi, once a sworn enemy of the American government, said that the United States had the right to retaliate after the 11 September 2001 attacks in New York and Washington, but advised that he would not brand Osama bin Laden a terrorist until there was an international agreement on the definition of terrorism. "America has the right to retaliate with direct military action; this is the right of self-defense," Gaddafi advised after the September 2001 attacks.[173]

The contrast may well be due solely to Syria's strategic importance in the Middle East, and the American need to work with Syria to secure a lasting peace in this volatile region.

The use of American military forces demonstrated a national will to deal with the, at that time, growing phenomenon of international terrorism. In 1985 it was written that "A decade ago, the world experienced an average of 10 incidents of terrorist violence per week—assassinations, bombings, air hijackings, kidnappings, maimings or attacks on facilities. The average now: Nearly 10 a day."[174]

The 1986 *Public Report of the Vice President's Task Force on Combatting Terrorism* noted:

> During the past decade, terrorists have attacked U.S. officials or installations abroad approximately once every 17 days. In the past 17 years, terrorists have killed as many U.S. diplomats as were killed in the previous 180 years.
>
> In 1982, a total of 57 attacks were directed against U.S. military personnel, resulting in two deaths. In 1983, even more incidents occurred (65), and 241 deaths resulted from one incident. In that bombing of the U.S. Marine barracks in Beirut, the United States lost nearly as many servicemen as the British lost in the entire Falklands campaign.[175]

America was, to some, acquiring something akin to a "siege mentality." This situation parallels the American sentiment that existed in the wake of the dramatic terrorist attacks in September 2001.

In the wake of America's attack on Libya the debate continued as to how nations could, on an individual basis, as well as in concert, upgrade their defenses against terrorist action. Suggestions from political, civil, military, law enforcement and lay sources spanned the spectrum of both passive and active measures. These included enhancing airport and airline security, expanding the role of intelligence, hardening targets, improving international co-operation, employing diplomatic pressure on countries that countenance terrorism, forming and using rescue teams, eliminating safe havens, and using government sanctioned *executive action* (assassination or murder)[176] and commando operations. As to the morality of the employment of "directed violence," Livingstone, a noted authority on these issues, has argued "such a policy is far more justifiable than the indiscriminate retaliatory bombing of refugee camps and villages since only the guilty are punished."[177]

There are no simple solutions to terrorism. Its manifestations pose a complicated, dynamic and multi-faceted problem for governments. Therefore, the design and implementation of national and international policies to provide an all-encompassing strategy remains a monumental and, for the most part, uncompleted endeavor. For those nations facing the challenge of terrorism, the United States has formulated a series of strategies that have been implemented or are being studied. Livingstone and Arnold have identified, in their thorough work on terrorism, the following key activities for improving national response capabilities:

1. Improving physical security.[178]

2. Train U.S. diplomatic and military personnel in personal security habits and to appreciate the terrorist threat.

3. Working closely with other governments to ensure that they meet their responsibilities for the protection of U.S. diplomatic and military personnel and facilities abroad.

4. Providing security to foreign diplomats and dignitaries in the United States.

5. Training foreign government officials in security and antiterrorist programs.

6. Working closely with other governments to collect, assess and share intelligence.

7. Improving the legal framework to enable better investigation and prosecution for terrorist offenses.

8. Improving the framework for international cooperation to deal with terrorism.

9. Increasing and sharing antiterrorism technology.

10. Exposing the involvement of states in sponsoring or carrying out acts of terrorism in every possible forum.

11. Cooperating with other countries to persuade or force terrorism-sponsoring states to end such activities.

12. Using force in a judicious manner to prevent or respond to terrorist attacks and to deter future attacks.

13. Searching for appropriate ways of solving legitimate grievances by non-violent means.[179]

Livingstone and Arnold go on to emphasize that there are long-term political implications that are too complex and in turn quite difficult to address. They appreciate that although the options of the overall strategy may appear simple, their application tends to be more problematic. These activities, noted above, depend upon the existence or creation of agreements or understandings, "for without creating the means to realize its objectives, any strategy, however well conceived, is reduced to bluster and hot air, and any country that embraces such a strategy runs the risk of being perceived as a paper tiger in the event a situation arises where it must act."[180]

These authors also incorporate some less savory options that are highly debatable for democratic governments. They leave no doubt as to the flexibility which decision-makers must bring to the choice of responses to meet the terrorist challenge and argue that policymakers must consider all possible options available even if some of the options, such as assassination, must be subsequently discarded as inappropriate or are prohibited at the time.[181]

Needless to say, the discussion of assassination is most contentious. Notwithstanding, in the war between Arab and Jew this method of "dealing" with enemies of the "state" has been employed. Israel's military and intelligence services have a ruthless reputation particularly in their use of kidnapping and assassination. These include the 1979 killing of Ali Hassan Salameh, who planned the 1972 Olympic massacre of eleven Israeli athletes. Salameh was reportedly killed by a remote-controlled car bomb in Beirut. Khalil al-Wazir (a.k.a. Abu Jihad), the second in command of the Palestinian Liberation Organization, was shot to death by an Israeli commando squad in front of his beachfront office in Tunis. (In another, less violent operation, Sheik Abdel Karim Obeid, an important spiritual leader of the Iranian-backed Hezbollah, was seized by Israeli operatives, kidnapped and transported from Lebanon to an Israeli prison facility.) Another Hizballah leader, Abbas Musawi, was ambushed and killed in occupied south Lebanon in 1992. In 1994, the well-known Islamic artist and writer Hani Abed was killed when his car suddenly exploded in the Gaza Strip. Another Islamic Jihad leader, Fathi al-Shiqaqi, was shot five times in a Malta street by two assailants who passed him on a motorcycle in 1995. A year later, Yahiya Ayyash, known as the "engineer" for his knowledge and skill in bomb making, was the target of a decapitation. It was reported that Ayyash was killed when fifty grams of high explosive, secreted in his cellular telephone, detonated during a call.[182] The question of "sanctioned or state-sponsored" assassination has recently resurfaced with the failed Israeli attempt on the head of Hamas's political bureau Khaled Meshal on 25 September 1997 by two Mossad agents using Canadian passports. Anton La Guardi noted in an *Ottawa Citizen* article that "Israel was unrepentant . . . over its bungled attempt to murder a senior member of the Islamic fundamentalist Hamas movement, saying it had a duty to 'fight uncompromisingly against terrorism.'"[183] The Israelis have continued their assassination initiative under the more innocuously named policy of "targeted attacks" which focuses on the liquidation of those Palestinians viewed by Israel as responsible for perpetrating terrorist attacks.[184] In tandem, Yasser Arafat has ordered his commanders to draw up their hit list of top Israelis in the wake of the assassination of Abu Ali Mustafa, the veteran leader of the Popular Front for the Liberation of Palestine (PFLP).[185] Moreover, it is the view of Prime Minister Ariel Sharon that assassination combined with arrests and limited incursions into the Palestinian territories, along with securing access in the territories and along the Green Line, were providing an operational answer to the terrorist threat. The policy of targeted attacks, sometimes referred to as "pinpoint prevention," which has focused on groups such as Hamas and the Islamic Jihad, has accounted for the deaths of up to thirty percent of their core operators, as seen in the actions against such small terrorist organizations such as Islamic Jihad.[186]

In the wake of the terrorist attacks against the World Trade Center and the Pentagon in September 2001, Vice President Dick Cheney promised a thorough reassessment of U.S. intelligence. Secretary of State Colin Powell advised that, considering the attacks, all American laws were under review, including the 1976 Executive Order 12333 signed by President Gerald Ford banning U.S. personnel from engaging in, or conspiring to engage in, assassinations. Moreover, when asked if U.S. or international laws would prevent the American government from assassinating Osama bin Laden, Cheney advised, "Not in my estimation."[187] In the wake of the September 2001 attacks, President George W. Bush gave the go-ahead to the CIA to do whatever was necessary to destroy bin Laden and his al-Qaeda network. This order effectively repealed Executive Order 12333.[188] This action, along with the offer of 175 million dollars (U.S.) for information concerning the terrorist suspects implicated in the 11 September attacks, is indicative that this conflict is unlike any before it, as the enemy does not represent a nation with armed forces. Rather, the American-led coalition of friendly and allied nations is confronted with an enemy that is a loosely structured terrorist network with hidden agents in dozens of countries and which is not dependent on state sponsorship from any one government. Moreover, the United States cannot afford to wage a conventional military campaign against all the countries that have, or continue to, harbor or sponsor terrorists. The list would include such sponsors as Iran, Iraq, Algeria, Syria, Sudan, Somalia, Yemen, Indonesia and Pakistan.[189]

The following chapter will study several examples of terrorist activities faced by Western governments in recent history, and will further explore the range of responses to which they have so far resorted.

NOTES

1. Wardlaw, *Political Terrorism*, 18. See also, Suter, "What Is Terrorism?"

2. Laqueur, *Terrorism*, 16. It is possibly no accident that the book includes the first definition of ideology.

3. Ibid., 18. See also S.G.F. Brandon, "The Zealots: The Ancient Jewish Resistance Against Rome," in Michael Elliot-Bateman (ed.), *The Fourth Dimension of Warfare, Volume 1: Intelligence, Subversion, Resistance.*

4. Ibid., 19.

5. Wardlaw, *Political Terrorism*, 18.

6. Laqueur, *Terrorism*, 22.

7. Ibid., 22–23.

8. Ibid., 50.

9. Ibid., 51.

10. Wardlaw, *Political Terrorism*, 19.

11. Laqueur, *Terrorism*, 55.

12. Wardlaw, *Political Terrorism*, 19.

13. Laqueur, *Terrorism*, 43.

14. Ibid., 44.

15. Wardlaw, *Political Terrorism*, 21.

16. Ibid., 22.

17. Ibid. For a thought-provoking view of the definition of terrorism and its evolution see Gearty, *The Future of Terrorism*. The issue of defining terrorism has been problematic since the word came into existence. For a view of this issue and the ramifications, see Gee, "I Know You Are, but What Am I"; and Edwards, "Islamic States Reject Terror Definition." The September 2001 attacks against the United States had a global effect as former "freedom fighters" were suddenly equated to terrorists and a number of "Muslim rebel armies found themselves on the wrong side of the global propaganda battlefield." See York, "World's Rebels Chilled by bin Laden Effect."

18. Kupperman and Trent, *Terrorism: Threat, Reality, Response*, 19.

19. Ibid., 20.

20. Marcus, "Arafat Shoots Down Hope: The Palestinian Leader Is Unable to Make the Switch from Guerrilla Warrior to Statesman."

21. St. John, "Analysis and Response of a Decade of Terrorism," 3. See also Wilkinson, "Terrorism: Motivations and Causes."

22. Ibid.

23. For an assessment of Ché's legacy see Diebel, "Disputed Legacy of a Revolutionary" and Kelly, "Curses and Dreams: Ernesto 'Che' Guevara, the Implacable Revolutionary," 1–14.

24. St. John, "Analysis and Response of a Decade of Terrorism," 3.

25. "Aviation: The Skyjackers," 29.

26. Ibid., 30.

27. Ibid.

28. Ibid.

29. Ibid.

30. Ibid.

31. "Airlines vs. Skyjackers," 13.

32. Ibid.

33. "Aviation: The Skyjackers," 30. For a more contemporary and realistic view, see "In the Mind of the Terrorist."

34. Ibid.

35. See "Profile of a Terrorist" and Hammer, "Portrait of a Terrorist." One Canadian woman who was among the passengers hijacked on an Indian Airlines jet for eight days in 1999 noted that the terrorists were, "intelligent, well organized and exceptionally cruel." See Wright and McGrory, "Kidnapper's Release a 'Disgrace'" and Schmetzer, "Spawning a New Breed of Terrorist: Religious Zealots Believe Their Deaths Will Be Rewarded, Experts on Islam Say." According to Schmetzer, "experts studying Islam's radical movements believe the missions will be carried out by a new breed of religious zealots indoctrinated in Islamic schools with the belief their sacrifice will bring them eternal life in paradise and instant martyrdom on Earth. Their determination to seek death makes them far more lethal than predecessors." See also Sprinzak, "Rational Fanatics." Sprinzak notes that the secretary-general of the Palestinian Islamic Jihad underlined the idea that, "Our enemy possesses the most sophisticated weapons in the world and its army is trained to a very high standard. . . . We have nothing with which to repel killing and thuggery against us except the weapon of martyrdom. It is easy and costs us only our lives. . . . human bombs cannot be defeated, not even by nuclear bombs." See also Potter, "Settlers Live under the Gun in Besieged Israeli Outpost; 'There Is No Defence Against Someone Who Will Kill Himself to Kill You,' Soldier Says in the Wake of Suicide Attack," and "Outsmarting Suicide Terrorists." The summer of 2001 saw a number of suicide bombings, underlining a religious fervor as well as the determination to inflict casualties upon the Israeli and American nations. See "Palestinians Are Not Afraid of Death"; Amr, "Militants Say Israeli Wrongs Drive Suicide Bombers"; Philps, "'Happy Man with a Bomb Strapped to His Waist." According to this latter article, sixty-eight percent of Palestinians support suicide bombing. Philps notes that, "the aspiration to be a suicide bomber is nothing outlandish. Iyad Nasr, a cousin, said: 'The Israelis have tanks, F-16s and Apache helicopters. We have only stones and our bare bodies. It is a way to create a balance of terror.'" See also Barr, "The World of a Suicide Bomber." Women will likely join the ranks of suicide bombers as some have responded to the *fatwa*, or decree, issued by the High Islamic Council in Saudi Arabia in August 2001, urging women to join the fight. Mahnaimi, "Israeli Fear as Women Join Suicide Squad." Moscow is also concerned that a long-term terrorist problem is the Caucasus, where Islamic suicide bombers are intensifying their operations. The first suicide attack occurred when two female terrorists drove a car fitted with a bomb into the Russian base at Alkhan-Iount, just south of Grozny. See "Second Wind for Moscow's Enemies," and "Polish Border Guards Arrest 3 Chechens With Explosives, Ammunition." See also McKittrick, "The Irish Bombers: What Sort of People Are They?," and MacFarquhar, "Portrait of A Suicide Bomber: Devout, Apolitical and Angry." For an insight into the suicide martyr phenomenon, see Goldberg, "The Martyr Strategy: What Does the New Phase of Terrorism Signify?" More recently, we have witnessed the evolution of what is known as *leaderless resistance,* part of the white supremacist methodology. Essentially, there are small cells and/or individuals, some working in pairs, acting independently. Such individuals have been called *lone wolves.* Experts argue this situation has come about as a consequence of new technology,

which in turn saw the disappearance of hierarchy. The novel *Hunter* by William Pierce, the head of the neo-Nazi National Alliance, dramatized the idea of the solitary white warrior. See Thomas, "New Face of Terror Crimes: 'Lone Wolf' Weaned on Hate." For an excellent article on recent views relating to a suicide bomber, see Lelyveld, "All Suicide Bombers Are Not Alike" and Schuler, "Inside the Mind of a Suicide Bomber." The use of a young female suicide bomber in January 2002 forced Israeli authorities to consider sweeping changes to their security policy. See Walker and Beeston, "Israel on Alert for More Female Suicide Bombers." See also, Gilmore, "Female Bomber Raises Israel's Security Fears."

36. "Mideast: Coup in the Sky," 41.
37. Ibid., 42.
38. Ibid.
39. "Algeria: Skyway Robbery," 52.
40. Ibid.
41. Ibid.
42. Doty, "Air Crimes Convention Supported Heavily," 60. The nations that had ratified the agreement as of November 1968 were the Republic of China, Denmark, Norway, the Philippines, Portugal and Sweden.
43. Ibid.
44. Ibid.
45. Ibid.
46. Ibid.
47. Wilkinson, *Terrorism And The Liberal State,* 220.
48. Watkins, "Air Transport: Federal Action in Hijackings Urged," 24.
49. Ibid.
50. Ibid.
51. Ibid.
52. Ibid.
53. Ibid.
54. Ibid., 25.
55. Ibid.
56. "The Search For a Way to Stop 'Skyjacking,'" 34.
57. Ibid.
58. Ibid.
59. Ibid.
60. Ibid.
61. "What Can Be Done About Skyjacking?," 20.
62. Ibid.
63. Ibid.
64. Ibid.
65. "Hijack Detector Tested by FAA," 53.
66. Ibid.
67. Ibid.
68. Ibid.
69. Ibid.
70. "Airlines, Government Accelerate Efforts at Hijacking Prevention," 33.
71. Ibid.

72. Ibid.

73. Ibid.

74. "Skyjacking: Holding Pattern," 34.

75. Ibid.

76. Ibid.

77. Ibid.

78. Ibid.

79. Ibid.

80. "IFALPA Mounts Anti-Hijack Drive," 22.

81. Ibid. See also Keyser, "World Must Wake Up, Israeli Pilot Warns."

82. Ibid.

83. Hotz, "More on Hijacking," 11.

84. Ibid.

85. Ibid.

86. "Death to Hijackers," 50.

87. Ibid.

88. "The Hijack War," 20. An untitled *The Christian Science Monitor* report (25 July 1996) noted that a small group of Middle Eastern men planned "Op Bojinga" aimed at blowing up a total of twelve American passenger airlines over a forty-eight–hour period over the Pacific in January 1995. This would have likely made a similar impact to the 1970 Dawson Field seizure, albeit this time with an estimated toll of up to 4,000 casualties. Also, in August 1999 a hijacker stabbed to death the pilot of an All Nippon Airways 747 after takeoff from Tokyo. After seizing a stewardess and threatening her with a twelve-inch knife, he gained entrance into the cockpit where he briefly flew the aircraft carrying more than 500 passengers. The hijacker was subsequently over-powered by crew members. See Hindell and Sapsted, "747 Pilot Killed as 500 Hijacked."

89. Ibid., 21.

90. Ibid.

91. "Terror Attacks on Air Travel—What Can Be Done," 17.

92. According to the American National Research Council, the machinery/technology is available to see through a traveler's clothes and determine if they have a weapon, a bomb or illegal drugs. This new technology, called "imaging," is a computer using electromagnets or X-rays to see through clothes and produce an image of the body and any foreign objects. This technology can generate images ranging from fuzzy body outlines to sharp X-ray pictures. Meanwhile, trace detection samples the air around the clothes and the person, identifying particles or vapors from explosives. What would keep this technology from being employed is that people may be very sensitive about using such intrusive means. See also Hoagland, "Americans Must Confront a New Age of Terrorism." Unfortunately, even with all the physical and technical methods of security in place, weapons still elude security measures. In July 1999, a woman carried a loaded .357 revolver in her carry-on luggage on a flight from Phoenix, Arizona to Toronto, Canada. Somehow the gun was not detected by security at the Skyharbor International Airport in Phoenix. Elton, "U.S. Woman Had .357-calibre Gun on Toronto Flight." Airport security became front page news following an incident with a passenger who successfully passed through airport security in Paris and boarded a flight for Miami. The

passenger, Richard C. Reid, had a bomb in his black baseball shoes. Reid was seated in a window seat and intended to blow a hole in the fuselage. See Shahin, "FBI Builds Case Against Shoe Bomber."

93. "Terror Attacks on Air Travel—What Can Be Done," 17.

94. Ibid., 18.

95. Ibid.

96. Ibid.

97. Ibid., 19. See also "Overseas: Guards, Detectors, Searches," 19.

98. "Washington Whispers," 8.

99. An untitled Associated Press report from 13 December 1996 argued for a more aggressive method of profiling. "Computer profiles of airline passengers would look at their travel histories and possible criminal pasts to identify potential terrorists under (new) airport security reforms." This and other recommendations were drawn from an FAA advisory panel that called for tighter airport security. For an example of cooperation in airport security, see "Anti-Terrorist Teams at Philippine Airports on Red Alert." On 17 August, an advisory was issued stating that Osama bin Laden had ordered the bombing of a U.S. airliner, thereby prompting increased security measures.

100. "When Armed Guards Ride Your Plane." 23.

101. Interview with senior British Parachute Regiment officer, London, England (4 October 1997). See also McKittrick, "The IRA's Grand Strategy."

102. La Guardia, "Israeli Commandos Killed in Botched Raid on Lebanon." A total of twelve naval commandos were killed in an Arab ambush. This incident appears to have sparked the establishment of an Israeli army school to teach guerrilla tactics. The school incorporates tactical training in mock Arab villages, and provides instruction in battle tactics. See Goldberg, "Israel Opens 'Rambo Academy' to Train Troops for Guerrilla War." One Israeli special operation was aimed at hunting down Mahum Abu Hunud, one of the key Hamas suicide bomb engineers. During this operation, three Israeli operatives from the Duvdevan brigade—consisting of specially selected Israeli soldiers who are trained to operate clandestinely in the West Bank and Gaza—were standing on a roof and were shot by their own comrades who misidentified them as Arabs. Unfortunately, Abu Hunud escaped, and an ensuing investigation ordered the dismissal of the Duvdevan commanding officer and most of their experienced officers. In October 2000, Duvdevan operators succeeded in capturing eight Palestinians suspected of partaking in the brutal lynching of two Israeli reserve soldiers at a police station in Ramallah. According to a report, volunteers for the Duvdevan use their language skills, knowledge of Arab culture and religious traditions, and appearance to assist them in operating in Arab society. Mahnaimi, "Israelis Risk All in Undercover Missions: Elite Squad Goes Behind Enemy Lines Posing as Arabs." Also, O'Sullivan, "Israel Captures Members of Palestinian Lynch Mob."

103. "Conference Exchanges Anti-Hijacking Data," 19.

104. Ibid. These included the U.S.S.R., Czechoslovakia, Poland and Hungary.

105. Ibid.

106. Ibid.

107. The Hague Convention for the Suppression of the Unlawful Seizure of Aircraft required contracting states to extradite apprehended hijackers to their country of origin or to prosecute them under the judicial code of the recipient state.

Significant clauses were included allowing political offense exceptions to the requirement of extradition.

108. "Pilots Spur Anti-Hijacking Drive," 19.
109. "Command Posts Manned by Key Braniff Officials During Hijack," 20.
110. Ibid.
111. Ibid.
112. "Axworthy Says 'Give In' If It Saves Lives."
113. "Hijacking Ordeal Ends in Baghdad." See also Farrell and Cobain, "Security Staff Were Behind Hijacking: Gun Brought Aboard in Pilot's Forgotten Travel Bag."
114. "Skyjacking: Death at the Terminal," 18.
115. "Skyjacking: 'A Calculated Risk,'" 24.
116. "Skyjacking: Death At the Terminal," 18.
117. "Progress in War on Skyjackers," 25.
118. Ibid.
119. Ibid.
120. Ibid.
121. "El Al Stresses Terrorist Security, Advises Other Airlines in Tel Aviv," 26.
122. Ibid.
123. Ibid.
124. Ibid.
125. United States, Department of State, "U.S. Deposits Ratification of Hijacking Convention," 371.
126. "Skyjacking: The Deadly Dilemma," 21.
127. Ibid.
128. Ibid.
129. "Skyjacking: Take Me Along," 47–48.
130. Ibid., 48. In January 2002, it was announced that armed plain-clothes members of the Royal Canadian Mounted Police are traveling on selected flights, both domestic and international. See "Armed Mounties Now on Many Flights."
131. Ibid.
132. Ibid.
133. Ibid.
134. "Costa Rica: Terrorizing Terrorists," 24.
135. Ibid.
136. Ibid.
137. Ibid.
138. Ibid.
139. Ibid.
140. St. John, "Analysis and Response of a Decade of Terrorism," 4. Needless to say, hijacking has continued unabated to this day. See also Sudam, "English, Trickery Help Pilots Foil Yemeni Hijacker," and "Mauritius: Alert over Possible Aircraft Hijacking by Hizbullah Supporters."
141. Malik, "Three Killed as Saudis Storm Highjacked Russian Jet." In another hijacking, the eleven Afghanis subsequently argued at their trial that they were legally justified in hijacking the airliner, passengers and crew to Britain because of the Taliban. In the course of the trial, prosecutor Bruce Houlder told jurors that they must decide whether, under British law, the terror, oppression and atrocities

of Afghanistan's ruling Taliban gave the orchestrators of the hijacking justification to take over the plane. "Taleban Oppression Justified Hijacking of Plane."

142. See Craig and Hosenball, "U.S. Agents to Patrol Airports in Britain."

143. Discussions with a Canadian intelligence officer, Ottawa, Ontario, Canada, (1 March 1999).

144. Ibid.

145. Bellavance, "FLQ Killing Was Used to Promote Unity in 1970."

146. Gelman and Thomas, "Banality and Terror," 60.

147. Ibid.

148. Ibid.

149. This aerial bombing finally saw the arrests of two men on 27 October 2000. The Royal Canadian Mounted Police, after a fifteen-year, $30 million investigation, arrested Ripudaman Singh Malik of Vancouver and Ajaib Singh Bagri of Kamloops. It was announced that more arrests are expected soon. Bailey, "Two B.C. Men Charged in Bombing That Killed 329." See also "14 Years Later, No Charges Laid in Bombing of Air India Jetliner. Legal Team's Only Decision Has Been to Double Number of Lawyers; Exasperated Sikh Community 'Sick and Tired' of Long-Drawn-Out Probe." The 1985 Air India Flight 182, en route from Toronto to Bombay, exploded over the Atlantic Ocean, killing 329 passengers.

150. The trial for the destruction of the Pan Am airliner over Lockerbie, Scotland in December 1988, which killed 270 persons, continues with the two Libyan suspects. A source close to the proceedings said the trial will last more than a year and the prosecution has prepared approximately 1,058 witnesses. Jamil, "2 February Set for the Lockerbie Trial." See also Nacheman, "Terrorist Takes Stand in Pan Am Bomb Trial." Due to the international complexity of this case, the trial is being held under Scottish law at a former American military base that has been declared by the Dutch government as Scottish territory for the duration of the trial. This was a complex, multinational agreement that persuaded Muammar Gaddafi, the Libyan leader, to hand over the suspects.

151. "Israel Hails Argentine Court Statement on Bombing." The Argentine Supreme Court has blamed the Islamic Jihad and the Hezbollah for the 1992 car bombing of the Israeli Embassy that killed twenty-nine people.

152. "Islamic Group Claims Bombing."

153. Gelman and Thomas, "Banality and Terror," 60. Trickey, "Six Months After Sept. 11, Life in the U.S. Returns to Normal." According to Trickey, the official death toll in New York City due to the September terrorist assaults is 2,830. Another 189 died in the aircraft that slammed into the Pentagon and 44 died in the plane that crashed in a field outside of Pittsburgh. For New York, these numbers are not finalized, and may never be.

154. Spinner, "Life Insurers Want Study of Future Terrorism's Cost."

155. "Hijackers Worked 'On Amazingly Little Money,' but Banking Hints Were Missed."

156. Mitrovica, "Terror Attacks Rare, U.S. Report Says, but Getting Deadlier." According to Paul Koring, "Since the end of the Vietnam War more than 25 years ago, terrorists have killed more U.S. soldiers and sailors than have died in combat in all U.S. military operations overseas during that same period, including the invasions of Grenada, Panama and Haiti, the Persian Gulf and Kosovo wars, air strikes against Libya and Iraq and peacekeeping missions in Lebanon and Soma-

lia." Koring, "U.S. Faces a Growing Terror: the Military Has Lost More People to Terrorism than in Wars since 1975, a Trend Paul Koring Writes, Expected to Escalate." According to this article, U.S. military killed or missing in action since 1975 totals 246 and the number of U.S. military killed from terrorist actions totals 319.

157. Ibid.

158. Rosenblum, "Think Again: This Is War."

159. Mitrovica, "Terror Attacks Rare, U.S. Report Says, but Getting Deadlier."

160. Bailey, "Hunt for Air India Bombs Has Cost about $26 Million." The 1985 Air India bombing has been the most expensive RCMP investigation to date.

161. "Lockerbie Crash: Syria Linked to Bomb." Per this article, "The bomb that blew up a Pan Am jet . . . may have been aimed at six CIA employees and arranged by a Syrian terrorist, not the two Libyans currently accused in the blast and being protected by Libyan leader Moammar Khadafy."

162. United States, *Public Report of the Vice President's Task Force on Combatting Terrorism*, 1.

163. Church, "Targeting Gaddafi," 22.

164. Ibid.

165. Ibid., 23.

166. Ibid.

167. Ibid., 22.

168. Ibid., 24.

169. Ibid.

170. Ibid., 25.

171. "Arens Says Syrians Bombed Marines' Building in Lebanon." It should be underlined that Arens is not an unbiased observer and it has since become apparent that Syria and Iran assisted the orchestrators of the bombing of the United States Marine Corps barracks; however, as noted above both went unpunished. See also Hodgson, "Terrorism Will Never Go Away."

172. Hodgson, "Terrorism Will Never Go Away."

173. Elmagd, "Gadhafi Supports U.S. Right to Retaliate."

174. "The Rise of World Terrorism," 27.

175. United States, *Public Report of the Vice President's Task Force on Combatting Terrorism*, 4–5.

176. During the 1999 NATO conflict over Kosovo, the issue of assassinating Yugoslav President Slobodan Milosevic surfaced. However, the American Deputy Attorney General Eric Holder told reporters that bombing Milosevic's home was within the guidelines provided to the military at the commencement of the bombing offensive. See "Cold War Legacy: U.S. Ban on Assassination." Some nations in the past have seemed less reticent to conduct such operations. For an overview regarding East Germany's Department IV (responsible for assassination), see Woodhead, "Stasi Spy Files Reveal Secret Hit Squad: High-tech Assassination Team Operated until the Fall of Berlin Wall in 1989."

177. Livingstone, *The War Against Terrorism*, 175.

178. This includes border checkpoints between nations. Recent media reports have underlined this situation along the Canadian-American border. See McKenna, "Porous Canadian Border a Menace, U.S. Legislators Told," Greenaway, "Canada 'A Gateway for Terrorists, Thugs,'" and Fife, "CSIS Insider Blasts Lax Security in Canada." See also Bellavance and Bell, "Canada Soft on Terrorism, Alliance MP

Charges: Jewish Congress Urges Ottawa to Step up the Fight," and Bronskill,
"Canada Won't Outlaw Terror Groups: Liberals Stop Short of Ban for Fear of
Alienating Ethnic Communities." A hijack attempt occurred at the Pearson Airport
in Toronto when a man bolted past security guards as he was going through a metal
detector. He subsequently charged onto a plane scheduled to go to Lisbon. Fortunately, he was unarmed and was seized by police authorities. See Green and
Mahoney, "Hijack Attempt Sparks Security Review." In the wake of the conflict
in Kosovo, Canadian authorities were greatly concerned over a possible terrorist
attack against NATO representatives as well as the possibility of violent anti-NATO
demonstrations. Magnish, "After the War Toronto Gears up for NATO Meeting
amid Concerns over Terrorism."

179. Livingstone and Arnold, *Fighting Back: Winning The War Against Terrorism,* 230.

180. Ibid.

181. Ibid., 231.

182. See "A History of Assassination."

183. La Guardia, "Israel Asserts 'National Duty' to Assassinate." In mid-August
1999, Hizballah's leadership accused Israel of assassinating one of their leaders,
Hajj Ali Dib, in a car explosion in south Lebanon. Marenko, "No Israeli Reaction
to Assassination of Hizballah Senior." See also "Hezbollah Commander Killed by
Bomb, Lebanese Guerrillas Blame Israel for Attack on Abu Hassan, Vow it 'Will
Not Go Unpunished.'" For an informative overview of assassination, see Rapoport,
Assassination & Terrorism. The Israelis continue to employ assassination as seen
in December 2000 with the assassination of Ibrahim Beni Ouda, an expert bomb
maker and member of the Ezzedine al Qassam Brigade of the military wing of
Hamas. Israeli intelligence—Shin Bet—feared that after his release from Nablus
prison on a weekend pass, Ouda would "go underground" and commence planning further terrorist activities. Reportedly, the Israelis detonated explosives in the
headrest of the car he was using, decapitating him. Mahnaimi, "Terrorist's Trip
to Oblivion," Rose, "A Time and a Place for Political Assassination," Harel, "Fear
Sends Hamas Men Back to Jail," Lahoud, "IDF Officer Confirms Tracking down
and Killing Militants," Kalman, "Israelis Kill Officer in Arafat Guard: Palestinian
Led Double Life as Head of Terrorist Cell, Army Says of Target," and Rudge, "Assassination Also Carries Risks to the Assassin." For more details, see Lavie and
Philps, "Israel Assassinates Palestinian Officer: Rocket Attack on Car; Barak Con-
gratulates Army on Death of Arafat Security Man," and Kiley, "Israelis Kill Guerrilla Chief: Hezbollah Kingpin Had Links to Arafat." It was reported that the Israeli
government had drawn up plans to assassinate a number of Arafat's closest aides.
According to the report, "Israeli sources insisted, however, that this was only the
beginning. They said Mr. Sharon had ordered the army and security services to
drawn [sic] up plans to kill senior Arafat lieutenants." The report further noted
that the targets were believed to include Marwan Barghouti, the head of the
Tanziom (Arafat's militia on the West Bank), Brigadier General Tawfiq Tirawi, head
of the Palestinian intelligence on the West Bank, and Mussa Afaraft, head of the
military intelligence service. It was reported that Sharon said that "Yasser Arafat
has remained a terrorist leader. This is well known around the world, and Israel
will defend itself against terrorism." Mahnaimi, "Israel Plans to Assassinate Arafat

Aides: Sharon Pledges to Strike 'Those Who Attack Us and Those Who Send Them.'" The summer of 2001 witnessed the saga of assassination orchestrated by the Israeli undercover units. Imad Abu Sneineh, 25, was reportedly eliminated in what Israel called an "early retirement" of those believed to be orchestrating acts of violence. Graham, "Israel Calls its Assassination of Enemies 'Early Retirement.'" Israeli authorities are split as to the effectiveness of the program; however, the assassinations do have a decisive effect on small organizations like Islamic Jihad, which has reportedly lost more than a third of its activist core. This "pinpoint prevention" policy remains focused on two highly dangerous groups: Hamas and the Islamic Jihad. Harel, "Sharon Says Killing Terrorists Works." According to Harel, the "present efforts are concentrated on suicide bombers and their operators. In most cases, those authorizing assassinations—the prime minister, the defense minister, the chief of staff and the head of Shin Bet—agree on the targets, but there have been a few cases in which there has been disagreement on whether a target is actually a 'ticking bomb' and whether it would not in fact be preferable to make an arrest." See also, "The Consequences of Selective Killing."

On the American scene, Christian Coalition President Pat Robertson has indicated that assassinating troublesome world leaders is an option and is preferable to the stated U.S. policy that prohibits assassination. Robertson critics took note that such a strategy would be contrary to biblical teachings. His response was "in my Bible, Jesus never said anything about assassinating heads of state." Rosin, "Robertson Espouses Assassin Solution." See McAllister, "Should He Just Be Killed? As Tempting as it May Be, Assassination Is a Bad Idea." Also, Beltrane, "'Let's Kill Saddam': Frustrated Americans Ponder Murderous Tactics." The reasons for not conducting an assassination were aptly underlined in Binyon, "Saddam's Foes Draw Line at Assassination." Binyon noted the difficulties of locating and infiltrating Saddam's entourage as well as the fallout from a failed attempt, which would provide Saddam with both a political and a propaganda victory. Moreover, such an action would pre-empt any attempt for a suitable diplomatic solution and, as well, provide Saddam with a reason for not negotiating. More importantly, however, should an assassination be successful the perpetrators would be responsible for maintaining political stability in the wake of Saddam.

Another subject that considers himself a target for assassination is Osama bin Laden, who has all but admitted to the 1998 bombings of the American embassies in West Africa; there are also indications that bin Laden was involved in the attack on the USS Cole in Aden in October 2000 and in the New York City and Washington bombings by suicide hijackers in September 2001. See West, "'Fingerprints of bin Laden Are All over These Attacks': Terrorist Strikes in Yemen Start of New Campaign by Saudi Millionaire, Western Experts Believe," and Taqui, "MI-6, CIA Accused of Planning to Assassinate bin Ladin." See also Zakaria, "U.S. Trying to Pry bin Laden out of Afghanistan"; Bone, Hussein, Binyon, Theodoulou and Evans, "The Hunt for Osama bin Laden; Russia and America Have Become Allies Against the Muslim Pimpernel," and Rachid, "U.S. Seeks Alliance with Moscow for Raid on bin Laden." To conduct an operation against bin Laden, Russian assistance would be critical, particularly given their knowledge and experience in operating in Afghanistan and their own considerable counterterrorist capability. A joint U.S.-Russia "snatch" operation against bin Laden would be considered an ideal way of dealing with this issue. Russia was infuriated in February 2000 by bin Laden's call for a jihad against Russia and bin Laden's call for global support by all Muslims for an independent Chechnya.

For an insight into the international aspect, see Leppard, Nuki and Walsh, "Britain's 'Murder Inc.' Plotted to Kill Rebel Leader." It has been underlined that American President Dwight Eisenhower had authorized the assassination of the Congolese premier Patrice Lumumba in 1960. However, the CIA was not able to "takeout" Lumumba before he was captured and killed by Congolese rivals on 17 January 1961. For other insights into assassination, see Nutter, *The CIA's Black Ops: Covert Action, Foreign Policy and Democracy*. The discussion of targeting continues in Weinberger, "When Can We Target the Leaders?" See also Schiff, "A Lack of Purpose in the Choice of Targets." This article notes that those who dispatch suicide bombers should be targeted for assassination. "Their inclusion in such a list would be in keeping with the biblical injunction that, when faced with a would-be murderer, you should strike first."

184. O'Sullivan, "Defense Officials Rethinking Terror Responses."

185. Mahnaimi, "Palestinians Draw up Israeli Hit List."

186. Harel, "Sharon Says Killing Terrorists Works."

187. Shala-Esa, "U.S. Vows Reassessment of Spy Operations after Attacks" and Krauthammer, "In Defense of 'Assassination.'"

188. Fletcher, Evans and Loyd, "CIA Licence to Kill Bin Laden"; "'Bullets Will Fly' in Terrorist Hunt"; and Woodward, "Bush to CIA: Do 'Whatever Necessary' to Kill Bin Laden."

189. Roslin, "When the State Turns Assassin."

2

International Aspects of Counterterrorism

TERRORISM AS AN INTERNATIONAL PHENOMENON IN RECENT HISTORY

Although it is well known that terrorist activities have been an integral part of conventional and guerrilla warfare, the type of political violence that we are experiencing today is, in reality, a relatively new phenomenon. Some observers argue that it should be considered "a distinct and significant new mode of armed conflict."[1] In fact, many analysts argue that since terrorist activity began increasing in the late 1960s, we have entered a new age of conflict. It has been stated that "terrorism represents a cheap and effective method of warfare against more powerful adversaries whose arsenals and weapons are of little comfort against small bands of marauding proxy forces armed with the latest technologies, imagination, and stealth. Today international terrorists and their patrons are, in effect, at war."[2] Today's terrorism comes under the rubric of "asymmetric threats," which is a term used to describe attempts to circumvent or undermine an enemy's strength while concomitantly exploiting his weaknesses. This is done by using methods and tactics that differ significantly from the opponent's usual mode of operations. This mode of threat is used to describe weapons and tactics that enemies could employ in order to negate or circumvent the technological, numerical, economic or military supremacy of a Western nation. In that regard, asymmetric threats run the spectrum from threat or intimidation, civil disobedience and criminal action to low-intensity conflict. The activities themselves range from computer hacking or computer warfare to terrorism, chemical, biological or nuclear threats, as well as other like or unlike issues. The key is the utilization of surprise in the use of weapons and concepts at hand but also employing these in ways not expected by the stronger nation. The attacks on 11 September 2001 underlined the destruction and psychological aspects of asymmetric operations by terrorists in a high-concept low-tech approach in their planning of such operations.

The twentieth-century theories of guerrilla warfare, including the *people's war* concepts fathered by Mao, combined with the turbulent political environment of the era following World War II, the advent of mass communications and the explosion of technology—especially the Internet—have been key determinants in producing the terrorism we know today.[3] For the most part, our technologically oriented age has thrust this type of violence upon us. Modern technological developments have made international terrorism possible. International jet travel provides global mobility enabling terrorists to strike on any continent. Modern media, thanks to the communication satellite, provide real-time access to a global audience. Meanwhile, modern weapons technology and high explosives are available to those who want them.[4] Indeed, as we are experiencing on a daily basis, modern society presents a spectrum of highly vulnerable targets, from airliners to nuclear reactors to our homes and bank accounts thanks to the computer and the Internet. Therefore, once the utility of terrorism was demonstrated it was inevitable that this mode of violence would be imitated on a global scale.[5]

Nations have become more aware of the high costs of conventional and nuclear warfare and the resulting impact of such activities on their societies. Terrorists, however, have few such restrictions:

> In contrast to the increased constraints on governments in the conduct of war, terrorists have adopted the concept of total warfare—they recognize no civilian noncombatants. Terrorists may attack anything, anywhere, anytime. Over the past . . . years, the spectrum of terrorist targets has expanded to include diplomats, embassies, airliners, airline offices, tourist agencies, tourists, hotels, airports, trains, train stations, reactors, refineries, restaurants, pubs, churches, temples, synagogues, nuns, priests, the Pope, schools, students, and nurseries. This widening of the range of 'legitimate' targets and the resultant narrowing of the category of innocent bystanders parallels and extends the twentieth-century concept of total war.[6]

The two world wars, Korea, Vietnam, the Gulf conflict, the air campaign over Kosovo, Afghanistan, and the ongoing war against terrorism reflect the industrial, nuclear and technological underpinnings of our global society. World Wars I and II were the wars of mass production in which superiority in forces and equipment prevailed. Korea was the reflection of the strategy of confrontation and limited war, while Vietnam demonstrated to all concerned the frustration of a super-power, technologically superior, engaging an enemy in a low-intensity war, winning militarily perhaps, but losing politically. More recently, the second Gulf War demonstrated the high-tech underpinnings of modern warfare and the importance of both coalitional warfare and force projection. Today major forms of international "warfare" are low-intensity conflict and terrorism.[7] This is easy to comprehend when one considers that a large

> portion of the economy is now devoted to the creation, collection, retrieval, transfer, and dissemination of information, and political power increasingly rests on the ability to create or control information. Terrorists are primitive psychological warriors in an information war. Terrorism reflects the current age of instant communications and rapid mobility.[8]

Brian Jenkins underlines that the success of terrorism has much to do with the perception of a nation's capability to deal with such crises, proposing that:

> Public perceptions of government standing and competence in combatting terrorism are based not on overall performance, but rather on performance in a few dramatic hostage incidents, where the government, of course, suffers disadvantages from the outset. The public sees the government only in crisis, demonstrably unable to provide security for its citizens, sometimes yielding to terrorists to save lives, unable to bring its enemies to justice. A rescue attempt that succeeds adds immeasurably to a nation's image of military prowess. An attempt that fails does incalculable damage.[9]

Many statistics exist to quantify the activities, numbers, types, locations and targets of international terrorists. It was reported in 1986 that "incidents of terrorism—those involving citizens or territory of more than one country—have doubled in number since 1975, to slightly over 800 last year [1985]."[10] Notwithstanding the bombings in August 1998 in Kenya and Tanzania, there are analysts who believe terrorism has been in decline in recent years.[11] *Patterns of Global Terrorism: 1997*, published by the American State Department, reported that there were a total of 304 acts of international terrorism, one of the lowest annual totals since 1971.[12] According to *Patterns of Global Terrorism: 1998*, the number of acts of international terrorism dropped to 273 attacks. However, in 1998 there was a record high toll of 741 people killed and 5,952 injured in terrorist attacks.[13] In 2000, there were 423 terrorist acts, an increase of eight percent from the 392 attacks in 1999. The death toll for 2000 was 405, and 791 were wounded.[14] The year 2001 witnessed a dramatic increase due to the audacious attacks on 11 September of that year.

Many commentators agree that terrorist violence is, and will likely remain, an integral part of international relations. As Scotland Yard's counterterrorist specialist George Churchill-Coleman stated, "Terrorism is with us now, whether you like it or not. You've got to adjust your way of life to that."[15] This mentality has now reached the American scene as the head of the newly created Office of Homeland Security, Tom Ridge, noted, "We need to accept that the possibility of terrorism is a permanent condition for the foreseeable future." He stated, "We just have to accept it."[16] At airports there is a "get on with the job" attitude and in daily living one must accept the need to be on guard, like steering clear of suspicious packages and reporting them to the local police. One columnist wrote, "By not surrounding the (terrorist) incident with hysterical posturing, we cut it down to size. We make it seem a nuisance rather than a cataclysm. We stifle its capacity to instill terror. We decline to be afraid."[17] In that regard, Great Britain is one of the few nations which is intimately familiar with terrorism and its impact. Lacking any other alternative, the British have essentially learned to live with the threats and the bombings. Moreover, the British have learned to live with intrusive surveillance cameras, the cost of bomb insurance (3.2 billion dollars a year), as well as a higher awareness of the threat that has been assimilated into the society over the years, particularly since the late 1960s. Accordingly, "The British approach to terrorism, developed over many years, seems natural in a culture that places great store on a 'stiff upper lip.'"[18]

The prognosis becomes ever more frightening as terrorists seek out softer targets, as witnessed in the 1998 bombings of the American embassies in Kenya and Tanzania. This is because international police and security agencies will, for the most part, strengthen the defenses of consulates, embassies and residences,[19] and will provide other forms of personal security for the more likely terrorist targets. Therefore, terrorist attacks will probably become more indiscriminate. The bombing campaigns in Paris during the summers of 1986 and 1995, aimed at government buildings, restaurants and cafes, the bombings in London during the spring of 1992 of commuter train stations and the financial district, and the use of sarin in the subway in Japan by the Aum Shinrikyo[20] in 1995, and the February 2001 reported discovery by the British police of a terrorist plot to release sarin into the London underground system[21] as well as the suicide hijacking of four airliners in September 2001 are examples of what we may expect.[22] (Other examples of indiscriminate terrorism are the strikes at airports such as those in December 1985, in Rome[23] and Vienna.[24]) Furthermore, targets abound in highly developed industrialized societies and analysts anticipate that terrorist groups will begin targeting vital points such as "computer systems, power grids and other key links of industrial societies."[25] Reports underline that terrorists are expanding their interests in nuclear,[26] chemical,[27] and biological weapons[28] as well as information warfare.[29] Some of these concerns were highlighted in December 1999 when the Solicitor General of Canada, Lawrence MacAulay, told the House of Commons that Canada needed to strengthen the government's capacity to address the threat of a nuclear, biological or chemical attack by terrorists. Although the possibility of such an attack happening was low, Mr. MacAulay felt all levels of government must be prepared to deal with such eventualities.[30] His concerns followed warnings by scientists of the Health Protection Branch that a release of the deadly anthrax bacteria in a major Canadian population center could kill upwards of 35,000 and cost 6.5 billion to the health care system, underlining the fact that medical facilities were not prepared to deal with such an incident. In the fall of 2001, a series of letters containing the anthrax virus were mailed to media centers in New York City. The letters were sent to ABC, NBC and CBS, and were orchestrated to attain the maximum amount of media coverage, while concomitantly stirring up popular fear and anxiety about these and other possible attacks. At the time of writing, anthrax had claimed only four victims; however, the fear and anxiety that it caused was well out of proportion to the threat posed. The media hype played directly into the hands of the terrorists.[31] Another issue that relates to this is that of bio-weapons scientists who represent a valuable resource to those nations developing bio-weapons, such as Iran.[32]

This type of weapon has been described, by some, as the *unseen arsenal.* Chemical and biological agents can take up to a minute to kill an adult and have been used by some unscrupulous nations as weapons. Sarin, for example, attacks the human nervous system and can kill a healthy human adult within two to fifteen minutes after initial exposure. The victim reportedly experiences blurred vision, tightness of the chest, nausea, as well as vomiting, convulsions, fluctuations in heart rate, a loss of consciousness, a seizure, eventual paralysis and death. In the case of anthrax, it takes one to six days and can kill within a day if left untreated. In the nascent stages, anthrax can be treated with penicillin. Pulmonary anthrax, the most deadly of the two main types of the disease, causes severe difficulty in breathing and is fatal about fifty percent of the time. Recent concerns in the media over smallpox continue and remain an issue for health professionals. Smallpox is a highly infectious viral disease that was declared extinct in 1980 by the World Health Organization. Symptoms are similar to influenza and are accompanied by a rash that spreads over the body and eventually develops into puss-filled blisters. This disease can be treated if a vaccine is administered early. The issue is that there are only limited amounts of the vaccine now available. The mortality rate in non-vaccinated individuals is thirty-five percent. Intelligence reports underline that Iraq is working with ricin, which is derived from castor beans. This agent takes effect in a few hours and can kill in seventy-two hours, with the individual weakening and developing a fever and cough. A rapid build-up of fluids in the lungs brings on respiratory distress and death. There is presently no antitoxin or vaccine available. Botulism and tularaemia are also of concern. Botulism is a toxin that causes progressive muscular paralysis and agitates the central and peripheral nervous system. Symptoms appear within eight to thirty-six hours after the onset of the infection. The individual may experience difficulty in swallowing and speaking, nausea, vomiting, and double vision, progressive muscle weakness, paralysis and respiratory failure. Prompt treatment with an antitoxin reduces the risk of death. The rate of mortality is assessed at sixty-five percent. As to tularaemia, it is also known as rabbit fever and is a disease that can be transmitted to humans. The symptoms include high fever, aching and swollen glands, but it can be effectively treated with antibiotics. Overall, this infectious disease is about five percent fatal. Without treatment, the mortality rate rises to more than thirty percent, depending on the form of the disease. No vaccination is available.

It should be underlined that genetic engineering can evolve a hardier and more deadly agent. More sinister, though, is that a malignant organism could be combined with a benign one in order to disguise a potentially fatal affliction with the symptoms of a different ailment so that the illness is misdiagnosed and mistreated. Rapid advancements, such as mapping the human genome, raise the possibility that bio-science could create weapons that target only certain segments of a population based on race, gender, or genetic predisposition to particular conditions.[33]

The issue of chemical and biological attacks surfaced in the wake of the Pentagon and World Trade Center attacks. Two Middle Eastern men were reportedly interested in finding work as crop dusters in Saskatchewan, Canada in June 2001. In the opinion of terrorism experts, crop dusters could be used to spray chemical weapons or deadly infectious agents such as anthrax or smallpox. As well, FBI investigators were concerned over the visit by several Middle Eastern men, including suspected suicide hijacker Mohamed Atta, to a crop-dusting company in New York City and Washington. It was further reported that Mr. Atta had sought a U.S. Department of Agriculture loan for the purchase of a crop-dusting aircraft.[34] According to reports, he was interested in the range of crop dusters and how much pesticide could be carried. Albeit, there remains much discourse among terrorist experts regarding the capability of terrorist groups to obtain, maintain and direct an effective biological attack. The anthrax letters sent in the fall of 2001 caused much panic and consternation. Gas masks were bought up from all stores that carried them and healthy people showed up at medical centers and doctors' offices demanding anti-anthrax antibiotics. Meanwhile, any powdered substances were deemed suspect. The American people struggled to guard themselves and their loved ones against the threat of the potentially deadly bacteria.[35] Concerns over anthrax initiated a stream of requests for vaccines,[36] particularly as details of the lax security at labs became public. According to one report, two germ banks in Mexico City had no guards, no security cameras and no health officials in germ-proof suits. Reports from several germ labs discovered hazardous spores being mailed out in hard-plastic travel vials to researchers. In contrast, since 1977, it has been illegal for labs to send any deadly microbes to destinations within the United States or any foreign country without the permission of the American Justice Department.[37] The anthrax panic was compounded by reports that Iraq had purchased from an American company eight strains of anthrax and admitted to weaponizing the strains. One report indicated that Iraq was working with Osama bin Laden on a joint operation aimed at attacking the United States. The Virginia-based American Type Culture Collection admitted the purchase of the anthrax strains to Saddam Hussein's government in 1985. According to sources, in late 1998, twelve Iraqi chemical experts went to Afghanistan to work with bin Laden's own chemical experts. Iraq made several technical declarations that it had constructed special nozzles that could spray liquified anthrax in a fine mist over populated centers to inspectors from the United Nations.[38]

Intelligence personnel and health experts continue to focus their attention on the possibility of attacks involving biological, chemical and nuclear weapons. Moreover, there is a history of previous use of biohazards. One of the earliest examples of employing biological warfare dates from the Scythian archers of 400 B.C. Apparently, Scythian archers dipped their arrow tips in the blood of decomposing corpses, creating a poisoned missile.[39] In late 1952, British authorities discovered that the Mau Mau terrorist groups operating in what is now Kenya used a highly toxic plant to poison thirty-three cattle. In February 1978, Palestinian extremists claimed to have poisoned a large shipment of Jaffa oranges with liquid mercury. The following year, in April and May 1979, anthrax spores were released at a Soviet military facility in Sverdlovsk, in the Soviet Union. Two years later, in October 1981, a terrorist group called Dark Harvest dropped off a package containing contaminated soil at the Wiltshire-based Chemical Defense Establishment in the United Kingdom. Fortunately, the anthrax used in the attack did not prove to be harmful. Three years later, in September and October 1984, 750 people were taken ill in Oregon after a member of a religious cult allegedly used salmonella to poison restaurant salad bars. In March 1995, the Aum Shinrikyo, a Japanese doomsday cult, attacked the Tokyo subway systems, releasing the agent sarin. This assault killed twelve commuters and caused 5,000 people to become ill. It was reported that the group had previously experimented with anthrax spores.[40] The fear of acquiring chemical weapons and the ease by which it can be done was demonstrated by a chemist at an American university. James M. Tour, a Rice University organic chemist, filled out a request to purchase the chemicals needed to make sarin and placed the order with the well-respected firm Sigma-Aldrich. The next day, he received by overnight mail the ingredients he had ordered. By closely following the recipe and properly processing the dimethyl methylphosphonate, phosphorus trichloride, sodium fluoride, and alcohol, Tour could have manufactured 280 grams of sarin for the cost of 130.20 U.S. dollars. Using an off-the-shelf pesticide sprayer or other effective means of distributing the sarin into a ventilation system, this amount of sarin could have killed a few hundred to tens of thousands of people.[41] The issue of a chemical attack surfaced in February 2002 in Rome when Italian security authorities arrested four Moroccans in possession of four kilograms of ferro cyanide and maps highlighting the American Embassy and other locations, as well as maps of Rome's sewer network.[42] It was later revealed that the Italian police had discovered a hole carved into an underground passageway next to the American Embassy. The chemical itself is harmless, but could have been turned into a deadly gas capable of killing large numbers of people.

There is a distinct psychological implication to biological agents, to the extent that the fear of a biological attack may be more damaging than the attack itself. A British medical journal article notes that the anxiety over the very idea of a biological attack could linger for years. Although there is much concern over chemical and biological weapons, neither, however, are particularly effective military weapons. Instead, the purpose of these types of weapons is to inflict fear via psychological means—by inducing confusion, uncertainty and fear into everyday life. One article notes that, in the event of a bio-terrorist attack, the immediate health problems would be surpassed by the long-term psychological effects, engendering the risk of mass sociogenic illness, which is a form of mass hysteria. The symptoms of sociogenic illness are anxiety, nausea, or vomiting.[43]

The issue of infrastructure protection also remains of vital concern, as was noted by Margaret Purdy, then Secretary to the Canadian Cabinet for Security and Intelligence. Ms. Purdy underlined that there are both physical and cyber threats from accidental disruption, computer hackers and disgruntled workers. Ms. Purdy warned that the worst is yet to come, as "everything is getting more malicious and more sophisticated. It is no longer about whether there will be an attack or not but when it will occur."[44] As well, terrorists are using the Internet to explain their manifestos. It has been reported that "12 of the 30 groups on the State Department's list of terrorist organizations are on the Web."[45]

Future terrorist operations will, in all probability, be conducted by the traditional groups belonging to militant Palestinian,[46] Islamic,[47] Kurdish,[48] Japanese,[49] anti-Turkish Armenians, Tamil,[50] Sikh,[51] Irish,[52] Peruvian Shining Path,[53] Colombian leftists,[54] German[55] and Italian right-wing and left-wing[56] elements, American militias,[57] British neo-Nazis,[58] single-issue terrorism[59] such as environmentalists,[60] anti-abortion and animal rights organizations,[61] bio-engineering,[62] and scores of other groups.[63] Less advertised terrorist groups such as the Tamil separatists[64] and militant black Muslim groups, such as the New Black Panthers, may attempt to launch themselves onto the world stage.[65] Some of these groups are acquiring advanced technical skills,[66] particularly in the employment of remote-controlled and timed explosive devices, such as the 1998 bombing of Omagh's main shopping street. The bomb killed twenty-nine people and consisted of 500 pounds of high explosives concealed in a car.[67] The IRA and the anti-West Islamic fundamentalists are bomb experts acknowledged by some as having "bombs of power unparalleled for a non-military organization"[68] as well as surface to air missiles.[69] This former issue became most noteworthy in August 2001, with the arrest of three IRA members in Colombia. The IRA team was reportedly assisting in the training of Revolutionary Armed Forces (FARC) guerrillas and secretly testing a "fireball mortar bomb" which was designed to destroy fortified buildings. One report noted that, according to British and Irish security sources, the IRA had completed preliminary tests near Omeath but needed a larger testing area that was free of surveillance. One of the IRA team members, James Monaghan, was said to be assisting the FARC guerrillas to improve the accuracy and power of a mortar that launches bombs loaded with homemade napalm.[70] This devastating technology[71] was proven in the August 1998 bombings in Kenya and Tanzania, in the February 1993 World Trade Center explosion in New York and the April 1995 bombing of the U.S. Federal Building in Oklahoma City.[72] This latter action by members of an American paramilitary group sadly brought terrorism home to Americans.

The advent and wake of the year 2000 celebrations had increased fears of terrorism from both traditional and non-traditional groups. The arrest of the Algerian Ahmed Ressam, who was driving a car filled with ingredients for a powerful bomb, fueled these fears and concerns. Mr. Ressam was being investigated for links with bin Laden. Meanwhile, the United States and Canada, as well as many other target nations, were on a heightened state of alert during the period prior to 2000 as well as in its wake.[73] In October 2000, bin Laden was alleged to have been a party to the attacks on the American destroyer USS Cole and the British Embassy in Yemen, as well as the World Trade Center and the Pentagon attacks in September 2001. These attacks were seen by some observers as signaling a new and prolonged terrorist campaign against American and British interests worldwide.[74] Employing asymmetric tactics, better known as the David effect, which utilizes a small force against powerful forces, essentially employing skill and cunning against a technologically dominant enemy. The low-tech, high-concept operations epitomized by the attacks in New York City and Washington are solid examples of what we may expect in the future. However, this issue, difficult as it may seem, may be surpassed by what can be called "ambiguous warfare," in which no perpetrator takes responsibility for a terrorist strike, as was witnessed in the wake of the 2001 anthrax attacks in the United States. The reality is what do targeted nations do when an enemy is not only skilled in asymmetrical warfare but is able to deny any responsibility in a compelling fashion.[75]

Today, the Casio computer watch can be turned into a timer for a bomb, and similarly liquid explosives can be easily hidden in travel luggage as hair shampoo. Today, detonator wire can be smuggled easily past sensors in shoes, as witnessed on 22 December 2001 by the arrest of twenty-eight-year-old Richard C. Reid who attempted to ignite explosives that were concealed in his shoes during a flight between Paris and Miami.[76] This is not to forget the threat posed by extremist elements who are known to use "suicide bombers,"[77] as seen during the wave of attacks in Israel in 1996 and again in 2001,[78] in particular, the terrorist assault by suicide hijackers in New York City and on the Pentagon in Washington. Hamas leader Shaykh Admad Yasin said in a telephone interview that he plans a wave of suicide operations against Israeli targets.[79] All of these provide an unsurpassed challenge to security authorities. Today's terrorism is evolving. The old style Marxist-Leninist–inspired terrorists have been in decline since the collapse of communism. However, they are being replaced by disciplined fanatics driven by extremist religious beliefs. Some are loners spurred by religious or personal beliefs with access to increasingly sophisticated weapons and in some cases unsophisticated methodology. Some are more indiscriminate working alone or in small groups motivated by single issues such as environmental degradation, abortion or animal rights. As to methodology, attacks on tourist sites, such as in Luxor, Egypt, and as well the ports in Yemen and Uganda, are not rare,[80] due in part to their ease of access.

With such relative newcomers to the global scene as the Islamic extremists,[81] the war against terrorism will broaden to incorporate other factions, such as al-Qaeda and individuals, such as Osama bin Laden,[82] who seek what they call justice through terror tactics. Along with established and evolving terrorist groups, there remains a number of extremely dangerous "shadow warriors," individual terrorists[83] with religious, political and ideological racial and ethnic concerns[84] that can inflict disproportionate damage to their targets. We may be witnessing the dawning of non-state terrorism on a global scale. In short, we will likely witness the continuation of terrorist violence,[85] a new targeting methodology and the advent of new groups. The reality is that nations who must deal with this style of warfare are re-evaluating what has gone on in the past and what indications there are for the present and future regarding the nature and intensity of the threat. Some observers have agreed that the tempo of the threat has petered off, others caution that it is intensifying due to post–Cold War proliferation of deadly materials, not to mention the easy access to information on how to formulate weapons of mass destruction. As one analyst opined, "We have seen in a few countries a level of fanaticism and sophistication as well as a willingness to undertake new and greater risks than in past decades."[86] These concerns have been underlined recently in the growing awareness of the potential threat from chemical and biological agents[87] as well as recent steps in preparing for such an eventuality.[88] The issue of a potential chemical or biological attack was evident when President Bill Clinton speculated in December 1999 that a germ (biological) or chemical attack on American soil was highly likely in the next century.[89] Sadly, he was correct in his speculation. It is noteworthy that sixty-six percent of the bio-terror cases from 1900 to mid-2001 were assessed as hoaxes or pranks. Twenty-one percent were threats of bio-attacks by those assessed as likely possessing bio-weapons; fortunately, the attacks did not occur. Only thirteen percent were actual attacks using a biological agent. Moreover, of the actual attacks using biological agents, twenty-four percent were within the United States. Of these attacks, there were no fatalities until mid-October 2001, when several deaths from anthrax occurred.[90] In an era where there is no other military force that can challenge American interests, the quandary of the world's most powerful military, in the aftermath of the USS Cole and the PENTTBOMB attacks, is not only how to prevent such strikes through increased "anti-terrorism training,"[91] but where and against whom to retaliate once a terrorist attack has been committed. We may now be witnessing the evolution of ambiguous terrorism on a grand scale.

The bio-terrorism issue struck home in early 2001 in the manner of an envelope mailed to the office of Canada's Immigration Minister Elinor Caplan.[92] According to reports, when departmental staff opened the envelope, a colored powder thought to be laced with bacteria spilled out, and initial thoughts were of anthrax. Although this was found to be a hoax, this incident underlined the ease and possibility of a bio-agent being unleashed as an act of terrorism. Should this situation be the case, the employment of biological or chemical agents would enable terrorists to enter into a new field of endeavor where governments will not have the necessary understanding, capability, or preparation to deal with such an eventuality. Particularly since the 1995 sarin attack on Tokyo's subway, resulting in a dozen deaths and thousands of casualties, there have been numerous threats against various abortion clinics, water supplies, military and government targets. In recent years, the FBI has opened several cases involving threats against American interests due to the procurement of chemical and biological materials. Reportedly, the number of cases has increased from thirty-seven in 1996 to nearly 200 cases in 1999. In 2000, there were 300 reported FBI cases of biological threat letters.[93] The unfortunate reality with nuclear, chemical or biological threats is that there can be no room for complacency. This situation was compounded when an article underscored the potential debilitating effects that an electromagnetic bomb (e-bomb) could have. Should a terrorist group with access to 1940s technology and $400 initiate such a project, and employ an e-bomb, it could "knock out electric power, computers and telecommunication and you've destroyed the foundation of modern society. In the age of Third World-sponsored terrorism, the E-bomb is the great equalizer."[94] The Ottawa hoax was followed only days later by the news that a Congolese woman who had arrived in Canada had been immediately hospitalized and put into an isolation room. She was bleeding from several sites on her body, and it was believed that she had the highly contagious Ebola virus.[95] The Ebola virus was named after a river in the Democratic Republic of Congo in 1976, and is known to cause a ghastly death. The virus is spread from human contact with bodily fluids. Once the virus takes hold, the victim initially suffers headaches, sore throat and fever, which then becomes a high fever, vomiting blood, and diarrhea, followed by hemorrhagic bleeding from bodily orifices, to the final stage of loss of consciousness, massive internal bleeding and death.[96] What would happen if terrorists could harness and effectively disperse such a virus?[97]

These two situations were followed by reports that the Canadian and American governments were courting disaster due to their lack of preparedness to counter chemical or biological weapons. Riem Gaade, a Toronto-based terrorism response specialist, advised that Canada is "greatly unprepared" to meet these threats. Health Canada documents also showed that the Canadian government would be unready to deal with an attack of bio-terrorism. The Health Canada report advised that Canada had dedicated neither funds nor personnel for such an eventuality. It was further noted that the medical system would be "rapidly overwhelmed" should a terrorist group unleash an agent such as anthrax in a heavily populated area. As an example, the report used the Ottawa suburb of Nepean to demonstrate the effects of an attack. Of a population of 100,000 being exposed to anthrax, 32,875 would be killed and the medical costs could be as high as 6.5 billion dollars. If the agent botulism was employed, 30,000 would die and hospital bills would total 6.8 billion dollars. The report was buttressed by citing a Canadian Security Intelligence Service document that stated that "Although it is impossible to estimate the precise likelihood of a mass-casualty terrorist using CBRN [chemical, biological, radiological, nuclear] materials . . . , it appears to be a case of not if, but when, the next event will occur."[98]

In the wake of the catastrophic attacks in New York City and in Washington, the threat of chemical and biological weapons surfaced once again with reports that one of the orchestrators of the suicide attacks on 11 September 2001 was interested prior to the attacks in aircraft capable of spraying pesticides.[99] The subsequent series of anthrax-laced letters in October 2001 demonstrated that this bio-terrorism scare was psychologically effective in disrupting work, and shut down the American Congress. The 11 September 2001 attacks claimed more than 3,000 lives, while, at the time of writing, anthrax had claimed five. The psychology of bio-terrorism is measured not by the number of deaths but rather the calculated, relentless and steady application of fear. In this light, military-type terror seeks to make the most dramatic statement as possible. In contrast, bio-terrorism is most effective when it is employed quietly, covertly, and when the deployment of a bio-agent is done over an extended period of time, so as to produce panic in the population. The aim is to damage a societal structure irretrievably; therefore, one must introduce a bio-agent that works stealthily and slowly. This type of bio-agent does not call for a direct response, as the damage is initially invisible; as time passes it becomes visible and the damage has already happened. Unlike acts of terrorism that seek to usurp people's belief in their safety at home, at work, and on the street, bio-terrorism undermines people's belief in the safety of their own bodies. One must breathe to live. Moon-suited bio-technicians may only further inspire fear that is already present in our nations.[100]

Another issue that has garnered attention is the vulnerability of the food supply to a bio-terrorist attack. This could be accomplished by the deliberate introduction of foot and mouth disease, for example. Although the Canadian government stepped up surveillance at the borders and at food processing plants after the attacks in September 2001, there was no guarantee that such initiatives could prevent a bio-terrorist attack, particularly when directed at Canadian farmers rather than at food processing facilities. The fear of a terrorist attack on the American food supply forced the Bush administration to look at making a single federal agency responsible for protecting the food supply from terrorist initiatives.[101] Also, this situation underlines the economic concerns, considering the costs of foot and mouth disease, which were reported to be in the region of 20 billion dollars.[102]

Today, we are experiencing what has been described as hyperterrorism, superterrorism and megaterrorism. Some have argued that subsequent to 11 September 2001, we must face the reality that the world is now threatened with the "megalomaniacal hyperterrorist." Looking back to the 1990s, the attacks that had the greatest effect were orchestrated by self-anointed individuals who had a belief in their respective destiny. The man who planned and orchestrated the 1993 World Trade Center bombing, Ramzi Yousef; the architect of the 1995 sarin gas attack in a Tokyo subway, Shoko Asahara; the 1995 Oklahoma bomber, Timothy McVeigh; and the man believed to be behind the PENTTBOMB attacks, Osama bin Laden,[103] are inextricably linked by their interest and capability to orchestrate devastating attacks. Terrorist experts were locked on classifying terrorism along organization or ideological lines, including left- or right-wing separatist, nationalist and religious terrorism as typical categories. The 1990s may have rendered this typology outmoded as analysts have disregarded the methodology of the megalomaniacal hyperterrorist. It has been argued that such individuals operate differently as they are "big thinkers" going beyond conventional terrorism and, unlike most terrorist groups, as well as nations, are apparently willing to employ weapons of mass destruction. Ramzi Yousef is arguably an excellent example of this as he openly discussed his intent relating to the World Trade Center, which was to blast the foundation of one of the towers so as to have it fall on the adjacent tower. Such a bombing, had it been effective, could have caused an estimated 250,000 casualties. Yousef was also the planner of Operation Bojinga, which was aimed at destroying twelve American passenger airliners in flight. If this is the trend, it is incumbent that we counter the rise of the megalomaniacal hyperterrorists by increasing human intelligence against these individuals as well as considering pre-emptive strikes.[104]

The following section discusses methods that might assist countries to deal with terrorism.

THE COUNTERTERRORIST REACTION

The Sovereignty Issue and Countermeasures

A major concern for countries involved in counterterrorist activities centers on the problems posed by national sovereignty and legal considerations, particularly as in the latter case any counterterrorist activity, at least in the democracies, must be subject to the law of the land. The nature of the application of law clearly varies, along with the responsibility for its enforcement, from country to country. In Norway, for example, counterterrorist activity is strictly and explicitly a matter for police, not the military. In contrast, Great Britain has employed not only the police and intelligence services but also military units to wage an undeclared war against terrorists.[105] For example, in 1988 an eleven-man jury ruled that the shootings of three IRA terrorists "on active service" in Gibraltar in March 1988 by members of the Special Air Service (SAS) were lawful. The jurists "decided that the soldiers had gunned them down, believing the IRA unit had planted a car bomb to blow up the Royal Anglian Regiment band during the weekly changing of the guard."[106]

As can be fully appreciated, such international counterterrorist actions by elite counterterrorist units are highly controversial. Due to the prickly nature of this issue, countries prefer to stay away from it rather than seeking solutions that might appear to erode their sovereignty. Sophisticated terrorists fully appreciate the conflict evolving from jurisdictional and sovereignty issues and have taken operational advantage of them on the domestic and international level, particularly in the Third World, where nationalism and anti-colonialist sentiment thrives. This trend continues, and any initiative to address sovereignty concerns and enhance co-operative counterterrorist actions, particularly in the employment of military and police, dissipates quickly once a terrorist incident is over.[107]

Moreover, countries do not wish to be seen as having "international death squads" wandering the world in search of terrorists. Therefore, states such as Britain, which maintain counterterrorist forces, must also maintain a high degree of control over their activities. Any deployment of counterterrorist forces abroad must be perceived to be a co-ordinated effort with the host country, as in the West German rescue of hostages in Mogadishu, or at least to have the sanction of the government targeted by terrorists, as in the Special Air Service (SAS) attack on the Iranian Embassy in London in 1980, the rescue of hostages in the Japanese Ambassador's residence in Lima, Peru in 1997,[108] and the July 2001 Russian success against Chechen terrorists.[109] Otherwise, it must be viewed as a humanitarian issue, as was the Israeli rescue of hostages in Entebbe (1976) and the ill-fated American mission into Iran (1980). By casting hostage rescue operations in such a light it is possible to diminish the problems that surround the issue of sovereignty.

Terrorism is becoming increasingly international at least in the sense that as more countries develop their national capabilities to deal with them, the terrorists will seek out states sympathetic to their cause, such as Libya, Syria and the Sudan, or look for less sophisticated countries which they can use as a base, such as Afghanistan. Such migration of terrorism increases the number of sovereignty hurdles that must be overcome. For many nations, it remains a complicated and emotional issue. As Paul Wilkinson points out:

> ... even those ... states which have been major targets of terrorism and have an obvious common interest in combatting it have been slow to agree [to] a collective approach. None of the international organizations, even NATO, has proved an easily acceptable framework in the sensitive areas of internal security, law and order. Traditionally governments have taken the view that here they must retain sovereign control. Western politicians and judiciaries are as chauvinistic in this respect as other states, despite the many moral and legal values they have in common with fellow Western governments.[110]

It is noteworthy, though, that since the New York City and Washington attacks, the situation has evolved dramatically in both security and political terms. In late October 2001, Canadian Prime Minister Jean Chrétien and Mexican President Vincent Fox pledged to pursue trilateral meetings with United States President George W. Bush so as to closely look at a common security and immigration policy, to ensure the security of the North American borders.[111]

COUNTERMEASURES AGAINST TERRORISM

In times of crisis, such as the Achille Lauro ship seizure in October 1985, the saga of TWA Flight 847 in June 1985, the Indian Airlines incident in late December 1999, or the Saudi jetliner in October 2000, the immediate attention of the governments involved is focused solely on freeing the hostages. Once this is achieved, they tend "to fall back in exhaustion."[112] Concerned governments must create an ongoing capability to deal with such outrages, and the capability must be in place before the crisis emerges. More importantly, governments must realize there is no panacea; that no security agency can forestall every risk. The October 2000 attack on the USS Cole and the PENTTBOMB in September 2001 underline the difficulties of pre-empting terrorist attacks as well as the obstacles in providing appropriate indicators of an impending attack.[113] Therefore, to combat terrorism, any concerned leadership "must take advantage of the breathing spells between terrorist attacks to invent stronger and more effective ways to protect itself. None of the available countermeasures is guaranteed to succeed; few of them are easy, and some involve moral and political adjustments that are sure to be controversial."[114] There are numerous countermeasures that could be implemented to ensure the safety of airports and to defeat terrorism.

As a global community, more governments could put political and economic pressure on lax national governments to ensure that their airports are safe.[115] For example, historically Athens and Beirut were two airports internationally acknowledged as having poor security. Today, some former Eastern European, Middle Eastern, African and Southeast Asian airports are noted for being lax; therefore international airlines associations such as the International Air Transport Association (IATA) should be made responsible for reviewing security operations and recommending changes as deemed necessary. More drastic national or international measures could be adopted, if required, such as halting all air traffic and imposing financial and legal penalties on those airlines that continue to use airports considered insecure.

Another countermeasure which may have to be reinforced is the installation of effective scanners,[116] detectors and management techniques, in concert with advanced technical measures, the physical checking of all baggage and passengers (with no exceptions) and the use of "sniffer" dogs.[117] In the future, we may even see the elimination of carry-on luggage. It has been argued that only passengers with tickets should be allowed access to terminal buildings. Such measures, including the employment of competent security personnel, would deter many potential aerial terrorists. In the wake of the still mysterious downing of TWA Flight 800 in 1996 a subtle fear still runs through all airline passengers. This concern is logical considering the last twenty-five to thirty years. As one writer stated, "This feeling of insecurity is justified. The minimal changes in travel habits that Americans accepted as a result of the first phase of aviation terrorism in the 1970s— metal detectors, cursory questioning of passengers at check-in, random use of dogs to sniff out explosives—have long since been overtaken by the engineering advances today's terrorists have made."[118] There are a number of initiatives to make airline travel more secure from terrorists that incorporate expensive and up-to-date "bomb sniffers," better trained guards and airport security personnel, and more passenger checkpoints. Biometrics, for example, is the emerging field where science and technology are employed to identify people. This computerized technology can, in a split second, identify individuals by their facial landscape, the gait of their walk and their voice tone. Meanwhile, researchers are also working on systems to identify people by the ridges of their fingernails, body odor and veins on their palms. Needless to say, these types of identification systems could provide a false sense of security, but also lead to fears of widespread public surveillance and the possibility of the erosion of personal privacy.[119] Recent technical advances in computers and cameras such as the Mandrake system have future potential. The Mandrake can automatically identify the facial features of suspects on the street. The close-circuit cameras take the images of a subject and digitally compare them against photographs of known criminals or police suspects that are held in the data banks of police/security forces. The system apparently latches onto key facial features and does a comparative analysis with information in the database.[120] The future airport terminal would be accessible only via one or two points, which would ensure easy monitoring. Notwithstanding the possible effectiveness of this technology, it does raise public concern over privacy issues, as was noted when the Royal Canadian Mounted Police (RCMP) employed the system at Toronto's Pearson International Airport.[121]

The future airport system could resemble the following. In order to prevent car bombs, the terminal area would be lined with concrete barriers. Upon checking in, travelers would present photo identification and would be questioned as to the content of their packages and if they packed their own luggage. At that point, each bag would be bar-coded and fed into a computer system along with the passenger's baggage claim ticket. All baggage would be searched or x-rayed before being loaded onto the aircraft. Once at the gate entrance, all hand-held parcels and carry-on luggage would pass through an x-ray and a "bomb sniffer" like the CTX5000, which has the capability of detecting both plastic and standard explosives.

As to security personnel, they have traditionally been poorly paid and educated, and have sometimes had criminal backgrounds[122]—this situation must change. Moreover, authorities or private companies that are responsible for security require regular refresher courses and upgrading, and should have all their inspection personnel security cleared. Furthermore, supervisors must maintain close watch over the quality and conduct of searches, and must be knowledgeable as to the latest "terrorist techniques" and methodology.[123] On the ground—and of serious concern to police and security forces—is the host of baggage handlers, fuelers and maintenance personnel who have access to the aircraft on the ground. As in Canada, these personnel must be subject to security checks and be restricted to certain areas and duties.[124] This situation has been a source of much concern due to reports of continuing lax security at international airports and the ease of access to sensitive areas, as well as attempts by terrorists to acquire airport security passes. It was underlined at the Lockerbie trial in January

2001 that the security at Heathrow in 1998 was so lax that nearly 800 passes issued to Heathrow Airport employees were unaccounted for and, as well, there was no system for checking the identities of baggage handlers.[125] The October 2000 seizure of a London-based Saudi Arabian Airlines Boeing 777 was reportedly commandeered by airport security officials employed to prevent such crimes. The two security officials included an undercover airport security guard and a border police officer. Apparently, one of these officials was thought to have brought a gun aboard concealed in a travel bag that the pilot had accidentally left behind in Jeddah.[126] Canadian reports have underlined attempts by members of various terrorist groups to infiltrate the nation's airport facilities, such as by applying for airport security passes as baggage handlers. Fortunately, Canadian Security Intelligence Service agents detected these initiatives.

It is important to appreciate that even after thirty years of airport security measures, undercover government agents were able to successfully breach the security measures at four of the largest airports in the United States. A Department of Transport report noted that government agents "carrying the fake bombs, and others participating in the investigation were successful in their efforts to sneak past security checkpoints in forty percent of their attempts, which occurred in 1995 and early 1996."[127] It was noted in December 1999 that U.S. Transportation Department investigators had penetrated the security barriers of a number of American airports, underlining serious gaps in security. These penetrations showed that FAA was slow to strengthen basic access control measures as well as to enforce existing controls allowing "piggybacking" through doors and gates. The report noted the poor training of security personnel, arguing for the creation of a professional force under federal government authority. In the future, recognizing that airports and airlines are, in reality, surrogate targets for terrorists, governments must enhance their security measures to meet future threats in conjunction with other concerned nations as well as strengthen border crossings. These could include one or all of the following:

1. Match all baggage to passengers and screen any baggage belonging to suspects using hand, x-ray and explosive detection apparatus;

2. Utilize blast-tested containers to hold baggage and cargo;

3. Develop an explosive detection system for personal and carry-on luggage. This would restrict the size and amount of hand-held luggage permitted on board;

4. Screen "profiled" passengers with hand searches and explosive trace detectors;

5. Scrutinize and closer define the definition of "known shipper" for cargo;

6. Focus on profiling both companies and individuals, such as looking at surface shippers who pay cash for shipments or request specific airlines or flights;

7. Have postal services acquire the authority to employ explosive detection equipment on air mail;

8. Access criminal records to check background and fingerprints to screen baggage, passenger and airport workers who have access;

9. Use of all national/international intelligence and police organizations to identify terrorists;

10. Search all aircraft deemed "high risk";

11. Require high-profile/high-traffic airports to have access to explosive-sniffing dog teams and other bomb detection equipment;

12. Implement regular evaluations at all airports, and report security lapses to FAA /Transport departments;

13. Ensure all airports have a security chief and set national standards for training security workers, who would undergo annual updating and testing;

14. Ensure all frontier ports and border areas have access to criminal/ terrorist databanks and are trained in questioning techniques.

15. Ensure the security of pilots throughout the flight.[128]

Since the dramatic aerial hijackings and the subsequent attacks in September 2001, United Airlines began installing steel bars on the cockpit doors of all their aircraft. The installation of steel bars and locks on doors in order to restrict cockpit access also brought on concerns regarding emergency evacuation of the cockpit. Moreover, some flight attendants worried about not being able to access the cockpit should the pilots become incapacitated.[129] One commercial airline company assured in late October 2001 that it would train their pilots to use stun guns that were powerful enough to deliver high-voltage shocks that can immobilize an individual for up to sixteen minutes. At the time, it was also noted that the U.S. Senate unanimously approved a bill that authorized the FAA to permit pilots to carry firearms in flight. Also, the Association of Flight Attendants advised that it wanted training for their members to learn how to effectively thwart a hijacker utilizing mace and other non-lethal toxins.[130] To enhance air security, American and Canadian authorities want airlines to turn over passenger lists so that they may be scrutinized by security and law enforcement under new anti-terrorism measures. This would be an integral part of an extensive prescreening process recommended by U.S. authorities. To aid this security initiative, American authorities hope to integrate electronic law enforcement and intelligence data with airlines and airport security systems.[131]

Government agencies must consider the protective hardening of targets such as embassies, residences and government offices. The destruction of the United States Marine Corps barracks in Beirut in 1983 resulted in an American government order to enhance security at diplomatic posts throughout the world. Secretary of State George Schultz asked in 1985 for some \$236 million in order to improve security at the State Department and at thirteen other establishments overseas.[132] This request included computerized control booths, barriers, rewards for information, bodyguards and security dogs. The use of a comprehensive identification system for employees, and bomb and weapon detection equipment (including nuclear, chemical and biological[133]) must also be considered.[134] After September 2001, there were concerns that bin Laden had obtained material for an atomic bomb. A former associate of bin Laden, Jamal al-Fadl, reportedly told an American court in February 2001 that he looked into acquiring uranium in 1993 or 1994. It was reported that he was shown a cylinder of the material, priced at 1.5 million dollars (U.S.), by a Sudanese contact. Arabian newspapers further reported that bin Laden had been successful in acquiring nuclear material. More disconcerting was a report from the *London Times* that quoted Western intelligence sources as saying bin Laden had nuclear material in his arsenal. A spokesman for the British government, however, advised that it was very skeptical that al-Qaeda was capable of making a bomb.[135] This information was contradicted when CIA Executive Director A. B. Krongard told a meeting of investors sponsored by Schwab Capital Markets that bin Laden may have nuclear material such as enriched uranium which could be fashioned into a crude radiological bomb.[136] The nightmare of a nuclear threat emanating from terrorists came to light in October 2001. American security officials received an intelligence alert advising that terrorists who were thought to have obtained a ten-kiloton nuclear weapon from the Russian nuclear arsenal were planning to bring the weapon into New York City. The agent who revealed this information was code-named Dragonfire and his information, along with a separate report from a Russian general who believed his forces were missing a ten-kiloton device, made the situation plausible. Fortunately, this did not happen. It has been estimated that a ten-kiloton bomb could kill upwards of 100,000 people and further irradiate 700,000, while totally flattening everything in a half mile diameter if detonated in Lower Manhattan.[137] As of 1996, the U.S. federal governme1t was reportedly spending more than seven billion dollars per year on programs to deter terrorism and protect American citizens.[138] A further two billion dollars in emergency funds have been dumped into counterterrorism in the wake of the devastation of two American embassies in eastern Africa during the summer of 1998. In the wake of the seizure of the Japanese ambassador's residence in Lima, Peru in December 1996, many nations began reviewing the security of their consulates and embassies. Moreover, due to the threat of terrorist activities in certain areas of the globe, many diplomats, business representatives and workers[139] live circumscribed lives. The construction of "hardened" buildings, security gates, guards, bulletproof glass, and armor-plated cars are now a part of everyday existence.[140] This also includes protection for computers[141] and computer databanks, and protection of these facilities from penetration and corruption,[142] and the use of websites by terrorists for recruitment and propaganda.[143] This includes a nation's cyber network, pipelines and power grids that are linked nationally and internationally. The security and protection of critical infrastructure[144] is vital to national interests and therefore a likely target. It is also likely that the protection of vital infrastructure will have an effect upon alliances, particularly as some nations share, to one degree or another, access to critical infrastructure. Canada has been identified as a "back door" to the United States and is reportedly unable to defend itself from sophisticated attacks, which then makes the American business infrastructure vulnerable to hackers, foreign interference, criminal and security threats.[145] This situation, and situations like this, can disrupt previously close economic relations and alliances and pose future problems.[146] Securing the national borders is an ever-present topic. Subsequent to the September 2001 terrorism attacks, the U.S. Congress and federal agencies examined ways to use new technology to identify arriving visitors and to triple the number of border guards on the Canadian border. The State Department will undergo a reexamination of six countries currently in the "visa waiver" program, will provide new access for immigration inspectors to a State Department database that includes photos of all visa applicants, and will reallocate more than 100 U.S. border guards from the U.S.-Mexico border to the Canadian-U.S. border. In addition, the American *Patriot Act* promises to triple the border patrols, as well as customs and immigration officials, and sink fifty million dollars into security screening technology.[147]

The expansion and coordination of a well-organized intelligence-gathering apparatus "is the critical element in defeating terrorist activities."[148] Winning the intelligence battle is vital if countries hope to reduce terrorist activity.[149] Unfortunately, this is easier said than done. The key is to break down the barriers that exist among national police and intelligence agencies. For despite the conclusion of the Cold War, there is still a reluctance on the part of certain intelligence organizations to provide needed information. For example, the CIA was reluctant to provide satellite intelligence in support for United Nations' peacekeeping operations or electronically gathered evidence of war crimes to the international tribunal in the Hague. The start-up of Europol—a European-wide police service—lost much impetus due to the reality that member governments are hesitant or reluctant to provide their intelligence to each other. This situation became more problematic when German Chancellor Gerhard Schröder and President Jacques Chirac of France proposed in December 1999 a "federalized" European

Union intelligence service to manage world crises. This initiative included Great Britain while excluding the Americans.[150] The thwarting of Palestinian attacks in the 1970s by Israel[151] and the United States, through the intelligence penetration of the Palestine Liberation Organization, remains an outstanding example of international co-operation, showing all security and intelligence agencies what can be achieved.[152] Notwithstanding, there is a dilemma. The recruitment of human sources also surfaces a number of serious "moral issues" due to the fact that some sources are "involved" with terrorist activity. The Central Intelligence Agency reportedly had "more than a hundred informants who the agency's [CIA] officers concluded were implicated in major crimes abroad, such as killings, assassinations, kidnapping or terrorist acts."[153] As well, those "humint" sources face certain death should they be compromised or discovered, as was the case in the execution of two Palestinians convicted of collaborating with Israeli authorities. It was reported that both men were accused of providing information that assisted Israeli intelligence in hunting down and assassinating suspected Palestinian terrorists. They were subsequently convicted and executed by a Palestinian Authority firing squad.[154]

In a Reuters report dated 30 October 1996 it was noted that "CIA Director John Deutch announced that he was boosting the number of case officers sent abroad, putting more foreigners on his payroll as spies and giving the president more possibilities for covert action." This initiative was aimed at increasing the number of humint assets in order to "further pre-empt, disrupt and defeat international terrorism."[155] One American, Senator Richard Lugar (R) of Indiana, has stated that "We have to come to grips with a different level of intelligence."[156] In that light, the infiltration of terrorist organizations is vitally important. One former field officer stated: "In counterterrorism, high-tech espionage is no substitute for a well-placed informant." Moreover, "you can photograph all you want. But you have to have somebody under that roof to tell you what's going on in there."[157] The call for better humint was only compounded in the wake of the World Trade Center and Pentagon attacks. However, this is not an easy option.[158] Therefore, a country must formulate a game plan to focus its intelligence efforts against terrorists, and to establish which government bodies are primarily responsible for counterterrorist intelligence gathering.[159] Livingstone and Arnold have emphasized that timely and accurate information has enabled security authorities to safely secure diplomats and other targets out of harm's way, warn governments of terrorist plans and expose the intentions of terrorist groups to friendly/allied governments. Moreover, a well-developed intelligence service can provide authorities with vital intelligence about a potential or upcoming terrorist action, permitting government and police authorities to initiate steps so as to pre-empt the incident or at the least minimize any damage. As well, a professional intelligence arm can assist authorities in tracking down the suspected terrorists and possibly identifying any support from sponsoring states.[160] This requirement for vital intelligence may also conflict with certain sensitivities such as dealing with "unsavory" foreign agencies that may have or have had poor human rights records. Albeit appreciating this, intelligence and security authorities must maintain a degree of pragmatism in dealing with such nations out of self-interest. Nevertheless, these initiatives must be properly monitored.[161]

More recently, an initiative introduced by the American government included the employment of rewards of up to five million dollars for the arrest of Osama bin Laden,[162] which was subsequently raised to twenty-five million in the wake of the 11 September 2001 attacks in New York City and Washington, as well as exchanging intelligence with U.S. allies in order to facilitate his apprehension. The FBI has said that bin Laden faces charges in New York following alleged attempts to acquire chemical and biological agents for terrorist activities.[163] Moreover, bin Laden was linked to Ahmed Ressam, an Algerian who had a false Canadian passport, and was discovered at a U.S. customs point in a car carrying explosives. Ressam was subsequently tried and convicted of international terrorism, using false documents, smuggling, and possessing explosives.[164] Apart from the monetary reward, the United States would likely offer safe haven and permanent residence for those who delivered bin Laden. More recently, the U.S. government has procured a "star witness" in Jamal Ahmed Mohamed Al-Fadl, a 37-year-old Sudanese who met bin Laden in Afghanistan. Al-Fadl rose through the al-Qaeda organization when he was involved in financial affairs. His information provided vital insights into the operation and financial organization of bin Laden. After defrauding the group, he turned to the U.S. to provide information as a federal witness against four alleged members of bin Laden's group who were convicted for the 1998 Kenya and Nairobi embassy bombings.[165] One of those sentenced described himself as a "soldier in the military wing of al-Qaeda." The four are the first to be convicted by an American jury of carrying out bin Laden's 1998 religious fatwa to kill Americans and their allies.[166] It is widely believed that American intelligence authorities played an important role in the tracking of Abdullah Ocalan, passing to the Turkish government his location at the Greek ambassador's Nairobi residence.[167]

There has been a suggestion that beyond "purely intelligence" issues, that *knowledge centers* focusing on terrorism be created. In the wake of the 1996 conference, the G-7 and Russia were expected to share, in a more systematic way, information developed in each of their countries to combat terrorism. Moreover, it was noted that "Britain, with its long experience of Irish Republican Army terrorism, has suggested that centers of excellence be set up in various countries through which this knowledge could be shared."[168]

Moreover, officials responsible for a nation's crisis-management function should be identified, formed into teams and given the opportunity to practice,[169] so that in the event of a terrorist attack, command and control measures can be implemented immediately. Officials, diplomats, civil servants, police and military personnel can be fully aware, ahead of time, of their duties and responsibilities. The benefits of such an approach were well demonstrated in the 1980 Iranian Embassy siege in London. The decisions were made by the Home Secretary, Mr. William Whitelaw, who acted as chairman of the Cabinet Office Briefing Room (COBR), the government's crisis committee. The committee included representatives from the Foreign Office, the Ministry of Defence, Scotland Yard and the security and intelligence (MI5) branch. COBR was assisted by specialist advisors. It was noted that:

> COBR did not go into the operation "cold." Everybody knew what they had to do and where to assemble when the codeword was given. This expertise came from the realization that such an incident was likely to happen and the team had conducted its own "war games" to prepare for the event.[170]

In contrast, the United States appears to have "more of a machismo attitude."[171] According to Robert Kupperman, the prevailing feeling is "that we don't need to prepare in that way for managing a crisis."[172] And in admiration of the British experience, Kupperman argues that "We have to get a regular program of crisis gaming going, and we have to make sure that at least cabinet-level people are involved in it."[173] It has been put forward that "If U.S. officials had done more advance planning in the Iranian situation, they might have reached different conclusions about Carter's rescue raid. Soon after the seizure of the U.S. diplomats in Teheran, the Israeli army war-gamed possible rescue operations."[174]

In the latter instance, there is no evidence that the United States operationally consulted with the Israelis to solicit advice or assistance, or for that matter any other allied country in their ill-fated Iranian adventure. Notwithstanding, the lessons learned from the British, French, German, American and Peruvian experiences, as well as others, can benefit those governments willing to learn from them and may assist in the safe release of hostages in future rescue operations.

The improvement of international cooperation to combat international terrorist activities is known to be "crucial to any effective effort to control and suppress terrorism."[175] This cooperation includes the control of immigration, which has been a point of contention between countries and more recently (December 1999) between Canada and the United States. It should be noted that once Fidel Castro undertook to extradite hijackers to the United States for legal proceedings, the hijacking phenomenon, with Cuba as a destination, diminished. The adherence to international agreements and the suspension of air services to nations suspected of harboring or support-ing terrorism, might assist in a coordinated approach to countering terror-ism. This saw success when sixteen Arab countries (a branch of the Cairo-based Arab League) met in Cairo during July 1996 to discuss greater cooperation in fighting terrorism. Headed by Egyptian Interior Minister Hassan el-Alfi, the meeting outlined a "code of conduct on terrorism," which states that member "lands will not be used to plan or carry out (ter-rorist) acts, and to hunt the terrorist elements, ban their infiltration through their borders and their residency." The code also bans any state from "re-ceiving, housing, training, arming or financing" terrorists.[176] One critical area where greater international cooperation could assist is in the sharing of intelligence. This could also include aiding friendly nations in training their intelligence, security, police and military forces in the various aspects of counterterrorism. Such cooperation may in the future include the possi-bility of creating "a multinational commando force that could be thrown into action in future terrorist emergencies."[177] The thought of creating a "multinational commando force" for specific military operations such as counterterrorism is far more likely than the creation of a United Nations–sponsored army, even in the wake of conflicts such as Haiti, Bosnia, Kosovo, Rwanda and Sierra Leone. Notwithstanding, joint special operations have been successful when the political will is there.[178] Furthermore, such co-operation would likely further enhance the effectiveness of those countries that now combat political violence on national and international levels.

Experience in negotiating with terrorists since the 1970s underlines "the importance of choosing the right negotiator—ideally someone who speaks the terrorists' language, understands their history and culture, is street-smart but also a good listener."[179] Other noteworthy negotiation aims focus on acquiring concessions, developing a trusting relationship with the terror-ists, and attempting to deprive the terrorists of rest.[180] Sadly, the terrorists themselves have rapidly assimilated these strategies and have evolved their own counters, such as taking along an extra gunman to keep negotiators off balance, as happened in Flight 847 between Beirut and Algiers. It is, therefore, vitally important that the negotiators be flexible and have the authority to develop means to overcome these terrorist ploys. Officials should understand that they must avoid declaring "publicly that they will not make concessions to terrorists. . . . Such statements may sound prin-cipled and tough-minded, but they constrain efforts to carry out the bar-gaining that inevitably takes place with hostage-takers."[181]

As one analyst has said, "The fact is that any government will negoti-ate, if not directly, then indirectly."[182] The release in December 1991 of a number of American and British hostages is proof that governments will directly or indirectly negotiate with terrorists for the safe release of their citizens.

For national leaders, ensuring the safety of the hostages should be of paramount importance. However, the negotiations that occur during a hostage crisis should not rule out "the option of a rescue mission [as this] keeps terrorists guessing—and may encourage them to make concessions more quickly."[183] The employment of elite military or police formations in hostage rescue attempts must be feasible. Since deployment to the crisis area must be rapid, special operations units could be based close to areas with a high potential for terrorist activities, i.e., the Middle East, Africa and Europe. These bases should have extensive training facilities, be reasonably private and maintained in secure surroundings. More information regarding the use of "final option forces" will be discussed in later chapters.

Western nations should seek agreements on ways of identifying and penalizing states which harbor or assist international terrorists. The economic influence of the West for instance could be brought to bear in fighting terrorist violence, particularly through economic sanctions and other means, such as the cessation of aerial traffic to those countries identified as sponsor nations.[184]

According to an American government report, seven nations are seen as recent supporter nations for terrorists: Iran,[185] Libya,[186] Iraq, Sudan, Syria, Cuba and North Korea. There are also individuals such as Saudi businessman Osama bin Laden,[187] a multimillionaire former Saudi citizen who was believed to have been residing in Afghanistan under the protection of the Taliban, prior to the counter-terrorist campaign in Afghanistan in 2001–2002. Bin Laden is suspected of financing the 1993 World Trade Center bombing, the attack in Riyadh in November 1995, the Khobar Tower bombings in June 1996, the bombings of the U.S. embassies in Kenya and Tanzania in August 1998, the attack on the USS Cole in October 2000 in Aden, and is linked to the daring suicide hijacking of commercial aircraft, and subsequent attacks in New York City and Washington in September 2001. The North Atlantic Treaty Organization (NATO) threw its full support behind British and American preparations to attack Afghanistan after the Bush administration presented a classified briefing by Washington's top counterterrorism official. The briefing confirmed the belief that bin Laden and his network al-Qaeda (the Base) supported the suicide hijackers responsible for the 11 September 2001 attacks. NATO members agreed—for the first time in their 52-year history—to invoke a joint defense clause known as Article 5. This clause underlines that an attack on one member state from abroad is viewed as an attack on all members. NATO had tentatively approved this initiative immediately after the 11 September attacks but could not put the Article 5 into effect until proof of the attacks' origin was provided by American officials.[188]

What is further disconcerting is that bin Laden is reportedly interested in obtaining weapons of mass destruction.[189] Jamal Ahmed al Fadl, a former aide of bin Laden, testified that he was sent to purchase uranium in 1993 and that bin Laden had been prepared to pay 1.5 million dollars U.S. on the uranium black market so that he could manufacture a nuclear weapon.[190] The financing of terrorists continues through bank robberies, kidnapping and drug money.[191] Therefore, in the wake of the New York City and Washington attacks, bin Laden's personal fortune, with estimates of wealth between 300 to 500 million, has become the focus of cutting off the monies that are believed to finance his terrorist activities. Using a complicated web of bank accounts and shell companies, it is believed that his holdings are scattered throughout the Arab states, Africa, Europe, Latin America and the United States. According to reports, he launders his money through Amsterdam and Luxembourg.[192] The financing of terrorists has become an issue for the United Nations. A draft international convention came up for adoption before the end of the 54th United Nations General Assembly.[193] In the wake of the American attacks in 2001, Canadians, for example, who raise money for or have dealings with individuals or groups that were identified on a new federal list of suspected terrorists will face up to five years of incarceration. The list will be updated as international and Canadian authorities access more information on terrorists' activities and their financial support base. These new financial regulations were described as an "interim measure" until the Canadian government can introduce amendments to the Criminal Code of Canada. The Canadian government introduced an omnibus bill that will create a new criminal offence, described simply as fundraising on behalf of terrorists, which may carry a stiffer sentence. The amendments will also allow Canadian authorities to seize assets of those linked to terrorist groups.[194]

Prior to the "successful" attack by American aircraft against selected Libyan targets in 1986,[195] the threat of precision reprisals such as bombings and assassination[196] was viewed with a jaundiced eye. Threats of retaliation[197] that aren't expeditiously carried out lead to the perception that the target nation is impotent. This apparent weakness encourages others to consider terrorism as an effective way to wage war. Although the option of retaliation creates many problems, it is one avenue that must remain open. As a deterrent measure, it may have limited effect, but it does demonstrate, as in the Libyan case, that the target sometimes fights back, thereby conveying a crucial message in the war against terrorists and the nations that support them.

As of 1999, President Clinton promised ten billion dollars for counterterrorism in his budget proposal. Forwarding his priority list to Congress, the President emphasized deterrence, prevention and preparedness.[198] Along with 2.1 billion dollars in supplemental funds, the 1998–99 fiscal year counterterrorism spending was more than eight billion dollars. Today, governments recognize that as long as terrorists operate they cannot defeat them totally, no matter how much money is appropriated, particularly since the foundations of much terrorist activity are embedded in deep-seated, highly emotional political grievances. Further, political violence will likely continue until these grievances are satisfactorily addressed. As democratic states place a premium on freedom, they will continue to remain vulnerable to such low-intensity violence.

In conclusion, nations will likely have little option but to be prepared to continue to experience a spectrum of terrorist violence well into the future. Therefore, these nations may be required to orchestrate all possible means to defeat terrorism—ensuring that they are employed with cautious fore-thought, and that there is no illusion as to their (limited) effect. Notwith-standing, President George W. Bush signed the *Patriot Act* into law on 26 October 2001. This potent anti-terrorism law gives police authorities new powers to spy on citizens and detain suspects. Under this act, police may detain, for seven days, anyone suspected of terrorist activity. It also allows roving wiretaps on all telephones used by a single individual. In addition, overseas banks must cooperate with U.S. investigators. The law also pro-vides stiff penalties for terrorist acts and possession of biological or chemical substances, as well as allocating funds to monitor visa recipients and funds for patrolling the U.S.-Canada border.[199]

Reflecting upon the international scene, no matter what a country may do to prevent a terrorist incident or hostage taking, terrorist acts which vary in scale and methodology will continue to occur. In that light, the follow-ing pages will turn to the experiences of three nations and how they devel-oped measures known to those in the field of counterterrorism as the "final option."

THE "FINAL OPTION"—THE EVOLUTION AND JUSTIFIABILITY OF ELITE COUNTERTERRORISM TEAMS

The evolution and deployment in the 1970s of elite counterterrorist teams in Israel and West Germany was in response, partly, to the frustrations of employing a series of so-called "non-force" methods against terrorists. Livingstone has argued that:

> governments have employed a variety of nonforce strategies in their efforts to resist terrorism, including diplomacy, negotiation, concessions, and cooptation. Occasionally such methods have worked, but more often than not they have failed or only provided a temporary prophylaxis to an endemic problem. It is widely recognized that, under most circumstances, making concessions to terrorists only invites further acts of terrorism. This fact, com-bined with the failure of the U.N. to take concerted action to develop effec-tive remedies to the problem of international terrorism, has resulted in a growing tendency on the part of national governments to resort to unilat-eral military action against terrorism in the belief that, if it is not possible to make terrorists answerable to the law, then they must be answerable to the gun.[200]

The terrorist assault upon the Israeli team during the 1972 Olympics in Munich combined with the failure to rescue the hostages in a subsequent action demonstrated to all observers the requirement for well-trained and equipped counterterrorist units. These units were created to meet the challenges of modern urban terrorism, which manifested itself in bombings, kidnappings, embassy and aircraft seizures, and hostage taking. Lacking in experience in these new areas, nations commenced developing these new units, as conventional military and police units were deemed too unwieldy and, in effect, not capable of dealing with this new mode of warfare. Not capable, in short, of dealing with well-organized and clandestine cells of dedicated terrorists. Hence, the evolution of highly flexible, rapid-reaction counterterrorist scenarios, manned by operators who have the desired qualities and traits for this type of police/military unit.[201] The employment of military options, under certain circumstances, is arguably justifiable under Article 51 of the United Nations Charter.[202] This article confirms that nations have the right to self-defense in the face of armed attack. Therefore, if one argues that terrorism constitutes an armed assault, every government has the inherent right to use military force as a defense against that assault.[203] Although the employment of military action by European NATO members against terrorists and supporters has been to say the least rare, there has been a number of incidents, some of which are described in this study, such as the GSG9 at Mogadishu, the French GIGN operations in Dijbouti and their dramatic rescue of 170 passengers and crew from Algerian Islamic extremists who seized an Air France airbus on 24 December 1994, and the April 1986 American strike against Libya, which stand as notable examples. This last example addressed a number of issues such as the demand, by the American public and government, for a tough response against terrorists and their sponsors. Through the infliction of a "heavy cost" on the perpetrators and their sponsors, the Libyan action provided the opportunity to deter future attacks and acted as a warning to terrorists and their supporters. Lastly, a military response can provide the opportunity of inflicting a psychologically damaging blow against the supporters of terrorism, thereby undermining their prestige, power and influence.

Although the "hard line" approach can be most attractive to the politicians and policy makers, there exist a number of issues that surface and cry out for a political stance or resolution. Reprisal operations by a nation or a cooperative expedition can be fraught with difficulty. First is the issue of acquiring the evidence and identification of the terrorist/sponsor nations that perpetrated the attack. This is easier said than done; more importantly, decision makers must be absolutely certain without a doubt as to who is responsible for a terrorist act. Moreover, the use of a military reprisal could expand the conflict, thereby outweighing the utility of the reprisal itself.[204] Collateral damage—the death of innocent civilians—could risk the loss of international support and the subsequent loss of the "moral high ground."

As with any military option, a unilateral response could witness the commensurate loss of support from one's friends and allies. Lastly, leaders, politicians and the military must appreciate that retaliation is not the panacea for terrorism and governments must not give their public false hopes and expectations in defeating terrorism. Such a situation could see an initiative to undertake greater military efforts and, in turn, spur rising public expectations.[205] It should be emphasized that, although military personnel, skills, equipment and expertise may assist in the "war" on terrorism, the military should *not* take the overall lead in the governmental campaign. It should be underlined that terrorism is an integral part of the spectrum of conflict which military force can be applied against when necessary, but it is "not fundamentally a military problem; it is a political, social and economic problem. The military, by its nature, is not suitably structured, trained or equipped to defeat terrorism."[206]

THE REQUIREMENT FOR THE ELITE COUNTERTERRORIST SOLDIER

It is apparent from recent twentieth-century history in Western countries that the responsibility for combating terrorism has been, for the most part, that of law enforcement authorities. On occasion, army units were tasked and, for the most part, were found to be operationally wanting in a number of areas such as strategy, methodology and structure. Conventional military forces and tactics have not met the challenge of terrorism: "Not only are contemporary weapons and tactics far too destructive to be employed in heavily populated urban regions, but also the deployment of large numbers of soldiers against terrorists simply increases the number of targets at which they can strike."[207]

General George Grivas, the famous Cypriot terrorist leader, noted that the level of terrorist operations is much lower than that of conventional military operations. Counterterrorist operations demand specially adapted and trained soldiers, tactics and strategy. He noted the "only hope of finding us was to play cat and mouse: to use tiny, expertly trained groups, who could work with cunning and patience and strike rapidly when we least expected."[208]

In short, one must use those same weapons and tactics belonging to the terrorists' inventory—psychology, stealth, speed, surprise and cunning—against the terrorists themselves. Moreover, candidates for such units must have motivation and determination, physical and mental stamina, initiative and self-discipline, be capable of operating in small groups during long-term isolated operations, and they must have the aptitude to assimilate a wide range of skills and think laterally.[209] This type of military operation[210] demands a different type of soldier, namely one who can develop a broad spectrum of skills. In short, "counterterrorism demands highly trained and motivated commandos, operating in small groups; skilled in electronics, communications, demolitions, marksmanship, deception, silent killing; and familiar with terrorist tactics and behavior."[211]

It should be underlined that two countries, in particular, were noted for their skill and audacious employment of counterterrorist forces in the mid 1970s. Israel and Germany are interesting examples: the former has extensive experience in commando and special operations and maintains a rather large corporate memory on military operations, since 1948, across the spectrum of warfare, especially in low-intensity conflict and terrorism. Germany, on the other hand, represents the other extreme, having little experience in "real world" special or counterterrorist operations, except for their experiences in World War II and since the subsequent creation of their counterterrorism force. Notwithstanding, Colonel Ulrich K. Wegener of Germany's GSG9 took the opportunity to study historical examples, observe and solicit the expertise of other countries, thereby making their experiences his own. While it is quite obvious that he drew much knowledge and skill from his own training, it is also quite apparent that his foreign training and attachments, as shall be seen, gave him the opportunity to gain valuable operational experience and more importantly the ability to call on the assistance of friendly or allied forces when required.

It is upon these two operations, at Entebbe and Mogadishu, that this paper shall embark, underlining the close international cooperation and assistance that Germany and Israel obtained throughout the course of these actions. It is the aim of this section to not only highlight the close cooperative effort of a number of countries to assist in these governmental responses but, concomitantly, to point out the various types of assistance that were forthcoming from the international community.

NOTES

1. Jenkins, New Mode of Conflict, 8.
2. Livingstone and Arnold (eds.), *Fighting Back: Winning The War Against Terrorism*, 1.
3. Jenkins, *New Modes of Conflict*, 9.
4. For a revealing look into the weapons available and where terrorists can obtain them, see Bell and Humphreys, "Terrorists' Supermarket: Canada Has Everything for the Discriminating 'Freedom Fighter.'" The authors note that Canada has been the location for such terrorist groups as the Tamil Tigers, Mujahedin, and Hezbollah to raise money in order to purchase equipment.
5. Ibid. Terrorist access to modern weapons continues to haunt police, intelligence and security forces. See Harnden, "IRA Testing Missiles, Clues Indicate." According to this article, the discovery of battery packs for a surface to air SAM-7, or "Grail"missile, may indicate the IRA are preparing to use them should the ceasefire end. The SAM-7 is shoulder fired, uses an infrared heat-seeking system and has a range of three kilometers. It was reported that a Russian-built anti-tank

weapon, believed to be an RPG-7, was employed in the 20 September 2000 attack on the London headquarters of Britain's MI6. The attack—launched by IRA splinter group—fortunately did not cause any casualties. See "Anti-Tank Projectile Hit London Spy HQ." In early March 2001, IRA dissidents allegedly bombed the British Broadcasting Corporation's television center in London. The car bomb, believed to be from the Real IRA, raised the specter of attacks by opponents to the peace process. The Real IRA is a splinter group held responsible for the 1998 bombing of Omagh, which killed twenty-nine people. See Freeman, "Car Bomb Explosion in London: Dissident Group Real IRA Blamed for Blast Outside BBC."

6. Ibid.

7. See Carr, "Terrorism as Warfare: the Lessons of Military History."

8. Jenkins, *New Modes of Conflict,* 10.

9. Ibid.

10. Hanley, "International Terrorism: Global Order Shaken by Wanton War."

11. "Terrorism: Fewer Incidents, Higher Casualties." See also Hoffman, "Keeping Mum: Terrorists Are Killing More, but Bragging Less."

12. United States, Department of State, *Patterns of Global Terrorism: 1997.* See also, Cooperman, "Terror Strikes Again: Attacks on U.S. Embassies Prompt Fear."

13. United States, Department of State, *Patterns of Global Terrorism: 1998.* See also, "Terrorism Took Record Toll in 1998, U.S. Report Says."

14. United States, Department of State, *Patterns of Global Terrorism: 1999* and United States, Department of State, *Patterns of Global Terrorism: 2000.*

15. Hanley, "International Terrorism: Global Order Shaken by Wanton War."

16. Calabresi and Ratnesar, "Can We Stop the Next Attack?"

17. McCabe, "Britain Learns to Live with Terrorism after Decades of Blasts."

18. McCabe, "Facing Terror with a Stiff Upper Lip."

19. "U.S. Targeting Terrorism with More Funds." The U.S. government has poured more than two billion in emergency funds into counterterrorism to bolster security and the purchasing of the latest in CT technology. This includes CAT scan equipment for airports to find explosives in baggage. Furthermore, the potential of chemical/biological weapons attack is also of governmental concern. See also Miller and Broad, "Clinton Describes Terrorism Threat for 21st Century." Even in the wake of the 1998 bombings of two American embassies in Africa many posts abroad are still far below optimal security standards. The improvements to security of the posts abroad include physical security barriers, blast walls, bomb detection units, metal detectors, x-ray equipment, CCTV and video recording equipment. Giacomo, "U.S. Still Has Much Work to Do on Securing Embassies." See also Emling, "'Remote Frisk' Seen as a Naked Assault on Human Rights."

20. For an interesting overview of the Aum Shinrikyo, see Watanabe, "Religion and Violence in Japan Today: A Chronological and Doctrinal Analysis of the Aum Shinrikyo," 80–100.

21. Hastings and Bamber, "Police Foil Terror Plot to Use Sarin Gas in London."

22. See Loeb, "Anthrax Vial Smuggled In to Make a Point at Hill Hearing." This article notes that William C. Patrick, a leading expert on biological warfare, walked through security carrying 7½ grams of powdered anthrax to a hearing on the House Permanent Select Committee on Intelligence. The aim was to demon-

strate the ease with which a bio-agent could be transported through government installations. More frightening has been the call by a Muslim cleric to use biological weapons against the West. See Maceskill and Ruford, "Muslim Calls for Bio-weapon Holy War."

23. For an overview of the violence in Italy, see Manwaring, "Italian Terrorism, 1968–1982: Strategic Lessons That Should Have Been Learned," 121–135.

24. Hanley, "International Terrorism: Global Order Shaken by Wanton War."

25. Ibid. See also Bruce, "Internet Is an Open Door to Crime and Terrorism." According to this article, "a U.S. intelligence officer brags that with twenty capable hackers and1 billion dollars, he could shut down America. "If that's true, so could a terrorist." See also Francis, "Cyber Threats Are All Too Real: Governments Fail to Comprehend Information Warfare," and "Hackers Launched 'Major Attack' on Pentagon Computer System." The threat to security, economic security in particular, was underlined in the actions of a teenage hacker who caused an estimate 1.7 billion dollars U.S. in damage by paralyzing major Internet sites in February 2000, including CNN.com, Yahoo.com, Amazon.com and eBay. The 16-year-old "Mafiaboy" brought down eleven Internet sites and shook confidence in electronic commerce. Hamilton, "Mafiaboy Pleads Guilty to Online Attacks," and Bronskill, "Canada Faces Cyber-threat, DND Warns: Forces Must Develop Ability to Counter New Forms of Attack." In February 2001, a report noted that hackers are attempting to break into Canada's electronic intelligence agency hundreds of times a month. Sallot, "Hackers Targeting Spy Computers: Sensitive Networks under Constant Attack Officials Tell Electronic Security Conference." According to one report, it was noted that "Disgruntled insiders and accounts held by former employees are a greater computer security threat to U.S. companies than outside hackers, according to a survey released on Tuesday." Abreu, "Tech-Security Survey—Insiders Are Main Computer Security Threat." See also Arquilla and Ronfeldt, "Fighting the Network War."

26. Jacobs, "The Nuclear Threat as a Terrorist Option," 149–163. For an excellent analysis of the nuclear, chemical and biological issues as they relate to terrorism, see Stern, *The Ultimate Terrorists* and Falkenrath, Newman, and Thayer, *America's Achilles' Heel: Nuclear, Biological, and Chemical Terrorism and Covert Attack*. See also Bremner, "Paris Trio Accused of Nuclear Smuggling." This report noted that French police and intelligence services are trying to trace the origin of a small quantity of highly enriched uranium that was seized on suspicion that the three men were selling it for nuclear weapons.

27. The possession of CW remains a serious concern. The Russian Federal Security Service (FSS) reportedly intercepted a telephone conversation between Chechen rebels. It was reported that the Chechens were preparing to produce and use toxic agents within the republic. "Chechen Plans to Put Domestic Chemicals to Test"; and Abd-al-Salam, "Sources Cited on Bin-Ladin's Possession of 'A Biological or Chemical Weapon.'"

28. The issue of biological and chemical terrorism is a real threat to all concerned. See "Experts: U.S. Not Ready for Germ Warfare"; Stern, "Taking the Terror Out of Bioterrorism"; Gorman, "Doomsday Bugs." This article notes that the "FBI has investigated 50 incidents of biological terrorism in the United States." For an overview see Kaplan, "Terrorism's Next Move: Nerve Gas and Germs Are the New Weapons of Choice." See also Venter, "Spectre of Biowar Remains: Al J. Venter

Analyses the Frightening Facts Revealed by Ken Alibek, the Most Senior Defector from the Former USSR's Biological Warfare Programme;" Babievsky, "Chemical and Biological Terrorism," 167–184, and "Report Catalogues Dangers of Anthrax as Weapon." The fear of biological warfare has spread to the agricultural area, where analysts and bureaucrats are awakening to the issues surrounding a chemical-biological attack on the nation's crops or animals. Such a situation would seriously impact the dairy, meat, chicken and other food industries. In fact, targeting farm animals would be low-tech, costing little in money, skills and equipment to deliver biological agents against farm animals. The plague of foot and mouth disease that occurred during the winter and spring of 2001 in the United Kingdom underlines the economic turmoil that could occur should a terrorist initiative wish to include biological terrorism against farm animals. "Facing up to the Agroterror Threat: How Biological Warfare Could Devastate Crops and Livestock." See also "A Large Dose of Terror: an Inside Look at How the Soviet Union Developed Lethal Germ Weapons, and Why the End of the Cold War Has Made the Threat of Biological Warfare Even Worse," Thomas and Waterhouse, "Britain Battles 'Ultimate Adversary,'" and de Bruxelles, "Moor Farmers Brace for 'Doomsday,'" and "Potent Virus Travelled the World for a Decade: Pan-Asia Strain 'Unstoppable.'" For an insight into the difficulties in employing anthrax as a weapon, see Spears, "Anthrax Difficult to Harness as a Weapon." See also Nickerson, "Bio-Terror Threats as Scary as Real Thing," and Thorne, "Consultations on Strategy Against Biological Threats Continue." This article notes that the Canadian government was attempting to develop a comprehensive strategy to address biological terrorism threats. See Hume, "Are We Open to Attack?" Garrett, "The Nightmare of Bioterrorism," Petrou, "Discovery of Deadly Virus Raises Fears of Biological Weapons." In one report, it was noted that the "U.S. government has contracted a biotechnology company to produce doses of a smallpox vaccine. The move was reportedly prompted by fears of potential bio-terrorist attacks, following the belief that samples of smallpox might have fallen into the hands of rogue states." "Bio-Terrorism Vaccine." *Jane's Intelligence Review* (October 2000). See also Miller, "U.S. Explores Other Options on Preventing Germ Warfare;" and Chyba, "Biological Terrorism and Public Health." See also, "Canada Deemed Ill-prepared for Chemical, Biological War," and Calamai, "Terrorism in a Test Tube." For an informative overview of the bio-terrorism issue, see Garrett, "Unprepared for the Worst."

    29. "'Terrorists Stepping up Operations,' Says U.S. Report." See also "Australians Warn of Computer Terrorism"; "White House Panel Warns of Infowarfare Threats, Computer Terrorism"; "Shoring Up Security Against Cyberterrorists"; and Regan, "Cyber Wars—Wars of the Future . . . Today." According to some observers China and Taiwan have commenced a guerrilla war in cyberspace and there are fears that such activities could escalate into open conflict. According to one report, Taiwanese computer experts were repairing damaged software and the mainframe computer. Suspicions are that this attack was inspired by mainland China and that key government agencies had gone on a cyber alert. Watts, "Tension Rises in Conflict 'That Surpasses All Boundaries': Virtual Warriors Fire Opening Shots in Cyber Battle." Also, "China 'Bombs' White House Web Site in Hacker War"; and Lungu, "Irregular Warfare and the Internet: The Case of the Zapatista Revolution." See also Lee, "Cyber-Criminals 'Now More Skillful.'"

30. Evenson, "Canada Poorly Prepared for Germ Warfare," and Munro, "Prepare for Bioterrorism Attack, Military Doctor Warns."

31. Vick, "Man in Kenya Gets U.S. Letter Containing Anthrax"; Lancaster and Dewar, "N.J. Mail Carrier, CBS Employee Have Anthrax"; and Moritsugu, San Martin and Chatterjee, "Anthrax Found in Second Capital Hill Office."

32. "More to Fear than Russian Germ Warfare: Brain Drain of Bio Weapon Scientists Threat to World Safety."

33. Abraham, "The 'Poor Man's Nukes'" and Bronskill, "Canada Not Ready for Terrorism: Ottawa."

34. McGregor, "Police Probe Reports of Aerial Poison Plot."

35. Mitchell, "How Stress and Illusion Breed Panic." See also, FBIS Has Athrax Suspect, Experts Says."

36. "Small British Firm Spearheads Production of Smallpox Vaccine."

37. "Security at Germ Banks Is Often Lax."

38. Lauria, "Iraq Bought Anthrax from U.S." See also, "Understanding Anthrax."

39. "The Early History of Contagion."

40. See Fialka, Chase, King and Winslow, "Deadly Biological Attack Feared," and Bone, "Gas Mask Sales Skyrocket in Wake of Terrorist Attacks."

41. Musser, "Better Killing Through Chemistry."

42. "Italy Arrests Four Moroccans with Cyanide, Maps." See also, "Chemical Bomb Attack Thwarted Italians Say."

43. Stonehouse, "Biological Agents 'Quintessential' Terror Weapons."

44. MacCallum, "Infrastructure Protection Key Issue."

45. Whitelaw, "Terrorists on the Web: Electronic 'Safe Haven'"; and Glaberson, "Guerrilla Warfare over the Internet."

46. See "Arafat Warns of Strife: PLO Chief Invokes Spectre of Hijacking." The article states that, "Arafat has warned of an escalation of violence in the occupied territories and of renewed plane hijackings if no progress is made on the Palestinian issue." The Palestinian situation has become increasingly violent. September–October 2000 witnessed numerous dead and wounded among both Israeli and Palestinian elements, to the extent that Yassar Arafat's Palestinian Authority has been blamed for orchestrating the violence, including a suicide bombing. See Willmer, "Arafat Blamed for Gaza Suicide Bomb: More Terrorism Feared." The threat posed by Islamic militants was explored during a presentation given by Michael Kelly of the Canadian Security Intelligence Service at a counter-terrorism symposium at the Royal Military College in Kingston, Ontario. Kelly re-affirmed to an audience of government officials, military personnel, and academics that "the threat is real, it's immediate, it's here." Stern, "Canada Faces 'Real' Terrorism Threat."

47. The fear of Islamic terrorism was noted in a report. See, "National Intelligence Agency Head Warns Indonesia 'Vulnerable' to Terrorism"; and Marcus, "Showing Arafat's True Colors."

48. The clandestine operation that saw the seizure of Abdullah Ocalan from a Greek embassy in Kenya and spirited away to Ankara has sparked a response from Kurdish communities worldwide. As Ocalan has been found guilty and should he be executed, this could ignite a wave of Kurdish-orchestrated violence similar to the Armenians' in the 1970s and '80s. See Wordsworth, "Ocalan Capture Sparks Global Kurd Protests." See also Hacaoglu, "'Baby Killer,' or Struggling Statesman";

and Knox, "Ocalan's Capture a Blow to Hopes for Autonomy." See also "Turkish Prosecutors Seek Death Penalty for Ocalan"; and Ersoy, "Turkish Court Sentences Ocalan to Death." In the wake of the sentencing Abdullah Ocalan called for his guerrillas to cease their fourteen-year-long battle for Kurdish home rule. Turgut, "Ocalan Calls on Kurd Rebels to End Struggle."

49. Hoffman, "Creatures of the Cold War: the JRA." This article notes that "Despite the fact that its last operation took place in 1988, the Japanese Red Army (JRA) cannot yet be discounted from further terrorist acts." In November 2000, Fusako Shigenobu, the founder of the Japanese Red Army (JRA), was arrested by the Japanese police as she left an Osaka hotel. She was charged with the attack and hostage-taking on the French embassy in the Hague. The JRA was responsible for a string of terrorist attacks in the 1970s and 1980s, including a 1972 machine-gun assault on the international airport outside of Tel Aviv that took the lives of twenty-four and wounded eighty. Ms. Shigenobu reportedly fled Japan in 1971 and was believed to have been living in Lebanon, where she was welcomed due to her support of the Palestinian cause. Sakurai, "Japanese Police Arrest Defiant Female Terrorist Leader: Red Army Group Killed 24 People in 1972 Israeli Attack." The group "Revolutionary Army" claimed the planting of a bomb to protest a middle school history text. The text had been criticized for white-washing the atrocities committed by the Imperial Japanese Forces during World War II. "Japan Textbook Explosion."

50. See "Sri Lankan Rebels Step up Attacks Suicide Bomber Strikes in Capital"; and "Lethal Tigers: No End Looks Likely in Sri Lanka's Long War." Since the 11 September 2001 attacks in the United States, the Tamil Tigers have been blacklisted along with a host of other terrorist groups, losing both their legitimacy and financial support. This situation caused their leader Vellupillai Prabhakaran to sue for a negotiated peace. Bell, "Sri Lankan Terrorist Group Agrees to Peace."

51. See "Sikh, in Punjab, Vows Flight for New Nation."

52. "INLA: the Deadly Hand of Irish Republicanism"; and Mullin, "Real IRA Re-emerges with New Name, New Threats." Although the Irish peace process continues, so does extremist activity. For an indication of the type of activities, see Smith, "Irish Security Sources Say Bomb Attack Thwarted"; Rosato, "Overnight Attacks Increase N. Ireland Tensions"; Cowley, "Republican Renegades Blamed for N. Irish Attacks"; Roddam, "Croatian Arms Haul Linked to Irish Guerrillas."

53. See "Peru: Shining Path." During the 1980s and '90s, the Maoist Shining Path insurgency waged a campaign of assassinations, sabotage and car bomb attacks. The activity decreased after the capture of Shining Path leadership in 1992. The insurgency has left 30,000 dead since 1980.

54. For an insightful commentary on the Colombian situation, see Klepak, "Colombia: Why Doesn't the War End?" Also Bugge, "Drugs, Colombia Preoccupy America's Defence Chiefs"; Adams and Whitworth, "Clinton Exhorts Colombia to Join War on Drugs"; Krauss, "In Visit to Colombia, Clinton Defends U.S. Outlay"; and Stewart, "Colombia Rebels Kidnap Senator's Family, 12 Others."

55. Warren, "German Army Plagued by Right-wing Extremists." According to this article, "High unemployment and the old regime's [East German] failure to confront history is encouraging support for neo-Nazis among young people." See also John, "German Neo-Nazis Flock to Internet-security Chief." According to this article, the number of far-right supporters in Germany has grown to eleven per-

cent in 1998 to 53,600. Of those, 8,200 are deemed violent. Authorities have attributed this situation to the high unemployment and the mistrust of foreigners. See also Simpson, "Germans Suspend Soldier over Racist Web Site: Investigation Launched"; Conradi, "Stasi Plot Lies Behind Neo-Nazi Revival: Report"; "Schroeder Says Not Enough Done to Fight Extremism"; "Germany Synagogue Attack"; and Hall, "Neo-Nazi Threat 'Played Down.'" This last article argues that the neo-Nazi threat in Germany has been underestimated by the government and the country could witness escalating far-right extremist violence on a scale not experienced since the urban terror of the 1970s. See also Boyes, "Germans Urged to Resist Neo-Nazis." The issue of race and the ensuring implications for immigration continue to be a problem not only for Germany but France, the United Kingdom, Italy and, as well, North America. See also Boyes, "We Do Not Need Any More Foreigners: Germany's Right Whips up Public Support for 'Culture' Rules Designed for Immigrants." See also Herman, "Skinhead Ranks Rising in Europe." This article noted that in Germany there were 430 violent crimes through the end of June out of 2,212 hate crimes that targeted people, mostly Jews and foreigners. Australia also seems to be concerned with illegal immigrants, warning them that they could be forced into prostitution, poverty and drug addiction if they go to Australia. This theme was dropped by the government due to pressure from human rights groups. However, another campaign featuring deadly snakes, sharks and man-eating crocodiles remains part of the Immigration Department's drive to discourage illegal immigration. Christie, "Australia Stands its Ground on Migrants: Man-eating Shark Video Has Deterred Boat People, Government Says," and "If Pimps Don't Get You, the Crocs Will: Australia Scraps Scare Campaign." The fear of religious issues has sparked a row over Italian immigration policy. Cardinal Gia como Biff, a Roman Catholic conservative, warned that "Christian Europe was in danger of being overwhelmed by a Muslim invasion" and urged the Italian government to allow only Roman Catholic immigrants to enter the country. This was in order to maintain the identity of the nation. Owen, "Italian Cardinal Attacks Muslim Immigration." For a different view on immigration policy, see Brouwer, "Don't Slam the Door."

56. "Red Brigades Announce Plan to 'Strike at the Heart of Imperialism.'"

57. Ousten, "Seized Explosives Ignite Major Hunt for Militia Groups." See also "Intelligence Briefs." This article notes that white supremacists are using the Internet to seek out recruits, initiating a substantial growth in America's "hate" groups, according to the Southern Poverty Law Center. The report counts the Klan, neo-Nazi, skinhead, Christian Identity, Council of Conservative Citizens, and black separatist groups as hate groups. Also, Laxer, "The Terror Within: The U.S. Fears Foreign Terrorism, but the Real Problem Is Closer to Home." This article notes that the idea of terrorism as something external to the United States avoids the reality that for the last few decades the American people have suffered serious assaults from home-grown para-military forces. For an overview, see Petrou, "Rebels Without a Cause."

58. See Syal, Craig and Bamber, "Neo-Nazis' Tactics Inspired by IRA: Group's Manifesto Urges Followers to Use Extreme Violence Against 'Invading Army'"; War, "Savagery in Soho: 2 Dead, 73 Hurt after Nail Bomb Rips Through Popular Gay Pub During Rush Hour"; and Williams, "Police Warn of Racist Campaign after Second London Bomb Blast." Recent articles underline the concerns of police and

security organizations regarding racist and anti-racist groups. Bronskill, "CSIS Targeting Anti-racists, Annual Report Reveals: 'Potential for Violence': Foreign Conflicts Could Bring Trouble Home to Canada Spy Agency Adds." Some other organizations are threatening the use of sabotage to achieve their objectives. One report stated that a radical anti-poverty group has vowed to sabotage the economy of Toronto. The Ontario Coalition Against Poverty threatened to target business, tourism and the film industry to strike back at Toronto's Mayor Mel Lastman, who campaigned against the homeless sleeping in parks. Benzie, "Anti-poverty Activists Vow Sabotage."

59. For an overview of single-issue terrorism, see Smith, "Single Issue Terrorism."

60. For an example, see the overview on the Earth Liberation Front in Saunders, "Suburban Guerrillas Fight Sprawl with Fires: Arsonists of the Earth Liberation Front Target Giant Homes and SUV Dealerships." Recent reports underline that the extremist elements of the U.S. environmental movement are becoming increasingly active. There are two defining concepts; one is biocentrism, which regards all organisms on earth as equal and therefore deserve moral rights and considerations. This philosophy identifies biodiversity and wilderness as an absolute good against which other actions should be judged. The other philosophy is deep ecology, which calls for a rollback of civilization and industrialization, the removal of pathogenic and exotic species. See Chalk, "U.S. Environmental Groups and 'Leaderless Resistance.'"

61. See Harrison and Foggo, "Terrorists Target Lab's Shareholders." This article noted that British police had advised the shareholders of a lab that conducts tests on animals that they were targets of a terrorist campaign.

62. Bronskill, "Protests over Modified Crops to Escalate: CSIS Confidential Report Spy Agency Warns over Bio-engineering."

63. The 1999 conflict in the Kosovo region underlined the threat to Americans at home. The FBI alerted the U.S. military to potential violence when several Serbian-American churches received faxed messages for Serb nationalists to kill American soldiers. Diamond, "Serb Letters Make Threats To Kill In U.S."

64. "State of Insecurity: Sri Lanka and the War That Lost its Way."

65. While some terrorist groups continue their crusade, the Red Army Faction has resigned from the international terrorist fraternity. The RAF—responsible for the kidnapping of Hans Martin Schlreyer and the five-day Lufthansa hijacking in 1977 that ended in the spectacular rescue of the crew and hostages—has lapsed into history. A letter sent to the Reuters News Agency announced, "Today, we're ending this project. The urban guerrillas who terrorized Germany during the Cold War said yesterday that it has given up its fight and disbanded." See "Red Army Faction Terrorist Group Disbands." The Faction killed fifty people between its operational years of 1968 to 1991 and lost twenty-six terrorists. The RAF rose from the radical anti-establishment student politics of the 1960s, taking inspiration from the Marxist 1959 Cuban revolution and Ché Guevara. See also Hoffman, "Intelligence and Terrorism: Emerging Threats and New Security Challenges in the Post-Cold War Era," 207–223. Hoffman underlines that there will be a proliferation of terrorism promoted by the religious imperative and related to this issue an increase in amateur terrorism action alongside the more professional terrorist. See also

Tendler, "Cleric Recruits Terrorists, Say MI5 Officers." Two senior MI5 officers have accused, at a special immigration trial, a Muslim cleric of recruiting terrorists for Kashmir. The British fear is that these jihad fighters may radicalize the British Muslim community.

66. For an overview of threats, see Gunaratna, "Transnational Threats in the Post-Cold War Era," and Gunaratna, "Terrorist Trends Suggest Shift of Focus to National Activities."

67. Sharrock, "Victim Turns on Police over Omagh 'Cover Ups'; Widower Demands Answers."

68. Hanley, "International Terrorism: Global Order Shaken by Wanton War." See Gunaratna, "Terrorist Trends Suggest Shift of Focus to National Activities."

69. For an examination of this SAM threat, see Hunter, "Manportable SAMs: the Airline Anathema." In 1993 for example, estimates of unused Stinger missiles in the hands of the Mujahedin were between 200 to 300. The CIA was reportedly offering $175,000 per missile.

70. Clarke and Rufford, "IRA Team Testing 'Napalm' Bomb," and Evans, "IRA Trio on Mission to Test Weapons."

71. The reality is that the information necessary to make the bombs is easily accessible on the Internet. This includes "The Terrorist's Handbook" with more than pages on how to make bombs. See "The Scourge of Terror."

72. Evans-Pritchard, "Case Collapsing Against Oklahoma Bomb Suspect." This bombing was noted to be "the deadliest act of terrorism ever committed on American soil." This has subsequently been surpassed by the 11 September 2001 terrorist acts committed in New York City and Washington. See also Smith and Thomas, "The Real Threat From Oklahoma City: Tactical and Strategic Responses to Terrorism," 119–138. The Oklahoma bombing legacy continues as the perpetrator, Timothy McVeigh, a 32-year-old Gulf War veteran, was subsequently executed by lethal injection. Campbell, "Oklahoma Bombing Saga Nears an End."

73. Labaton, "National Security Adviser Warns of Risk of Terrorism"; and Whitelaw, "The Ball Goes Up, but What Comes Down? Assessing Terrorists' Plans for the Millennium." See also Knickerbocker, "U.S. Goes on Alert for New York's Terrorists; Security Is Widespread, Intense as Nation Readies for Trouble from Inside and Out"; and "Trends In Terrorism." For a threat assessment in the wake of the USS Cole, see Burns, "U.S. Forces on High Alert in Gulf: New Indications of Terrorist Threats." The article underlines that the U.S. forces in Saudi Arabia and Kuwait are on the highest alert following new indicators of terrorist threats in the Persian Gulf countries. Moreover, U.S. officials have noted that since the USS Cole attack on 12 October, no American ships have gone through the Suez Canal. The threat of a water-borne or sub-surface attack remains a reality. Experiences drawn from the Achille Lauro and the USS Cole, as well as information indicating that certain terrorist groups have trained and are prepared to conduct scuba or swimmer attacks against civil or military surface ships underlines the potential threat. Moreover, the thought that small boats with a low radar signature, packed with high explosives, and targeted against high value surface vessels might be deployed is most disquieting. Discussion with General Ulrich K. Wegener, Royal Military College, Kinston, Canada (7 March 2002).

74. West, "'Fingerprints of bin Laden Are All over These Attacks': Terrorist

Strikes in Yemen Start of New Campaign by Saudi Millionaire, Western Experts Believe." See also Karon, "Bin Laden Rides Again: Myth Vs. Reality"; and Gershberg, " Israel Says Bin Laden Seeks Local Operatives."

75. Lake, 6 *Nightmares: Real Threats in a Dangerous World and How America Can Meet Them.*

76. Wapshott, "Telltale Signs Failed to Stop Shoe Bomber."

77. The issue of suicide bombers has been of great concern for authorities due to the immense damage that can be wrought by these individuals as well as underlining their respective groups' determination to pursue their political aims, particularly in the wake of the September 2001 attacks. Suicide terrorism is defined as the readiness to sacrifice one's life in the process of destroying or attempting to destroy a target, be it a person or place, in order to advance a political goal. The aim of the suicide terrorist is to sacrifice himself, to die, while destroying the enemy target. A profile of Palestinian suicide bombers notes them to be between 19 and 25 years of age, from large families and, therefore, not the principle wage earners. For the most part, they are not married and have no children. Their families are Muslim, devoutly religious, with those enticed to become suicide bombers coming from poor refugee camps or villages in the West Bank or Gaza Strip. See Hunter, "Bomb School: International Terrorist Training Camps"; Hassan, "An Arsenal of Believers"; and Nolen, "What Motivates Suicide Bombers?" According to Hunter, Iran teaches "suicide bombing techniques." See also La Guardia, "Suicide Bombers Kill 7, Wound 192 in Jerusalem." The October 2000 suicide attack on the USS Cole underlines the seriousness and effectiveness of this methodology. The suicide terrorists responsible for the 11 September 2001 attacks in New York City and Washington reportedly appear to have led happy family lives. It was further noted that the suicide hijackers were well-educated and skilled, and not hopeless young zealots, which is dramatically different from previous stereotypic suicide operators. In one case the suicide hijacker was reportedly a happy family man. It has been underlined in the Palestinian case that the "steady stream of hostility, carefully cultivated and implemented over the past decade, has conditioned the average Palestinian in society to justify launching vicious acts of cruelty against it." "A Culture of Hate." See also Blair, "Investigators Probe Yemen Blast Site"; Kiley, "'I Want to Die as a Martyr,' 12-year-old Says: Thousands of Youngsters Trained in Warfare at PLO Camps"; and Sprinzak, "Rational Fanatics." In one instance, suicide bomber Dia Tawil videotaped his intent. In his mid-twenties and a student at Bir Zeil University, Tawil noted that "I am the twelfth of the martyrs the Izzedine al Qassam Brigades have prepared to turn their bodies and their bones into shrapnel that will kill the Zionist occupiers." Tawil blew himself up on 27 March 2001 next to a bus in Jerusalem, injuring more than two dozen Israelis in the attack. "Suicide Bomber Left Video Confession." Another suicide bombing took place in late April 2001, when a man wearing a belt which contained explosives and packed with fifteen-centimeter nails joined a lineup for the bus, blowing himself up and killing an Israeli doctor. Kalman, "Palestinian Bomber Targets Bus Queue." See also, Robinson, "Four Die in Suicide Bombing in Northern Israel." Recent articles noted a negative backlash in the world's civilized community. Television viewing audiences were appalled at the "overall glorification of suicide bombers. On Arab children's television programming, Palestinian youths as young as eight or nine are shown with mock dynamite strapped around their waists, reciting lines that say they

want to grow up to be suicide bombers." Landy, "Martyrs or Murderers?" In the wake of the dramatic World Trade Center attack, it was reported that the Tamil Tiger guerrillas launched a suicide attack on a ship carrying 1,200 government troops. "Rebel Suicide Boats Attack Sri Lanka Troop Ship." See also, Gunaratna, "Terror from the Sky." This article discusses the evolution of suicide terrorism and the recent employment of airborne suicide terrorism. To appreciate the motivation of suicide bombers is critical in creating a strategy to deal with this lethal type of attack. For an overview into the background and motivation see Eshel, "Israel Reviews Profile of Suicide Bombers." The threat posed by suicide bombers remains of considerable concern to Western security authorities. See Adams, "Young, Keen and Ripe for Recruitment." See also, Gabor, "Fighting Fair: The Geneva Convention Set Strict Rules on War and How it Is Conducted." Female suicide bombers have raised Israel's concerns and such activities will create a more problematic security environment for Israeli authorities. See Gilmore, "Female Bomber Raises Israel's Security Fears."

78. In the early summer of 2001, one suicide bomber from the terrorist group Hamas blew himself up in the middle of a group of teenage girls outside a popular disco in Tel Aviv, killing twenty-two, including the bomber, who reportedly was infected by hepatitis B. His body parts may have infected some of the survivors! See Goldberg, "The Martyr Strategy."

79. "Hamas Leader Threatens New Suicide Operations Against Israel"; Philps, "Israel Warns of Revenge for Suicide Bombing," and Kalman, "Blast Kills Three Israelis, Suicide Bombers." For a valuable insight into suicide bombers, see Sprinzak, "Rational Fanatics," 67–73. After a month-long cessation in assassinations, a Palestinian militia leader was targeted by Israeli authorities and killed by a bomb that was reportedly hidden in a wall and detonated from a helicopter. The target, al-Karmi was supposedly responsible for the shooting deaths of nine Israelis. Philps, "Palestinian Militant Leader Assassinated."

80. Binyon, "Terrorist Profile Identifies New Threat."

81. For an excellent article on fundamentalism as a threat to the West, see Pipes, "Behind the Will of Islam: Once a Religion of Worldly Success, Islam Has Endured Two Centuries of Trauma. Solutions Have Presented Themselves in the Forms of Secularism and Reformism, but It Is the New Option of Fundamentalist Islam That Presents a Threat to the West."

82. See "Bin Laden's Long Tentacles of Terror," and "Time Interview: Bin Laden Says He Instigated Terrorist Attack." As to the future, a German intelligence report warns a wave of fundamentalist terrorism could engulf Germany and Europe, posing a serious problem to both Islamic and Western nations. This anticipated surge in Islamic violence will take the form of attacks against "easy targets" predicated upon the ease of access, low cost and the potential for psychological and media impact, as seen in the suicide attacks in New York and Washington in September 2001. Notwithstanding these operations, we may see Islamic terrorists employing airliners, small helicopters, pilotless reconnaissance planes, and weapons of mass destruction. This may be augmented by the 700 Russian-made SAM-6 Igla missiles which were reportedly sold to Iran. See Azulay-Katz and Amit, "Russian Missiles Sold to Iran Might Reach Hizballah, Endanger IDF Planes 'Know-How' to Iran to Continue." As for targets, the United States and Israel hold places one and two, respectively. As well, European nations could be targeted if

they extradite fundamentalists. The report added that Europe is seen as, and has become, a safe haven for fundamentalists. Al-Khatib, "German Intelligence: Fundamentalists Are Preparing New Terror Campaign in the West." There have also been unconfirmed reports that bin Laden is supporting a terrorist school in Chechnya. According to one report, there is a center for the preparation of "underage saboteurs." "Bin Ladin Said to Fund Terrorism 'School' in Chechnya." Also, "Bin Laden Said Sending More Fighters to Chechnya, but Facing Curbs in Afghanistan," and West, "Bin laden's Fingerprints All over These Attacks." It was reported that a letter supposedly authored by bin Laden expressed the resolve to create a "Global Islamic State." Ikramullah, "Usama bin Laden 'Letter' Calling for 'Global Islamic State.'" More recently, it has come to light that bin Laden had attempted to create the equivalent of a terrorist NATO alliance. Grier, "A Terrorist Version of NATO?" It should be underlined that many of the Islamic terrorists linked to bin Laden have had what could be described as sophisticated training. In a report on the terrorist training manual linked to the 1998 Tanzania and Nairobi U.S. embassy bombings, the text is notably detailed, operational and methodological throughout. It describes the importance of information gathering as it relates to the target, personal deception measures so as to not disclose Islamic orientation, tips for setting up assumed identities and how to rent apartments, assassination techniques, and training exercises to teach Islamic spies to avoid detection. Weiser, "Word for Word: Tips for Terrorists: Lose the Toothpick, Don't Talk to Cabbies, and Watch Where You Park." For an excellent overview of bin Laden's network al-Qaeda, see Gunaratna, "Blowback." In fact, the suicide operatives who conducted the terrorist attacks in New York City and Washington appeared to have been "sleepers" who portrayed, for the most part, a quiet unassuming lifestyle. It is notable that during the Second World War, the employment of Japanese Kamikaze aircraft sank thirty-four ships and damaged hundreds of other vessels. In the Battle of Okinawa, they killed almost 5,000 men. Gordon, "When an Open Society Is Wielded as a Weapon Against Itself." In the wake of the New York City and Washington attacks, an eleven-volume handbook, reportedly used by Osama bin Laden, contains "how to" information about everything one needs to known to be a Muslim terrorist. This includes everything from poison gas and explosives, to hand-to-hand combat with religious exhortations. The eleven-volume series, entitled "Manual of Afghan Jihad," is essentially a guide to the "basic rules of sabotage and destruction." According to intelligence analysts who read parts of the manual, they reported that its highly technical detail, including diagrams, underlines that the authors represent a new level of operational skill and sophistication in the training of bin Laden's operators. The preface notes that these series of manuals are meant for use in war against "the enemies of our movement, the enemies of Allah, and for any Islamic group." Gannon, "Bin Laden Manual Lists 'Rules of Destruction.'"

83. "New Style Terrorist Is a Lone Fanatic." The article notes that the modern terrorist is likely a loner driven by personal or religious motives with access to chemical and biological agents with the potential for causing more destruction than his 1970s predecessors. A United Nations' investigator has argued that religious extremism is "an ever-growing scourge" that is epitomized by Afghanistan, where Taliban rulers had "taken an entire society hostage." Goodman, "UN Report Re-

ligious Extremism Is 'Ever-growing Scourge.'" It became apparent that nations and interests other than the U.S. were at threat from al-Qaeda. Both Germany and Great Britain, as well as Canada, were seen as potential targets for bin Laden's operators. Graham, "Berlin Fears Imminent Attack" and "Notebook Contains Plan for Bombing London." To garner an insight into the issues of concern to bin Laden, see Gerecht, "The Gospel According to Osama bin Laden." For an interpretation of the reasons for Osama bin Laden's attacks on America, see Doran, "Somebody Else's Civil War."

84. Fife, "Terrorists, Spies Using Canada's Immigrant Communities, CSIS Says"; and "Spy Agency Urges Watch on Refugees, Immigrants." This article notes that "Canada is vulnerable to terrorist activity by a few immigrants and refugees who bring their homeland struggles here, the Canadian Security Intelligence Service says in its annual report." For an overview of the immigration crisis in Southeast Asia and the Middle East, see Davis, "Riding the Wave of Illegal Immigrants." See also Blatchford, "Canada and Terrorism."

85. See French, "Terrorist Threat Growing: Just When You Thought it Safe." The article states, "The world is becoming a more dangerous place to do business, but cutbacks in media coverage may be masking the threat to the entrepreneur, a U.S.-based terrorism watcher warns." Of note is that the article complains that the "'media threshold is now so high that most terrorist acts don't meet it.'" Moreover, "People are being lulled into a false sense of security that terrorism has gone away. . . . In reality, the hard, cold evidence demonstrates it hasn't gone away."

86. Discussions with a senior intelligence officer, Ottawa, Canada (22 June 1998). See also Miller, "President Steps Up Efforts Against Terrorism."

87. Miller and Broad, "New York City Developing Plans to Counter Chemical, Germ Attacks." See also Garrett, "Bioterrorism Frightens the Experts." This article underlines that the public health infrastructure in both Canada and the U.S. would be devastated by an attack using modern germ technology. One scenario employed smallpox as the biological agent, and in the exercise this agent left an estimated 15,000 dead over a two-month period and 80 million dead over a year due to a lack of global vaccines. This concern over a biological attack was underlined when Alberta public health experts noted that Canada is poorly prepared to deal with a bio-terrorist attack due to a lack of co-ordination amongst the authorities responsible for defending Canadians against such initiatives. See Walker, "Canada Unprepared for Attacks by Biological Terrorists, Experts Say: Poor Coordination, Limited Resources Hinder Effective Response to Anthrax, Ebola Attacks." See also Venter, "Biological Warfare: the Poor Man's Atomic Bomb," 42–47. It has also surfaced that current agricultural practices in North America can provide an opportunity for terrorists to conduct acts of bio-terrorism and chemical warfare. Large farms could pose an easy target for terrorists. To destroy ninety-five percent of the American beef industry, a terrorist would have to target just a 200-mile radius. Like crops and cattle, agricultural supplies are now being controlled by fewer companies, providing opportunities for terrorists and disenfranchised employees to do substantial damage by putting chemicals or bio-agents into the food supply. Beaudin, "Terrorists Could Try to Poison Our Food: Sabotage Gets Easier Symposium Is Told to Be Set for Attacks." The foot and mouth disease crisis in 2001 in Great Britain and Europe underlines the potential for economic or agrarian

terrorism. British scientists say the current strain of foot and mouth disease is a new and virulent version of the virus that causes painful blisters on the hoofs and mouths of the animals. Walton, "Virus Last Came to Canada with Migrant."

88. "Report: U.S. Unprepared for Bioterrorism." See also Fox, "Be Afraid, Be Very Afraid about Bioterrorism, Experts Tell U.S. Conference." The article notes that modern societies are vulnerable and that both American defense and health officials have agreed since the mid 1990s that the risk of a bioterrorist attack was high enough to warrant taking countermeasures and building a credible response. The issue of possible terrorist use of chemical or biological agents was surfaced in New York City and Washington. This was compounded by earlier reports that twenty Iraqi soldiers were killed and up to 200 admitted to hospital when a chemical weapons exercise went wrong. "20 Iraqis Die During Weapons Training." For an excellent overview, see Rauf, "Future Trends in CBRN Terrorism to 2010." Canadian studies underlined the seriousness of the threat from a nuclear, chemical, or biological attack, as well as the realization that the Canadian Forces could not respond quickly enough should an attack occur on the capital city of Ottawa, Mofina, "Military Ill-Prepared for Attack on Ottawa" and Pugliese, "Only 11 Nuclear Bombs to 'Take Out' Canada." Nuclear, chemical, and biological threats pervaded the thoughts of security and intelligence authorities, particularly in the wake of the discovery that al-Qaeda had low-grade uranium and cyanide, both of which were discovered by American Forces in a storage facility near the Kandahar airport. It was believed that al-Qaeda intended to use the uranium-238 for dirty bombs, which would consist of conventional explosives married to radioactive material. Such an explosion would spread radioactive material over a wide area. The results would kill people in the bomb blast area, poison others with radiation, and would render large areas unusable, Brown, "Al-Qaeda Cache of Low-Grade Uranium, Cyanide Found Near Kandahar Airport"; Dutter and Fenton, "Uranium and Cyanide Found at bin Laden Base"; and Loyd, "Al-Qaeda Tested Terror Weapons." The threat of chemical strikes permeated the Christmas of 2001, both in Israel and the United Kingdom, McGrory, "Israel Fears Chemical Strike by Hamas"; "British Troops Storm Ship"; and Leppard, "Spy Chiefs Hunt for 20 'Terror Ships.'"

89. Gearan, "Clinton Predicts Century of Technological Advances." See also "Chemical, Biological, Radiological and Nuclear (CBRN) Terrorism"; and Purver, "The Threat of Chemical/Biological Terrorism." For an interesting view of Aum Shinrikyo's mission failure, see Rosenau, "Aum Shinrikyo's Biological Weapons Program: Why Did it Fail?" For further information pertaining to the Aum Shinrikyo's test with anthrax, see "AFP Reports Japanese Sect Aum Conducted 'Trial Run of Anthrax Weapon.'"

90. "Biothreats: Just the Facts: II."

91. The Pentagon's Cole commission argued for improved U.S. intelligence gathering and insistence on better protection for U.S. forces. In fact, "the commission recommended that anti-terrorism and force-protection training will be given to all troops with the same intensity that they are trained in other areas," one defense official advised Reuters. This awareness training is to make troops more conscious of the possibility of a biological, chemical or bomb attack as a natural result of the expanding threat from "asymmetrical warfare" against American and indeed Western interests. Aldinger, "Anti-terrorism Training Recommended for U.S. Troops."

92. Bronskill, Mofina and May, "Bio-Terrorism Risk Hits Home." This threat is also felt in India. See Vaidya, "Defence Forces Focus on Threats of NBC Warfare."

93. Roman, "Threat of Germ Warfare 'A Reality'"; Evenson, "Canada Poorly Prepared for Germ Warfare, Thousands Could Die: Biological Agents 'Uniquely Effective as Terrorist Weapons,'" and "This Week: Special Delivery: Does This Package Contain Anthrax?" *Saturday Night* 21. For an excellent overview of the CBW threat in the aftermath of 11 September 2001, see Latter, "After 11 September, CBW Threat Looms."

94. Wilson, "Electromagnetic Pulse Bomb: It's Called the E-Bomb." As societies become more high-tech, there is also a cruel paradox in that this leaves these same societies vulnerable to crippling terrorist cyber attacks which could result in financial and psychological damage, Homer-Dixon, "The Rise of Complex Terrorism."

95. Abraham, Bourette and Foss, "Ebola-like Case Sends Authorities Scrambling."

96. Ibid. [Abraham, et al.] See also Picard, "Disease Fit for a Stephen King Thriller."

97. For an interesting view of disease as a threat to national security, see Fox, "Phantom Warriors: Disease as a Threat to U.S. National Security," *Parameters,* 121–36. The option of a smallpox bio-terrorist assault was a persistent shadow to security and governmental authorities, particularly in the wake of revelations that al-Qaeda elements toyed with chemical and biological agents, Spears, "Smallpox is the Most Dangerous Virus Ever."

98. MacKinnon, "Canada Blind to Bioterror, Critic Warns." See also Rose, "The Trouble with Biological Weapons."

99. See Weiss and Blum, "The Man Who the FBI Believes Flew an American Airlines Plane into the World Trade Center Sept. 11 Apparently Walked into a U.S. Department of Agriculture Office in Florida Last Year and Asked about a Loan to Buy a Crop-duster Plane." This article notes the "apparent interest in the spray planes has heightened fears that the United States may be at risk of an aerial assault involving biological or chemical weapons." This interest was compounded by a report that a suspicious person wanted to buy and fly the planes belonging to a Regina-based crop dusting firm. This situation was exacerbated when two people were detained who had transport licenses for chemical and hazardous material. See "Crop Dusting Firm Raises Alarm" and "Germ Warfare Fears Grow." It has been argued that the events of 11 September 2001 were unthinkable; however, considering the events of the last century, this is not so. The horrific events of WWI, WWII, the Holocaust, Cambodia, Rwanda, and a number of other events were also unthinkable. In reality, every human act is coldly thinkable, from the highest to the lowest.

100. Vedantam, "Bioterrorism's Relentless, Stealthy March."

101. "Bush Worried About Terrorist Attacks on U.S. Food Supply."

102. Thompson, "Food Supply Vulnerable to Bioterrorism, Agency Head Says."

103. Bamber and Blanchfield, "Bin Laden Takes Credit for Sept. 11."

104. Sprinzak, "The Lone Gunmen."

105. In the last few years, the British military began studying the expansion of its roles to tackle organized criminal activity, the drug trade and international ter-

rorism. This included greater assistance to MI5, the employment of the Special Forces in customs operations, and the employment of submarines and aircraft to monitor ships and motor vehicles suspected of carrying contraband. See "Army Set to Join Battle on Crime." According to one report, Scotland Yard's Special Branch is positioning itself from its historic duties of counterterrorism and political crime to fight organized crime. See "Special Branch Is Set to Join War on Organized Crime." Canada was further criticized for not being able to handle a biological or chemical terrorist attack. Moreover, it was highlighted that "few Canadian Forces personnel are interested in becoming specialists in chemical or biological defense." The reason was that this was seen as a career-limiting move and outside the mainstream career path! See Monchuk, "Canada Not Ready for Bio Attacks."

106. "SAS Killings in Gibraltar Ruled Lawful."

107. Paul Wilkinson, "Trends in International Terrorism and the American Response," in Freedman, et al., *Terrorism and International Order*, 49.

108. "Confident They Had Defeated Guerrillas, Security Forces Let Guard Down"; and Diebel, "Guerrilla Leader Captivates the World." According to some sources the Japanese government was not advised prior to the Peruvian assault of the embassy. It should be noted however that Peruvian authorities and its counter-terrorist team had available a number of "foreign advisors" on site to consult with as needed. Needless to say, the Peruvian success has brought about further cooperative efforts in South America. Recently Peru offered to assist the Colombian government with its experiences in dealing with terrorists and guerrillas. "Foreign Minister: Colombian Guerrillas Pose 'Threat.'"

109. Karpukhin, "Commandos Storm Seized Russian Bus, Kill Hijacker."

110. Freedman, *Terrorism and International Order*, 48–49.

111. Tibbetts, "PM Considers Security Perimeter."

112. Whitaker, et al., "Ten Ways to Fight Terrorism," 26.

113. Burns, "Attack Alert Ignored, Spy Says Congress Told Officials at Pentagon Failed to Heed Warning of Terrorism Expert: Senators"; Zakaria, "U.S. Intelligence Analyst Quits over Cole Attack"; "Lessons from USS Cole." In the wake of the USS Cole attack, a Defense Intelligence Agency counterterrorist analyst resigned, claiming that his superiors had failed to pass on information that would have helped to anticipate the terrorist attack.

114. Ibid.

115. See "Security and Civilian Airports." Racial profiling is a politically charged issue as well as the focus of an interesting and balanced article that underlined that the number of suicide bombers is not large and that racial profiling is a logical security tool, Krauthammer, "The Case for Profiling."

116. See Grey and Haynes, "Police See Knife Carriers at 60ft with X-ray Spy Cameras." This articles notes that "cameras deployed by Britain's police forces will, in future, have the power to see through our clothes. An 'x-ray' version of the CCTV camera is being developed to detect hidden guns and knives from up to 60ft away." Airport security remains a top issue for both politicians and bureaucrats. In the aftermath of 11 September 2001, Canada created The Canadian Air Transport Security Agency (CATSA) within Transport Canada; it will likely be responsible for passenger screening and other security duties. The Canadian government will ensure that airport security companies will have to meet new certification standards and the December 2001 federal budget set aside funds for the purchase of explo-

sive detection systems. Moreover, Transport minister David Collenette was convinced by airline pilots to request that armed air marshals (RCMP officers) fly aboard selected flights as a precaution, McGregor, "Airport Security Redesign 'Work in Progress.'"

117. See Schere, "New Antiterrorist Weapon: Lassie vs. 'Carlos the Jackal.'" The articles notes that the FAA "with an annual K-9 budget of $1 million, currently used dogs to search suspicious objects and for spot-checking luggage." Moreover, they are mobile and can climb over luggage, walk a line of people and are capable of detecting smells beyond the sensitivity of machines to measure.

118. Hoagland, "Americans must Confront a New Age of Terrorism"; and Landay, "U.S. Takes Global Precautions To Stem Threat of Terrorism."

119. Munro, "Lasting Impression."

120. "British Spy Cameras Can Identify Terrorists."

121. Walters, "Mounties Use Secret Cameras at Pearson: System Looks for Criminals but Raises Privacy Worry."

122. The fallout from the September 2001 PENTTBOMB attacks included a series of security reviews aimed, in part, at the security of airports and passenger aircraft. In one case, a security company allegedly hired criminals to staff security at Philadelphia International Airport. The company reportedly did not perform the required security checks; it was noted that last year eighteen guards were known to have convictions ranging from drug possession to burglary, as well as resisting arrest. The company has 25,000 employees who work at all major American airports. See "Terrorist Security Company."

123. Walters, "Mounties Use Secret Cameras at Pearson: System Looks for Criminals but Raises Privacy Worry."

124. See Bowers, "Ground Personnel: Gap in Airport Security System." This article notes the high rate of turnover of these employees (more than fifty percent) and the low wages paid as a source of the retention problem. The employees themselves are "mobile" as they are mostly students, retirees or people with poor education. Airport security was to include background checks on baggage screens and everyone authorized to be in "secure" areas with access to terminal ramps. This includes mechanics, flight attendants, gate agents, catering-truck drivers and baggage workers. Also, bomb-detection scanners were to be purchased so as to equip U.S. airports to screen all checked baggage. Phillips and Nakashima, "FBI to Check More Airport Workers."

125. Cramb, "Lockerbie Bomb 'Was Put on at Heathrow.'"

126. Farrell and Cobain, "Security Staff Were Behind Hijacking: Gun Brought Aboard in Pilot's Forgotten Travel Bag."

127. Belluck, "Airport Inquiry Faulted Security Before Explosion."

128. For a view of how Ahmed Ressam became involved in terrorism, see Jiwa, "How I Became a Terrorist." Since the arrest of Ahmed Ressam in December 1999, raising a number of serious questions regarding the security of the Canadian-U.S. border, President George W. Bush has pledged more money and personnel to combat the flow of drugs and immigrants from Canada. Notwithstanding official assurances that the Canadian and U.S. authorities are co-operating, there is a persistent concern among American elected officials that Canada has become a haven for foreign criminals and terrorists whose intention is to target the United States. These politicians and others have argued that "unless Canada toughens up its

immigration policy, the Canada-U.S. border must be tightened." Ottawa allocated forty-eight million dollars for better screening of immigrants and more immigration officers abroad. The associate commissioner for the U.S. Immigration and Naturalization Service noted that "illegal immigration, and terrorism in particular, the challenge for U.S. and Canadian officials is the rapid and timely exchange of information on such individuals who pose a common threat." Essentially, underlining the importance of intelligence and cooperation in defeating these threats. Koring, "Some Border Security Gaps Plugged, Many Remain." This border security issue becomes more problematic as calls for erasing borders becomes more economically driven and, therefore, influential. See "Canada–U.S. Borderless."

129. "Airlines Begin Installing Steel Bars, Locks on Doors to Restrict Access to Cockpit."

130. Kehaulani Goo, "Some Pilots to Receive Stun-gun Training."

131. "Canada Likely to Follow U.S. Air Security Process."

132. Whitaker, et al., "Ten Ways to Fight Terrorism."

133. "The Man Who Protects America From Terrorism." This article underlines the concern regarding the potential terrorist employment of weapons of mass destruction, "the possibility of an assault from nerve gas, bacteria and viruses, and from . . . an electronic Pearl Harbor." For a report on a test scenario which underlines American concerns over the threat of bio-terrorism, see Neergaard, "How Bioterrorism Nearly Wiped out the U.S."

134. Ibid.

135. Knox, "Probe Stirs Specter of Bin Laden A-bomb."

136. Landers, "CIA Says Terror War Not for Faint-hearted."

137. Calabresi and Ratnesar, "Can We Stop the Next Attack?"

138. Untitled, *Reuters* (2 December 1997).

139. Sankey, "Terrorists Target Oilpatch: Security Specialist Gives Warning." Mr. Alan Bell—an internationally renowned security consultant with Globe Risk Holdings—underlined the problems and issues surrounding overseas hostage-taking aimed at the resource industry. "Guerrilla groups seize foreign workers and ransom them. This issue of security has become more relevant in the wake of a series of hostage takings in Colombia and Ecuador. It has been noted that there are 202 Canadian oil and gas exploration and service companies working overseas and are potential targets for terrorists interested in parlaying hostages for ransom."

140. See "Protecting Diplomats Increasingly Complex."

141. Security authorities have underlined concerns over the threat of computer hackers and cyber-terrorists attacking the nation's vital electronic systems as they access the tools to breach secure systems. Bronskill, "Canada Becoming More Vulnerable to Hackers: CSIS"; Bronskill, "'Hactivists' and Cyber-Outlaws Growing Threat: CSIS." Computer hackers changed the logo on the web page of the Canadian Security Intelligence Service in August 1999 to read "Canadian Security Illegal Service," underlining the vulnerability of all websites. See Canadian Broadcasting Corporation, "Interview with J. Lee and Richard Reynolds." See also Campbell, "Russian Hackers Steal U.S. Weapons Secrets" and Rose, "Terror Has a New Name: The Internet: 'The First Web War.'" Moreover, it has been revealed that the website of the Hezbollah was manipulated by Israeli hackers, who amended the site to include an Israeli flag and a tiny piano playing "Hatikva"—the Israeli national anthem. This assault was parried by a counterassault led by pro-Palestinian

cyber-soldiers who attacked the Israeli websites of the army, the Foreign Ministry, the prime minister and the Parliament. It is the opinion of Gilad Rabinovitch of Net Vision, an Israeli Internet provider, that this situation represents the "first full-scale war in cyberspace." Hockstader, "Fly in Mideast Cyber-War." Canada, for one, has created a new federal agency tasked to protect national electronic infrastructure: The Office of Critical Infrastructure Protection and Emergency Preparedness (OCIPEP) is the first new national security organization since the creation of CSIS in 1984. The purpose of this new agency is to counter activities to crash Canada's electrical power grids, air traffic control, natural gas pipelines, and the Toronto Stock Exchange. Interestingly, the new agency is being established under the Department of National Defence, which sends a clear signal that the issues to be addressed by OCIPEP are deemed to be as important as protecting Canada from physical attack. Sallot, "Guarding Canada's E-frontier: New Federal Agency Aims to Protect Critical Infrastructure from Hack Attacks." This issue is further compounded with the reports that underemployed, highly skilled Russian computer experts and hackers have increased the probability that they could be employed for more sinister purposes. Alvey, "Russian Hackers for Hire: the Rise of the E-mercenary." The threat posed by cyber terrorism in the aftermath of the 11 September attacks was described in an article by Michael Petrou. See Petrou, "How Canada Is Boosting Cyber Security."

142. Macleod, "Mounties Fear Y2K Terrorists' Cyber-Attacks: Computer Crisis Ties up Experts, Risks Security."

143. The terrorist employment of websites was further exposed when the terrorist group Islamic Jihad began claiming responsibility for attacks against Israeli civilians while glorifying the suicide bombers. The sites operated out of Toronto, Ontario. It was further noted that an Islamic site in Montreal posted an "invitation to Jihad" and called upon Muslims to train for holy war at paramilitary camps in Afghanistan. See Bell, "Mideast Terrorists Run Toronto Web Site"; "RCMP Probe Terrorist Link"; and Bell, "Web Site Used to Recruit Terrorists Moves to U.S."

144. Mofina and Blanchfield, "Utilities Most Likely Terrorism Targets."

145. During the Ahmed Ressam trial in April 2001, it was noted that Canadian authorities were not very thorough in their examination of the bona fides of Ressam. He received a Canadian passport using a fake student card, forged Quebec baptismal certificate, and a 300-dollar payoff to a shady middleman. Bell, "Passport Office Did Little Checking, Ressam Trial Told." The issue of forged passports was raised again in the wake of the attacks on 11 September. The security implications of the forged/stolen passport business are readily identifiable. Moreover, the situation is of particular concern in the areas of terrorism, human smuggling and identity fraud. Smith, "The Terrorists and Crime Bosses Behind the Fake Passport Trade." Canada reportedly plans to comply with the U.S. legislation requiring disclosure of personal information and other pertinent information. This data will be forwarded to U.S. Customs and Immigration before the flight lands. Baxter, "Canada to Comply with U.S. in New Airline Security Act" and Schmidt, "Canada to Give U.S. More Details on Travelers." As the situation evolves it is likely that we will see the evolution of a fully integrated continental defense structure within Canada, the United States, and possibly Mexico. This will have some sensitive sovereignty issues.

146. Akin, "Canada's Computer Security Loopholes Called Threat to U.S.:

Branch Office 'Back Door': Teens, Foreign States Represent Threat Conference Told." That said, the American Government Accounting Office noted in an audit that lax computer security poses a serious and growing threat to a spectrum of critical U.S. government operations and property underlining a number of security lapses at twenty-four U.S. federal agencies. The audit noted that a broad array of federal operations and assets were at risk of fraud as well as misuse and disruption. Wolf, "U.S. Government Computer Security Said Lax," and "U.S. Gets Low Grade for Computer Security." Concerns were underlined in the summer of 2001 when analysts allowed that for "two weeks last spring, hackers wormed their way inside a computer system that plays a key role in moving electrical power where it is needed around California." The deregulation of the energy industry also brought with it less secure computer networks that could be hacked into to disrupt power transfers. Piller, "Hackers Could Worm Way into Power."

147. Sheridan, "U.S. Moves to Tighten Security on Borders"; and O'Neill, "100 More U.S. Guards Sent to Border with Canada."

148. Interview with a Canadian intelligence officer, Ottawa, Canada (26 February 1999). See also O'Ballance, "Terrorism & Intelligence," and Bell, "Better Spies Needed Overseas—Senator: Law Agency Called For: Canada Now Relies on Allies for Foreign Intelligence." According to this article, "The urgency for such a service comes mostly from Canada's continued attractiveness to foreign terrorist organizations, which have been sending agents here disguised as refugees."

149. Intelligence is the vital thread in the national and international war against terrorism. In November 2000, the British Security Service foiled a bombing plot by dissident Irish republican extremists. Reportedly, the intent was to detonate a large bomb in central London during a major event. The bomb weighed 227 kilograms—twice the size of the Omagh bomb that killed twenty-nine people in 1998. "British Security Foils Plot to Bomb London: Report." The same month, French police arrested, in Paris, seven key members of the Spanish left-wing extremist group GRAPO. Spain's Interior Minister Jaime Mayor Oreja said that the arrests had dismantled the executive and guerrilla branches of the Spanish terrorist group. During the raids, the French authorities discovered bomb-making equipment, detonators and forged travel documents. Deiller, "Europe's Last Marxist Army Dismantled: Seven Spanish Arrests." Intelligence cooperation is vital, particularly in order to discover the organization, capabilities and terrorists involved. Blanche, "Arabs Likely to Aid U.S. Efforts to Track down Terrorists." Although some nations did not consider themselves as possible targets for al-Qaeda, this perception changed as the campaign in Afghanistan evolved. Bell and Jimenez, "Canada On al-Qaeda Hit List, Officials Say." The issue of al-Qaeda operatives working throughout the West was further reinforced with revelations that there were a number of supporters and sympathizers in Canada. Bell and Jimenez, "Al-Qaeda Operatives in Canada." Good intelligence enabled the seizure of 50 tons of weapons taken from a Palestinian ship. The seizure caused much concern among Israeli and Palestinian officials as the weapons were reportedly supplied by the Iranian government. Gershberg, "Ships Deadly Cargo Seized by Israel."

150. Wallace, "The Fear Factor, Governments Grapple with a New Anonymous Style of Terror," 27. Co-operation is vital in the intelligence field and for the most part is taken for granted. One article noted that "the British and Israeli secret services failed to prevent terrorist attacks, including 'hits' by Palestinians on the streets

of London, because of inter-agency feuds." Lashmar and Elam, "MI5 Was Feuding with Mossad While Known Terrorist Struck in London." During the course of the American-led military operations it became evident that American and French, as well as other nationalities, were involved with al-Qaeda. See Sage, "French al-Qaeda Fighter Was 'Brainwashed,' Father Says"; Newton, "U.S. Talib Defends Terrorists in Interview"; and Taylor, "Bin Laden's Balkan Connections." This discovery was further compounded when the twenty-one-year-old French citizen Abdur Rehman was captured and questioned. Rehman had received military training at an al-Qaeda camp. These discoveries of white/Western Muslims, now known as white al-Qaeda, are an important discovery. "Frenchman Was al-Qaeda Member."

151. Unfortunately intelligence success can be fleeting. Israel, as well as other nations, has been caught off guard for a myriad of reasons. For an interesting insight into the Israeli failures and their ramifications, see Blanche, "Israeli Intelligence Agencies under Fire."

152. Whitaker, et al., "Ten Ways to Fight Terrorism."

153. Smith, "CIA Dumps Over 1,000 Informants."

154. Hockstader, "Firing Squads Execute Palestinians," and Kalman, "Convicted Palestinian Spy Sentenced to Death."

155. Untitled, *Reuters*. After a number of intelligence problems, particularly the bombing of the Chinese Embassy in Belgrade in May 1999, the House of Representatives approved funding to increase the number of intelligence personnel and humint sources. "U.S. House Votes CIA Funding for More Spies"; "C.I.A. Picked a Bombing Target Only Once: The Chinese Embassy"; "CIA Chief Takes Responsibility for Chinese Embassy Bombing"; Fenton, "Wanted: Trainee Spies, Starting at $34,000 (US): CIA Espionage Is Back in Vogue Around Washington"; and Pincus, "Top Spy Retiring from CIA: Downing Led Revamp of Clandestine Service." Jack G. Downing stated that the CIA is in the midst of its greatest recruiting drive for case officers in its history. Moreover, the CIA intends to complete the rebuilding of its clandestine capability by 2005. "Spies, Damned Lies and Information."

156. Landay, "U.S. Takes Global Precautions to Stem Threat of Terrorism."

157. Bowers and Landay, "Terrorist Threat Spurs New Debate on 'Human' Spies." See also "Racist Groups Hard to Penetrate—UK's Straw" and "U.S. Clandestine Service Steps in When All Else Fails, Says CIA Deputy Director." This last article notes that "the challenge is to infiltrate groups that are small, hidden and connected to each other in a labyrinth of ways."

158. For an insight into the frustrations relating to developing "humint," see Gerecht, "The Counterterrorist Myth." This article was published just before the 11 September attacks in the United States and underlines, in rather surprising terms, the "intelligence gap" that had evolved in the CIA.

159. Livingstone and Arnold, *Fighting Back: Winning the War Against Terrorism*, 232.

160. Ibid., 231–232. See also Johnston, "1985 Arab Hijacker Faces Penalty Today." FBI agents took into custody Omar Mohammed Ali Rezaq, the lone survivor of a three-man terrorist team that commandeered Egypt Air Flight 648 on 23 November 1985. The FBI apprehended the terrorist in Lagos and brought him to the U.S. for trial. More recently, Musbah Abulgasem Eter, a former member of the Libyan secret service, was arrested by the Italian authorities. This individual

was wanted for the 1986 Berlin disco bombing that killed two American service-men and a Turkish woman and wounded 200. See "Libyan Arrested for '86 Bombing." In the pursuit of justice, four former East German intelligence officers were put on trial for assisting some of the West's most wanted terrorists. These officers reportedly helped the Red Army Faction members obtain new identities and begin new lives in the East. See Drozdiak, "Ex-East Germans on Trial for Helping Terrorists: Security Officers Say They Reduced Violence."

161. Bell, "CSIS Works with 'Unsavoury' Foreign Agencies: Watchdog."

162. "U.S. Tries New Tack in Hunt for bin Laden." See also "FBI Puts Osama bin Laden on 10-Most-Wanted List." For an overview on bin Laden, see O'Ballance, "Osama bin Laden and His al-Qaida Organization."

163. "FBI Working with U.S. Allies on bin Laden—Freeh."

164. In April 2001, Ahmed Ressam was convicted. The verdict came the same day as a Paris tribunal sentenced Ressam (in absentia) to five years for trafficking in false passports and aiding Islamic militants in France. Five other members of the Montreal jihad cell, including the leader Fateh Kamel, were also handed prison terms. Bell, "Ressam Convicted of Terrorism," and Duffy, "Ressam Came Perilously Close to a Terrible Success." Ressam has since co-operated with American authorities against Mokhtar Haouari, accused of scheming to set off bombs with Ressam. According to reports, Ressam's target was the Los Angeles International Airport. Bronskill, "Ressam Makes Deal, Agrees to Talk."

165. Wordsworth, "Low Pay Drove Laden Aide into Arms of U.S. Law," "Defense Grills Terror Witness on bin Laden," "Witness Tells How bin Laden Group Works: Embassy Bombing Trial Hears from Defector," and Appleson, "Bin Laden Supporter Tells of Order on Americans."

166. Powell, "4 Bombers Get Life Sentences."

167. Scott, "PKK Is Down but Not Out as Leaders Talk of Three-Front War." See also Ersoy, "Turkish Court Sentences Ocalan to Death."

168. Drohan, "Tougher Air-Travel Security Likely: G7 Ministers Expected to Agree Today to Beef up Antiterrorism Measures."

169. Bindman, "Mock Terrorist Attack Set to Roll near Border." This article stated that "Canada and the United States will stage the largest-ever test of their ability to respond to a terrorist attack in a mock hostage-taking somewhere along the border later this month." See also "FBI Conduct a Terrorism Attack Simulation." In the wake of the suicide attack on the USS Cole, there were numerous reports noting that there had been indications of an impending attack, but to what level of detail has not, at the time of writing, been revealed. According to one report, American intelligence had been advised in May 2000 that a militant Islamic group was preparing to attack an American target in the Middle East. See Miller and MacFarquhar, "American Intelligence Officials Said Yesterday That They Received Reports in Late May That a Militant Egyptian Islamic Group Was in the Final Stages of Preparing a Terror Attack," and "U.S. on Alert after Threats of Terrorism: Mideast, Jakarta Embassy Warned of Possible Attacks." Canada and the United States conducted an exercise called "Thin Ice" which envisaged an anthrax attack by terrorists on Vancouver and Seattle. The aim was to bring representatives from different departments and agencies together in order to manage a crisis of this type. Bohn, "Vancouver, Seattle Targets in a Mock Anthrax Attack."

170. Dobson and Payne, *Terror! The West Fights Back*, 39.

171. Whitaker, et al., "Ten Ways to Fight Terrorism," 28.

172. Ibid.

173. Ibid. It is unfortunate to note that many nations still do not employ and practice their elected representatives and decision-makers in these exercises.

174. Ibid.

175. Livingstone and Arnold, *Fighting Back: Winning the War Against Terrorism,* 237. A notable example of international co-operation is the discovery of a Basque bomb factory in the south of France in March 1999. According to one report, French "anti-terrorist investigators found 250 kg (550 pounds) of chemicals used to make explosives." "French Police Uncover Basque Bomb Factory." In June 1999 indications of further international co-operation came in the form of a pledge by ministers of Algeria, France, Italy, Morocco, Portugal, Spain and Tunisia. These countries agreed to stem the flow of illegal immigration. Discussion focused on cooperation on security, border surveillance and drug smuggling. "Eight Mediterranean States Vows [*sic*] to Fight Terrorism."

176. Untitled.

177. "Global Force Proposed to Fight Terrorist Threat." See also French, "Talking a Tough Line on Terrorism."

178. Trickey, "'The World Is Not Ready for a UN Army,' Ambassador Laments: Fowler Says Global Fear of 'World Government' Makes UN Unable to Stop Genocide Before it Starts." The article notes that the Canadian ambassador to the U.N., Robert Fowler, advised that the American fear of "world government" makes it impossible to mount a U.N.-sponsored force capable of stopping a war before it starts. Mr. Fowler said it is virtually inconceivable that a U.N. force will be created to pre-empt genocidal threats of violence because of the fear of supernationalism.

179. Whitaker, et al., "Ten Ways to Fight Terrorism," 28.

180. Ibid. See also Nordland, et al., "Were the Deals Worth It?", 38.

181. Ibid.

182. Ibid. It should be noted that a moral case for not negotiating can be made, but the real issue is that governments must be pragmatic and, therefore, they will bargain with the aim of winning the negotiation. Although *not* negotiating with terrorists is stated government policy for many countries, government officials, as well as politicians and diplomats, soon discover that this *official policy* is in fact, seldom honored. See "What Will Make the Terrorist Go Away?" The article states that "the apparent position of democratic governments has been simple: We never bargain with terrorists. Simple in rhetoric, muddled in reality."

183. Ibid.

184. Livingstone, *The War Against Terrorism,* 164–165. Today, there are individuals such as bin Laden, a multimillionaire former Saudi citizen who was operating from Afghanistan under the protection of the Taliban. He is suspected of financing the 1993 World Trade Center bombing, the attack in Riyadh in November 1995, the Khobar Tower bombing in June 1996 and the bombing of the U.S. embassies in Kenya and Tanzania in August 1998, as well as the PENTTBOMB attacks. Moreover, the financing of terrorism continues through bank robberies, kidnapping and drug running. See "Cash for Carnage: Funding the Modern Terrorist." For a most informative article on bin Laden, see Bergen, "Terrorism's Dark Master." Also, Watson and Evans, "U.S. Targets Bin Laden's Fortress," and Jiwa,

"Osama Bin Laden's Global Network." For an overview of how Osama bin Laden nearly fell in U.S. custody see Wedgwood, "The Law at War: How Osama Slipped Away." See also, Anderson, "Is This the Way bin Laden Escaped?"

185. U.S. government officials subsequently removed Iran as a terrorist sponsor nation. See "State Department Drops Iran as Terrorist."

186. "Libya Remains a Pariah State to U.S.: Suspension of Sanctions Unlikely to Affect Frozen Assets or Washington's Ban on Trade, Travel." Recent initiatives may see Libya and Syria dropped from the Clinton administration's list of countries that allegedly sponsor terrorism. "Report Says U.S. May Drop Libya from Terrorist List."

187. It was reported that "Osama bin Laden, . . . has been foiled in at least seven attempted attacks on American outposts around the world since his involvement in bombing two U.S. embassies in Africa." According to this article, the targeted embassies were in Uruguay, Uganda, Ivory Coast, Tajikistan, Azerbaijan and Albania. "Washington Foils Seven bin Laden Bomb Attempts." See also Levy and Scott-Clark, "Back with a Vengeance: Bin Laden Is Training Recruits to Unleash a Fresh Wave of Terror Against the West." The article notes that bin Laden has rebuilt his "terrorist universities" and his agents are in the process of preparing the administrative requirements and personnel to undertake a "new jihad." Bin Laden said in a recent televised interview that he seeks to incite the Islamic nation to liberate its land and to conduct a "holy war" against the "Crusader-Jewish aggression" against Islamic lands. "Bin Laden Vows to Continue Holy War Against the United States." Recently, Pakistani clerics warned the West that reprisals will be taken against foreigners living in Pakistan, should the United States mount a strike against bin Laden's bases in Afghanistan. West, "Diplomats Fear 'Massacre of Foreigners': Attack on bin Laden Will Lead to Reprisals, Clerics Warn." For an overview of Osama bin Laden, see Bodansky, *Bin Laden: the Man Who Declared War on America.*

188. Stackhouse, "Bin Laden Evidence Satisfies NATO Allies."

189. It has been underlined that Osama bin Laden has actively sought weapons of mass destruction for the past six years and is apparently prepared to spend money, time and effort to obtain these types of weapons. The aim is that "bin Laden wants a lot of people watching and he also wants a lot of Americans dead." Leader, "Osama bin Laden and the Terrorist Search for WMD." In some quarters, there is a belief that he has a chem-bio capability and access to suitcase nukes.

190. Hays, "Bin Laden Sought Uranium, Trial Hears; Ex-Aide Testifies in Embassy-Blast Case."

191. "Cash for Carnage: Funding the Modern Terrorist," and Francis, "The Most Dangerous Nation on Earth." According to Francis, the Colombian guerrillas "are the best-paid terrorists in the world. Financed by the narcotics industry, they have so much power that Andres Pastrana, the country's president, is considering giving them political input in exchange for the return of their lucrative drug fields."

192. Vincent, "Bin Laden's Greatest Asset Is Ability to Handle Money"; Doran, "CIA on the Trail of Terrorist Cash," and "Global Efforts to Find Bin Laden's Millions Could Come up Short." For an insightful view of the financial structure of Al-Qaeda, see Roule, Kinsell and Joyce, "Investigators Seek to Break up Al-Qaeda's Financial Structure."

193. "Terrorism: UN Works to Stamp Out Funding." The article states:

> The initial draft, sponsored by France, was inspired by a number of terror-
> ism cases in which certain governments were found to have provided sup-
> port to organizations funding terrorism. Article 2 of the draft convention
> described such support in following terms: a misdemeanor is committed by
> anyone who, illegally or intentionally, provides funding for a person or or-
> ganization in the knowledge that the money will or could be used, all or in
> part, to prepare or commit an act destined to cause death or serious bodily
> harm to a civilian or all other person [*sic*] unconnected to an armed conflict
> when, by its nature or context, the act constitutes a means of intimidating a
> government or civilian population.

The committee appeared to exclude violence linked to civil war or carried out
by independence movements from the convention. To be sure, article 3 indicates
the text doesn't concern acts carried out inside a single country by one of its inhabitants.

In the recent past a number of countries fearful of standing up to terrorist movements have cited religious freedom or the rights of people to associate with one
another as a reason for allowing organizations to bankroll terrorism. In this respect, article 5 stipulates that acts covered by the convention can in no way to be
justified by considerations of a political, philosophical, ideological, racial, ethnic,
religious or any other related nature.

Some of the draft's twenty-five articles focus on how to stamp out such funding, laying down obligations particularly toward tax havens. Article 17, for instance,
calls on signatory states to take measures that make it compulsory for their financial institutions and other professions involved in financial transactions to clearly
identify their usual or occasional customers. To that effect it said, countries should
consider adopting regulations that outlaw anonymous bank accounts or the opening of accounts with obviously fictitious names. As well, it called on financial institutions to keep a record of all transactions for at least five years.

Developments are being seen in various countries with regard to terrorist
fundraising. The Liberation Tigers of Tamil Eelam (LTTE) is reportedly using front
organizations in Canada to raise funds through so-called cultural functions. Jiwa,
"Board Probes Fund-raising for Terrorists in Schools." According to CSIS, associations affiliated to the Tamil Tigers raised approximately 2 million dollars Canadian
for the LTTE war chest. In an effort to address this issue, the Canadian government
considered a politically sensitive recommendation to give CSIS a powerful new
weapon in countering terrorism. A bill before the House of Commons in the spring
of 2001 would allow CSIS to effectively strip charitable status from those groups that
provide clandestine support for terrorist groups. See Travers, "Past Time to Curb
Terrorists," and "Bill C-16: An Act Respecting the Registration of Charities and Security Information and to Amend the Income Tax Act." 37th Parliament 1st Session.
Reid Morden, a former director of CSIS, stated that the Canadian government was
reluctant to take strong measures against groups that raise funds for international
terrorism due to the fact that ethnic communities are some of the Liberal Party's greatest supporters. "Politics Trumping Security: Ex-Spy: Former CSIS Chief Accuses Liberals of Being Timid on Terror for Fear of Losing Ethnic Votes."

The United Kingdom has created anti-terrorist legislation that came into force in February 2001. The Terrorism Act empowers the United Kingdom to outlaw groups that commit violence abroad and to crack down on those who support such groups, channel funds, or recruit for terrorist organizations. "Britain Draws Weapon Against Terrorism"; Johnston, "Terrorists to Be Expelled from British Bases," and Evans, "Britain Moves to Outlaw Tamil Tigers: Terrorist Organization, Group among 21 to Be Banned under New Legislation." See "Terrorism Act 2000" which is Chapter 11 in the 2000 Acts of Parliament.

194. Leblanc, "Terrorist Fundraisers Will Face Jail," and Bill C-36.

195. For a review of the April 1986 U.S. air raid on Libya (Operation El Dorado Canyon), see Prunckun, Jr. and Mohr, "Military Deterrence of International Terrorism: An Evaluation of Operation El Dorado Canyon," 267–280. This study indicates "that the level of activity of Libyan-associated terrorist groups and, after a brief upsurge, the frequency of attacks against U.S. targets both declined after the raid." This study also notes "a shift from acts of medium and high severity to acts of low severity in violence."

196. "U.S. Army Seeks OK to Kill Terrorists." According to this article, "'Using military force against terrorists to protect U.S. citizens or the national security of the United States is a legitimate exercise of the international legal right of self-defense and does not constitute assassination,' the army's legal opinion concludes." Recently released declassified material underlined that the CIA considered the assassination of fifty-eight Guatemalans including President Arbenz. In 1953 the CIA prepared plans for "K" groups, or assassination teams, to work with the rebels. CIA HQ sent twenty silencers for .22 caliber rifles to the rebels, who were being trained in Honduras according to an 11 January 1954 cable. See Pincus, "CIA Had Hit List of 58 Guatemalans in the 1950s: Agency Reveals Details of Covert Action Against President Arbenz, Overthrown but Not Killed." See also Travers, "Covert Action Will Be Nasty." This report underlines that "assassination and covert operations banned in better times will be part of a long, dirty underground struggle that will begin after the world witnesses the first U.S. military response to the Sept. 11 attacks."

197. For an interesting, yet dated, view of the issues pertaining to retaliation, see "The Problems with Retaliation: Four Ex-CIA Chiefs Weigh the Options for Countering Terrorism."

198. "U.S. Targeting Terrorism with More Funds."

199. Ibbitson, "Bush Signs Antiterror Legislation into Law."

200. This section draws on the book by de B. Taillon, *The Evolution of Special Forces in Counter-Terrorism*. Livingstone, *The War Against Terrorism*, 176. See also Alexander, "The Force Option: Using an Often Overlooked Weapon in the Counterterrorism Arsenal."

201. See Meys, "Counter-Terrorist Intervention Units."

202. See Osmanczyk, *The Encyclopedia of the United Nations and International Agreements,* 838. Article 51 states "Nothing in the present Charter shall impair the inherent right of individual or collective self-defense if an armed attack occurs against a Member of the United Nations, until the Security Council has taken measures necessary to maintain international peace and security. Measures taken by Members in the exercise of this right of self-defense shall be immediately reported to the Security Council and shall not in any way affect the authority and responsi-

bility of the Security Council under the present Charter to take at any time such action as it deems necessary in order to maintain or restore international peace and security." This article has been highlighted by a number of academics, security experts and Clinton administration spokespersons as an instrumental aspect of the defense of President Clinton's launch of cruise missiles against suspected terrorist sites and facilities in Sudan and Afghanistan on 20 August 1998.

203. See Beltrane, "U.S. Bombs Terrorist Outposts," and Stackhouse, "U.S. Bombs Terrorist Training Camps." On the other hand, the United States in executing the attacks has been accused of being a terrorist itself. The political critic Noam Chomsky is among those who view the United States as a main practitioner of terrorism in regularly using violence for political motives. See Thompson, "Is it Terrorism to Attack Terrorists?" According to the Afghan Foreign Minister Maulvi Abdul Wakeel Mutawakkil, if the United States launched an attack on Afghanistan, "it would be given a crushing reply." Moreover, he advised that Osama bin Laden is not a terrorist but rather a mujahid [holy warrior] and that "the United States has unnecessarily turned Usama into a symbol of terror." See Khalil, "Afghan ForMin Promises 'Crushing Reply' If U.S. Attacks." Some analysts have offered that we may face a clash of cultures and religions. See Kaplan, "Looking the World in the Eye."

204. Dyer, "Bombing Attacks Just Spitting in the Wind."

205. See Wilkinson, "The Role of the Military in Combatting Terrorism," 7–8.

206. See Gotowicki, "Confronting Terrorism: New War Form or Mission Impossible?"

207. Livingstone, *The War Against Terrorism,* 176.

208. Taber, *The War of the Flea: Guerrilla Warfare Theory and Practice,* 118.

209. Interview with a senior counterterrorist operator, Ottawa, Canada (4 May 1998). There is also a *stress* element as was underlined in an article by James Clark and Adnan Nathan, where it was noted that a number of SAS troops suffer fatigue and flashbacks. See Clark and Nathan, "SAS Men Seek Help to Stem Wave of Suicides."

210. The tactical principles that drive this type of operation consist of surprise, synchronizing multiple entries, and the saturation and domination of the target, so as to neutralize threats and to evacuate the aircraft/premises rapidly. The reality that must be underlined is that a deliberate assault offers a greater chance of success than an immediate action. Interview with a former SAS operative, Ottawa, Canada (24 February 1999). For a view of what is known as the "War on Terrorism," see Vest, "Fourth-Generation Warfare," and Perry, "Preparing for the Next Attack."

211. Livingstone, *The War Against Terrorism,* 176.

3

Entebbe and Mogadishu: Lessons in Successful Hostage Rescue

An examination of two successful hostage-rescue incidents of the 1970s at Entebbe and Mogadishu, and one failure at Malta in 1985, highlight some of the key factors[1] that may determine success or failure in this type of *surgical operation*. These include contingency planning, preparation and coordination of the rescue forces, overall command, control and communication, the assembling of the intelligence picture (C3I), and, in particular, international collaboration. As this section shall reveal, neither of these missions could have been successful without considerable international cooperation.

Although the degree of co-operation may vary due to the locations of the incident and various political considerations in the countries involved, Western countries have continued to assist each other even though they have experienced the normal ups and downs of relations between states. Many of these countries have developed elite counterterrorist forces of some description and these units have been used to train similar organizations in other countries. The United States, Canada, Israel, Germany, Great Britain and France[2] have assisted each other and others in developing anti-terrorist techniques and counterterrorist forces. These include cross-training in weapons and tactics, demolitions, as well as insertion and extraction methods. Such skills are, in turn, incorporated into the training of units in collaborating countries. The advantages accruing from such cooperation are heightened by personnel exchanges. As will be shown, personnel from these counterterrorist forces have traveled to the sites of terrorist incidents to advise, assist and even participate with their foreign counterparts in domestic and foreign counterterrorist operations.

ENTEBBE RESCUE

The Entebbe rescue, code-named "Thunderbolt" and later renamed "Operation Jonathan,"[3] was described by the historian Richard Deacon as "an astonishing epic of military adventure and enterprise carried out in a spirit of medieval buccaneering by a team trained in the arts of both the military and espionage."[4]

This was indeed a daring and dangerous mission where the lives of 103 hostages hung in the balance. However, this operation probably could not have succeeded had it not been for the assistance given Israel's intelligence and military agencies by several "friendly" governments. This close co-operation spanned the spectrum from international moral support to having a foreign paramilitary representative providing intelligence for the Israeli rescue force. Without this co-operation, the rescue attempt might well have failed. Worse still, Israel may have had to succumb to the terrorists' demands. Today, Operation Thunderbolt represents a fine example of the international efforts that can assist in the successful execution of a rescue mission. The following extended narrative will underline how international assistance was vital, particularly at critical junctures throughout this operation.

The incident began on 27 June 1976, when Air France Flight 139 from Tel Aviv to Paris was seized in midair by seven members of the Popular Front for the Liberation of Palestine (PFLP) just after a scheduled stopover in Athens.[5] In the aircraft there were a total of 256 passengers and twelve crew. According to one witness, two men left their seats and, brandishing revolvers, said, "We are revolutionaries and this airplane is now our property. We are going to take you where we please."[6] Other terrorists joined in to assist their comrades in seizing the aircraft. Once the task was completed, their West German leader, later identified Wilfred Boese of the Red Cells, made the following announcement: "This is the Che Guevara Brigade of the Popular Front of the Liberation of Palestine. I am your new commandant. This plane is renamed Haifa. You are our prisoners."[7]

The plane flew on to Benghazi, Libya for a brief refueling stop. There, one pregnant passenger, a 30-year-old British subject, was allowed to deplane.

Soon after departure from Libya, Flight 139 attempted to land in Sudan but was refused permission. It continued its flight to Entebbe International Airport in Uganda. On arrival in Entebbe, the passengers and crew occupied an unused passenger terminal.[8] It was then that the first indications of collusion between Idi Amin and the PFLP became apparent to some of the hostages when they were met by additional Palestinian terrorists and units of the Ugandan army. One hostage, Akipa Lasker, a lawyer from Tel Aviv later stated:

> "When we reached Uganda and got off the plane we saw more Palestinians there," he recalled.
> Lasker said he saw five or six of the latter. "They were definitely not on the flight," he stressed. "When we got off the plane we saw them waiting and looking at us."[9]

The purpose of the hijacking was initially obscure. However, the aim became quite apparent when the terrorists announced that they sought the release of fifty-three Palestinians or pro-Palestinian comrades incarcerated in Israel, Switzerland, West Germany, France and Kenya.[10] The hostages taken from the Air France flight were a mixture of Israelis and non-Israelis including a number of French, Greek, American, Canadian and New Zealand citizens. Once it had been confirmed that German terrorists were involved in the operation, the West German government rapidly deployed Colonel Ulrich Wegener, of the GSG9, to Entebbe. The aim was to keep the West German government and, in turn, the Israelis, apprised of the activities in and around the airfield, as well as to garner any on-site intelligence. This information was reported directly to the West German authorities, and was subsequently forwarded to Israel to assist in the planning of the rescue operation. As well, British government representatives assisted in the provision of critically important intelligence.

On arrival in Uganda, the terrorists subsequently selected a negotiator. He was Hashi Abdullan, Somalia's ambassador to Uganda. He, in turn, requested that the French government name its own representative. During these first delicate negotiations, President Idi Amin Dada refused Ambassador Pierre Renard's intervention on behalf of the French government. Instead, Amin himself would negotiate directly with the terrorists.

By 30 June it was apparent to some diplomatic observers that the Israeli government's policy was not to yield to the demands of the terrorists. One country, Canada, supported the Israeli stance; this was greeted by one Israeli official "with satisfaction having heard news broadcast that Cdn govt [Canadian government] would not/not be requesting govts [governments] of Israel, West Germany, Switzerland, France and Kenya to accept terrorists demands."[11]

This was a departure from previous Israeli policy. In 1969 for example, Egyptian and Syrian nationals were freed in return for two hijacked TWA passengers held in Damascus and for two imprisoned Israeli pilots who had been downed over Egypt.[12] As for the demands for the release of the fifty-three jailed comrades, Kampala Radio had announced on 29 June that once

these prisoners were freed, Air France was to bring "all these freedom fighters to Entebbe International Airport, to be exchanged with the hostages and
the aircraft. Air France to transport the freedom fighters held in Israel to
Entebbe International Airport and it should only carry the freedom fighters
and the crew."[13]

The PFLP, via Kampala Radio, set an 8:00 a.m. deadline for Thursday,
30 June and stated that there would be "severe and heavy punishment"[14]
if their demands were not met. The same day, the hijackers released forty-
seven non-Israeli hostages who were taken by an Air France 707 to Nairobi.

As events unfolded, it became clear to all concerned that although this
terrorist action began as an international incident, it was clearly becoming
an Israeli issue. Until then, it had been argued that the "allegedly" firm
Israeli commitment not to bargain with terrorists could be ignored. According to observers in Jerusalem, there were several reasons for this:

1. [The] lives of non-Israeli nationals are in danger.
2. Neither the plane nor the hijackers are within striking distance of
   Israeli troops.
3. Israel had not been directly involved in negotiations.
4. Other governments are directly involved.[15]

The New York Times reported that "Israel's policy in the past has been to
refuse to negotiate with terrorists on the ground that that [sic] will lead only
to further terrorist attempts. Senior officials conceded, however, that the
Uganda situation faces Israel with an specially [sic] difficult dilemma."[16]

The following day, a further 100 non-Israeli passengers were freed. This
release of passengers by the hijackers allowed Israeli intelligence to acquire
vital pieces of information regarding the terrorists, the airport, security and
weapons. They learned also that the transit lounge that held the hostages
was not wired with explosives. Moreover, the freeing of the non-Israeli
passengers mobilized Israeli public opinion. As one writer noted: More
importantly, these reports provided information about the daily routine
within the terminal, the accommodations, the location of the various con-
veniences, and guard routine. As to their captors, the released passengers
provided a profile of their guards and their overall behavior toward the
hostages, as well as where the terrorists and the Ugandan soldiers were situated in the building and surrounding area. All of which were critical for
the planners. This act galvanized Israel as it gave the first indication that
the Jews were the target and their lives were the focus of the negotiations.[17]

During the questioning of the freed passengers by French and Israeli intelligence personnel, President Amin emerged not as a mediator, but as an
accomplice. This information strengthened the Israeli feeling that Uganda
was working with Dr. Waddieh Haddad, the terrorist chief.[18]

The Israeli government, upon notification of the hijacking, had rapidly organized a crisis management team consisting of the prime minister, members of the Cabinet and the chief of staff of the Israeli Defense Force. Each crisis management team member was supported by a variety of people with specialized expertise, such as on anti-piracy tactics, as well as military, political, and diplomatic experts. More importantly, the team members and the experts rapidly joined forces, as they had all dealt with similar emergencies, although never on this magnitude.[19]

A series of suggestions were forthcoming, including the capture of Idi Amin while en route to Mauritius to attend a conference of the Organization for African Unity. Some argued that Moshe Dayan should be sent to confer with Amin. More radical ideas included holding relatives of PFLP members, should any hostages be murdered.[20]

Two options were obvious to all concerned. The first was to negotiate; the second was to undertake a military action of some type to rescue the hostages. It was vital for the Israeli government to be seen to be seeking a peaceful resolution to the problem. According to Chaim Herzog Lieutenant General Mordechai Gur issued orders for a feasibility study on the evening of 28 June to prepare a force to parachute into Entebbe, or to infiltrate across Lake Victoria. The aim was to seize the airport terminal with the view of neutralizing the terrorists and defending the hostages until an arrangement could be made with the government of Uganda to release the Israeli hostages. Apparently Prime Minister Yitzak Rabin at this point did not want to contemplate the feasibility of a military operation and the inherent risks that it carried.[21] On 29 June, Prime Minister Rabin asked Lieutenant General Gur,[22] "Do we have a military option?" In response Gur related that "he lacked adequate intelligence about the airfield layout at Entebbe, the number of hostages, the military and human risks. 'At the moment,' he replied, 'we do not have a military option.'"[23]

Rabin called for a vote and received unanimous agreement from his Cabinet that the Israeli government would pursue negotiations.[24] Notwithstanding, Defense Minister Shimon Peres, on his own initiative,[25] began the search for a viable military option.[26] It was his contention that Israel must refuse to surrender to the terrorists, for if Israel did succumb it would constitute a serious political and moral defeat, not to mention set an exceedingly dangerous precedent for future governmental leaders in the war against terrorism. The tasks of planning and commanding an operation, should it come to that, were given to Brigadier General Dan Shomron, the chief infantry and paratroop officer in the Israel Defense Forces.[27] Shomron had successfully commanded an armored brigade in the Sinai in 1973 and had already commenced the planning process on his own to assess the potential for a rescue operation.

In preparing options, Shimon Peres ordered Gur to determine if the French government would assist Israel by allowing the latter's aircraft to use the refueling facilities at Djibouti. As Stevenson notes, "Nobody had to ask what he [Peres] meant. If a military operation became necessary . . . planes must fly around hostile Arab territories, evade Somalia's Russian detection systems, and complete flights beyond the normal range of Israel's existing military aircraft."[28]

Of interest during this period was the fact that Kenya held five imprisoned Palestinian freedom fighters, three of whom had been apprehended as they attempted to down an El Al airliner with a Soviet-made anti-aircraft missile when approaching the Nairobi airport on 18 January 1975.[29] This missile system and an array of other weapons had been seized by Kenyan security personnel. The weapons used were traced to Uganda.[30] On 21 January 1975 a man and a woman arrived in Nairobi hoping to discover the fate of the three terrorists. These individuals had been arrested, searched and interrogated by both Kenyan and, in February, Israeli intelligence. The woman was reportedly carrying orders written in invisible ink on her stomach. These orders included an attack on an aircraft belonging to El Al.[31] All five were then sent to Israel and were put on trial on 6 July 1977.[32] At the time of the Entebbe incident, however, the PFLP hijackers openly threatened to take reprisals against the Kenyan government if it did not comply with their request to release their incarcerated members.

By Wednesday, 30 June it became readily apparent from the information gathered through the interviews of released hostages that Amin and his army were working in concert with the PFLP. Nevertheless, Colonel Baruch Bar-Lev, who had once been on friendly terms with Amin, maintained close contact in a futile attempt to relay to the Ugandan president the gravity of the situation and to remind him of his personal responsibility for the hostages.[33]

By 30 June Shomron and his staff had devised a plan to land a commando force at Entebbe, liquidate the terrorists, release and evacuate the hostages. The focus was not to capture the whole terminal and airfield; rather it was to strike at the terrorists and emanate outward, securing the building and airfield approaches. The Israeli Air Force advised Shomron's planning staff that their C-130 aircraft could reach Entebbe, however, there was the requirement to either refuel at Entebbe or somewhere en route back to Israel. The requirement now for the staff was time to prepare the forces and work out the details in exercises and to secure a refuelling point. A deadline extension was critical.[34] The terrorists extended their deadline to Thursday, 1 July. The Israeli government proposed a joint Israeli-French negotiation team to the French government. The proposal was accepted.

Regarding this extension Prime Minister Rabin has said that "Thursday was critical,"[35] due to the fact that he "had to report that we [the Israelis] had no military option that could be applied before the Thursday deadline set by the terrorists."[36] On Thursday, according to reporter Michael Elkins, the Israeli government:

decided to open negotiations for the release of all the hostages with a readiness to release prisoners. The reference being to prisoners held for terrorist acts in Israel whose release had been demanded by the hijackers and it was generally accepted here that there was no other alternative. Official sources are saying that the government fully intended to negotiate.[37]

Moreover, "I could not resist the demand to negotiate," said the prime minister. "Military operations depended upon accurate intelligence and proof, by way of full dress rehearsals, that a commando strike could be conducted with success."[38]

By the morning of 1 July, Prime Minister Rabin was under severe pressure to release the hostages held by Israel and received the approval of the Defense and Foreign Affairs Committee of the Knesset, and Menachem Begin, the leader of the opposition and the Cabinet. That afternoon, Shomron presented his reserve plan to Defense Minister Peres, General Gur (chief of Operations), General Adam (chief of the Air Force), Major General Benjamin Peled and the Assistant Chief of the Operations Branch Avigdon Ben-Gal. Shomron's plan called for the operation to land at the Entebbe airport at 11 p.m. on Saturday, 3 July with rehearsals scheduled for 2 July.

At the conclusion of Shomron's presentation, Peres requested the views of the audience. The responses varied. Shomron underlined that there was one serious vulnerability in the plan, and that was to land the first aircraft without arousing the suspicion of either the terrorists or Ugandans. It was Shomron's contention that if this initial landing was possible the operation was assured of success.

After much discussion, Peres approved the plan, pending the final approval of the Cabinet. Meanwhile, planning was to continue unabated. Peres agreed that Shomron was to command the operation and begin selecting the personnel and units to execute the plan, with a final exercise on a model of Entebbe to be conducted on Friday evening. Shomron commenced assembling his forces soon after his briefing on 1 July. This force consisted of some 200 troops from the 35th Airborne Brigade, the Golani Brigade and elements of the Sayaret Matkal, better known as the General Staff Intelligence Reconnaissance Unit. All were highly trained with an exceedingly high proportion being battle-hardened regulars. The General Staff plan, according to Herzog, required:

1. A force to illuminate and secure the runway;
2. A force to occupy the old terminal and release the hostages;
3. A force to take control of the new terminal;
4. A force to secure the airfield and destroy the Ugandan fighter aircraft;
5. A force to evacuate the hostages from the terminal to the aircraft.[39]

While negotiations continued, planners recognized that the military option would require detailed intelligence for any chance of success. A seventy-two–hour deadline extension, granted by the terrorists, was given at noon on 1 July. This gave the military the opportunity to exercise their plan and to amass the information needed to plan the rescue operation.[40] "Prior to the extension Thursday of the deadline, officials said, there had not been enough time to prepare and mount an operation that had any realistic prospect of success by midday Thursday, when the hijackers said they would kill the hostages and blow up the plane."[41]

To this day the reason that the PFLP allowed so much time is unknown. The Israelis believed that it may have been due to Amin's departure for Mauritius.[42] The Israeli intelligence effort continued to acquire information germane to all aspects of the planning phase, including the compiling of character profiles on President Amin and the terrorists. Some Israeli intelligence officers in Kenya were reportedly discreetly met by a series of senior Kenyan representatives. This included the head of Nairobi police, Lionel Bryn Davies, Bruce McKenzie,[43] a close friend of President Kenyatta, as well as the commander of Kenyatta's General Service Unit, Geoffrey Karithil. They agreed that there would be no objection to Israeli Air Force planes transiting Kenyan air space—and that President Kenyatta would not "notice" should any aircraft land at the Nairobi airport for refueling.[44]

The importance of this strategically located refueling stop cannot be overstated.[45] Kenyan authorities offered full assistance in this regard: "The commander of Kenyatta's GSU strong-arm units . . . was able to give assurances that his president would turn a blind eye if the GSU and Nairobi airport police isolated the rescue force during a stopover—provided this phase of the operation was conducted as a routine matter under cover of El Al charters."[46]

It should be underlined that Kenya's assistance to Israel had to be perceived as legal from an international viewpoint. Therefore an opinion was sought: from Charles Njojo, Kenya's attorney general, who offered a legal opinion that noted that as long as the laws of international civil aviation were properly observed, as perceived by the Kenyan airport authority, the airport facilities could not be legally refused.[47]

It should be pointed out that Kenya had been the brunt of a series of threats from Amin, and these threats were given credence by Uganda's Soviet-made MIG fighters and its well-equipped army. Ironically, thanks to Israeli military assistance, Uganda had quite a formidable armed force for a Third World nation. Richard Garrett states that:

> Uganda had come a long way since Israeli experts had raised its armed forces from the slough of inefficiency. According to a sufficiently accurate estimate, they now consisted of 21,000 well-armed and well-trained soldiers equipped with 267 armored troop carriers, SAM ground-to-air missiles, howitzers and

mortars. In addition to this, the Ugandan Air Force had well over fifty combat planes . . . It was thought that about half of the army was concentrated between Entebbe and Kampala (twenty-one miles away). Twenty-one of the fighter planes were at Entebbe airport.[48]

Information, both domestic and foreign, assisted in the training of the assault force. The Israeli firm, Solel Boneh, which had built the new airport terminal[49] as part and parcel of an Israeli aid program, produced in preparation for this mission, an Entebbe Airport replica for rehearsals. (This model may have been modified through intelligence derived from the released hostages, Israeli reconnaissance aircraft and information drawn from American satellites.[50]) Moreover, intelligence regarding the location of the terrorists, the airport layout and the defensive positions of the Ugandan forces was being forwarded by Colonel Wegener (who was sent to Uganda when the West German government thought that West German terrorists were involved) and a British diplomat in a joint effort to assist in gathering all the on-site intelligence necessary for a successful rescue. All communications went through the West German and British governments, respectively, and then on to Israeli authorities.[51]

According to one official, the Israelis, during this time, continued to negotiate in good faith, "But it quickly became obvious that we weren't getting anywhere."[52] Support for a military rescue operation became increasingly strong by Friday, 2 July. It was on this day that there was a dramatic increase in the area of international cooperation, particularly between Israel and the Western intelligence community. Information on Wilfried Böse, believed to be the German who was declaring himself as captain of the hijacked aircraft, was supplied by West Germany. Canada sent a mass of intelligence material. It should be noted that Guy Toupin, coordinator of security for the 1976 Olympic Games which had been held in Montreal, had worked for more than a year with the numerous police forces of a variety of countries in preparation for the Olympics. Toupin remembered quite clearly the massacre of Israeli athletes during the 1972 Olympic Games in Munich.[53] With the assistance of the West, the vitally important intelligence picture began to take shape. This intelligence flow increased the chance for a successful military option, particularly as new intelligence from the French Direction de la Surveillance du Territoire (DST), Scotland Yard, the CIA and FBI, and the security branch of the Royal Canadian Mounted Police (RCMP) reached the Israeli authorities, and additional information was received from released hostages and Israeli informants within Amin's government. The hostage rescue team members were also given photographs and identikit details to memorize. In that regard, the Israelis were to proceed on the basis that action would be taken.[54]

The Israeli government, in maintaining a negotiation posture, as well as planning a military operation, was keeping its options open. Israel, in fact, cloaked itself with the aura of a country desiring to negotiate. This evolved into a highly sophisticated strategic deception plan.[55] In this regard the importance of international cooperation and support became more apparent once the Israeli leadership realized the high costs of submitting to the terrorist demands. France soon became, although Paris did not realize it, an integral part of the total Israeli deception plan. The French government remained an equal negotiating partner up to the last minute of discussions. More importantly, this Franco-Israeli negotiating team provided further evidence to the terrorists that the Israeli government was concerned only with achieving a peaceful settlement to this hostage crisis. This ruse, as shall be seen, worked.

The vital intelligence provided by the United States, France, West Germany, Canada and Israel allowed the military planners to reduce the unknowns of the mission. However, international cooperation did not cease there, and one could argue that this assistance, at a critical juncture, assured the success of the military option. On 2 July there were three critical developments. First, the Pentagon provided the Israeli government with aerial and satellite photographs of Entebbe Airport. Meanwhile, Colonel Wegener and a British diplomat had penetrated Entebbe, brought out, and forwarded critical information. Lastly, Kenya provided assurances that an Israeli strike force would be allowed to land at Nairobi to refuel and care for the wounded on its homeward bound trip from Uganda.[56]

This assistance needed the support of foreign governments. Without reconnaissance and satellite photographs, and without the permission of the Kenyan government to land in Nairobi, the probability of success would have been greatly reduced. The satellite photographs, in particular, were essential as the rescue force planners had to know if the terrorists had obstructed the runways with vehicles to prevent any rescue aircraft from landing safely.[57] With this American information and that provided on the ground by Wegener and his British diplomatic counterpart,[58] and the Kenyan agreement to assist, an Israeli government official said, "Militarily, the situation on the ground now looked easier than when the Palestinians held hostages here in Israel."[59]

The deception plan continued and was extremely effective. Internationally it still looked as though Israel would have to give in—and the Israelis continued their attempts to keep up that impression. The morning meeting of the crisis group on July 3 was held up while Foreign Minister Allon kept a scheduled breakfast with Daniel Patrick Moynihan, former American ambassador to the United Nations. "It was an amazing performance," Moynihan said later. "I thought I'd be out as soon as we finished coffee, but Allon went on and on, as if he didn't have a care in the world. He told me: 'We have great hope that the French will be able to negotiate something. We're waiting.' And he gave me a tour d'horizon that lasted an hour."[60]

Moreover, Herzog notes that on 2 July Israeli television broadcasted a film, taken by a foreign press correspondent, that showed the new terminal in Entebbe. From this they learned that the new terminal was a two-story building and from photographs shown of the old terminal, they saw where the Israeli hostages were being held.[61]

On Saturday, 3 July at 8:00 a.m., Gur briefed the Israeli plan to Peres and both briefed Prime Minister Rabin. According to Herzog, Gur opened his remarks by saying "I present to you a plan for execution this evening. The troops are on their way, and the entire operation is now in motion according to a pre-arranged plan." The Prime Minister gave his approval, subject to the approval of the Cabinet. Three hours later the final briefing of the troops took place. Take-off was set for 15:30 hours.[62]

At 2:00 p.m., the Israeli crisis group met and agreed to recommend the military option to the Cabinet. Here again the deception had succeeded so well, with the unwitting assistance of France, that the Cabinet members were for the most part unaware of the military preparations that had taken place.[63] Finally, they believed that Israel was negotiating to the end. During this meeting, Cabinet members expressed concern over the possibility of casualties. The tide was turned by Rabin, who argued forcefully for a rescue, "even if we lost 10 or 20 or 25 killed."[64]

The Cabinet voted. The result was unanimous.[65] The hostages were to be rescued. General Gur gave the necessary orders to the 35th Airborne Brigade, the Golani Brigade and elements of Sayaret Matkal (better known as General Staff Intelligence Reconnaissance Unit[66]) that would comprise the strike force.

Great Britain was also a source of continued support and intelligence for Israel. The British offered "the fullest cooperation within limits set by the fact that British citizens were still living in Uganda."[67] More important, it was information originating from British sources that suggested:

> for reasons ranging from President Amin's return from the African summit to the growing unease among some of the PLO strategists in Kampala, the risk had increased considerably that execution of hostages would begin early on Sunday morning. If Thunderbolt was to be launched, the time frame was reduced drastically. The equation was now simple. Risk losing 35 Israelis [estimate of casualties] by taking action, or face the possibility of 105 dead by the sin of omission.[68]

With respect to the operation, the force commander, Brigadier-General Shomron, was fully prepared. During rehearsal, his troops had successfully completed the rescue exercise in fifty-five minutes, from the time the aircraft landed to the time they were airborne again. The ground force contingent, tasked to enter the old terminal and retrieve the hostages, was led by the 30-year-old Lieutenant Colonel Jonathan Netanyahu,[69] a well-respected leader, who was unfortunately to become the only Israeli military fatality.[70]

The passage of intelligence and preparations for the operation continued unabated, while in Paris Major General Rehavam Zeevi, who was responsible for negotiations, reported to Rabin that they were experiencing difficulties. Rabin requested that Zeevi continue to negotiate. Zeevi himself was unaware that he too was an integral part of the Israeli ruse.[71]

Operational Planning Aspects

Entebbe is some 2,500 miles from Israel. Fortunately, a number of Israelis had intimate knowledge of the Ugandan armed forces, and others had acquired detailed plans of the airport and its facilities. The task for the military planning staffs was to sift through the information and intelligence available, determine the facts, incorporate them into an "operational appreciation," and in turn produce a suitable plan. The logical outcome of the "operational appreciation," in simple terms, was that troops would be clandestinely flown to Entebbe in order to rescue the hostages.

The Israeli planning staffs had long believed that special operations, such as hostage rescue, require planners with experience and a flexible attitude toward unorthodox situations. Moreover, the skills and experience of the Israeli forces gleaned over a number of years in military and special operations assisted greatly in the success of this action, as shall be seen.[72] They sought opinions and proposals from likely and unlikely sources. As Richard Deacon has noted in his study of the Israeli intelligence services:

Israel's Army and Secret Service are not hamstrung by too much bureaucracy or emphasis on that self-destroying military myth, the divine right of seniority. All ranks had the opportunity to press plans and suggestions over the heads of their immediate superiors to the C-in-C. . . . In turning "Operation Jonathan" into a practical proposition this was a tremendous advantage: some excellent ideas came from minor agents in the field and non-commissioned soldiers and airmen.[73]

Israeli experience in special operations underlined that the central problem in conducting the rescue was speed. Could Israeli troops execute the mission before the terrorists could kill any of the hostages? Information gleaned from the non-Israeli passengers, who had returned to Paris, gave the Israeli intelligence staffs the opportunity to assess the hostage situation in the Entebbe terminal.[74] This data was further supplemented by satellite photographs supplied by the United States. Although the employment of technical means was vital, "humint" (human intelligence sources) from the released hostages was critical. Slowly the intelligence picture became clearer, thanks to the cooperation and intelligence from friendly nations, and the highly versatile and productive Israeli intelligence service. Deacon states, "As a result of all this the military planners in Tel Aviv were able to report that, providing they could land at Entebbe, without arousing suspicion, the rescue of the hostages would be a relatively simple operation."[75]

The Israeli planners were well aware of how rapidly the intelligence picture could change as the situation evolved, and were most sensitive to these issues. The chief of operations understood the need for the latest intelligence.[76] This aspect of Operation Thunderbolt ensured the success of the plan.

The need for the aircraft to refuel somewhere along the route was a major problem. The aircraft employed would be operating at their maximum ranges. The air fleet consisted of five C-130 Hercules transport aircraft and two Boeing 707 passenger planes. Another, a fuel-carrying C-130 aircraft, was to fly ahead of the rescue force, landing at a Kenyan airbase near Mombasa, where it was kept in reserve in case of an emergency. The difficulty for Kenya was that, should any of the rescue aircraft land at a Kenyan military station, the government could arguably be held accountable for co-operating in the rescue. In contrast, if the Israelis successfully landed at the Nairobi runway, and if, as was the case, the formation was flying under the appropriate civil registration, as requested by the Kenyan government,[77] Nairobi could *plausibly deny* any complicity.

The assault force was to depart Israel from Ophir airbase on 3 July in four C-130s, as would a command and control Boeing 707. The use of the Boeing 707 in this raid apparently tipped off the Central Intelligence Agency (CIA) that there was something in the offing. According to one source:

> At noon on Friday, the American CIA . . . discovered that two IAF Boeings were parked at Lod Airport, swarming with fitters and painters. Different insignia were being painted on the planes. [Further] . . . a coded cable was at that time on its way from Tel Aviv to the CIA in Washington: there are indications of operational activity in Israel, though it is difficult to assume that Israel will operate in Uganda.[78]

The 707, which carried General "Benny" Peled and a team of communications officers, served as the aerial command post (ACP).[79] The generals could monitor the mission and maintain the communications links with the assault force. Meanwhile, a second "medical" 707 was destined to land in Nairobi and await the rescue force in a secured area.

A deception plan was carefully executed, both to assist the rescue force and for the benefit of Kenya. In particular, "All four Hercules were camouflaged by civil registration numbers and followed the same commercial route. Pilots followed normal civil aviation procedures."[80]

This deception provided Nairobi with a degree of "plausible deniability" so it could eschew any accusations of a *co-operative effort with Israel* in a military operation against a fellow African state. Moreover, to avoid detection by Arab and Soviet surveillance vessels, the rescue force flew at extremely low altitudes. This type of flying demanded much from the professional skills of the crew: "'There were times when we flew them [C-130s] like combat planes,' reported an airman. 'We did everything but dogfight. We made sudden sharp turns to dodge the Russian-built radar pickets on sea and land, then had to climb fast to get over the mountains.'"[81]

The pathfinder aircraft, a C-130 fitted with the latest electronic and navigational aids, led the assault force aircraft safely to their objective. On the way in, inclement weather forced the rescue fleet to approach Sudanese airspace. As the aircraft approached Lake Victoria, it encountered a massive front of storm clouds rising to 13,000m.[82] As time was of the essence, the force proceeded directly through the front, the lead pilot fully aware that he was solely responsible to get "his cargo of 86 officers and men and the forward command post of Major-General Dan Shomron with all their vehicles and equipment . . . on the ground according to a precise timetable."[83]

According to Herzog, the lead aircraft landed at 11:01 p.m., only thirty seconds behind schedule and, opportunely, dovetailed behind a scheduled arrival of a British cargo aircraft, arousing no suspicion. The Israeli plan was to land in the wake of a scheduled British cargo flight in the hopes of not arousing any Ugandan or PFLP suspicions. The flight approach was made over Lake Victoria in a heavy rainstorm, and as the British aircraft landed the first Israeli Hercules followed close behind. The Israeli pilot slowed his aircraft down according to plan, allowing elements of the vanguard force to depart the aircraft while it was taxiing along the runway. As the commandos moved parallel along the tarmac they placed lights alongside the runway in anticipation that the Ugandan authorities might attempt to douse the airfield lights and thereby prevent the landing of the follow-on Israeli aircraft.

Meanwhile the first C-130 aircraft taxied to a quiet corner of the field where the rest of the initial landing force deplaned, along with a black Mercedes similar to the one driven by President Amin, which was escorted by two Israeli Land Rovers. The vehicles now drove slowly but deliberately toward the main terminal building where the hostages were being held. The terminal was well lit and as they approached the control tower two Ugandan soldiers on security duty came into view. As one Ugandan approached the convoy he was quickly silenced. At that point the Israeli commandos disembarked from their vehicles just a short distance from the terminal building. It was quickly discovered that one of the entrances to the terminal had been blocked, forcing the initial assault force to enter through a secondary entrance. Upon entry a number of terrorists were found lying on the floor sleeping. At this point four terrorists were rapidly engaged and quickly neutralized. An Israeli commando called out in both Hebrew and

English for the hostages to remain on the floor. Unfortunately, one hostage stood up and was immediately shot. The rescue commander Jonathan Netanyahu followed in the wake of the initial assault unit; however, as he paused just before the entrance he was shot in the neck.

Seven minutes later a second Israeli aircraft landed and was followed by three more Hercules transports in rapid succession. More vehicles were disembarked and they immediately headed toward the terminal area to reinforce the initial assaulters and to secure the area for a hostage extraction. At this point two terrorists attempted to pass unnoticed out of the terminal; fortunately, an Israeli commando took immediate notice as one of these terrorists had a grenade on his belt. Both terrorists were killed when they were engaged by Israeli small arms fire and the grenade exploded. Meanwhile, commando reinforcements commenced searching and clearing the new terminal building while numerous Ugandan soldiers quickly fled the area on foot.

Sporadic fire from some Ugandan troops on the control tower was quickly suppressed and it was soon possible to commence evacuating hostages from the terminal. Located with the first evacuation aircraft was a small medical team tasked to provide assistance and treatment of the wounded. At this point, shots erupted in the old terminal; this situation was quickly remedied by a team of Israeli commandos. Shortly thereafter, the refueling was to commence, however, the Israeli squadron commander recommended that the aircraft not be refueled at Entebbe. The on-site commander, General Shomron, considered the proposal, accepted the recommendation, and immediately forwarded it to the advance headquarters circling above in a Boeing 707. The order came back to immediately depart for Nairobi and to refuel at the airport facilities there.

Fifty-seven minutes after the first Israeli aircraft landed, the first Hercules departed for Nairobi at 11:54 p.m. Just forty-two minutes later the last aircraft departed, leaving in its wake the burning hulks of numerous Ugandan Air Force Mig fighters that were based at the Entebbe airport. The flight of Hercules aircraft safely landed in Nairobi for refueling and then continued their return flight back to Israel. It was reported in the wake of this operation that a total of thirty-five Ugandan soldiers and thirteen terrorists were killed, along with one Israeli commando officer.

The three main tasks[84] as described in a briefing by Major General Gazit were:

1. Move as soon as possible to old terminal bldg. [building] to kill or capture those guarding hostages. IDF knew that guards were a mix of terrorists (ten or eleven) plus Ugandan soldiers.
2. Move to new terminal bldg. [building] and control tower and ensure no counteraction was implemented from there.

3. Secure approaches to airfield and prevent entry of any opposing forces (from outside airport or from mil [military] camp located within airport perimeter).[85]

Time and speed were crucial. The post-operation briefing noted that task (A) was "accomplished within 7–8 mins [minutes] of IDF arrival."[86] Further, in just twenty-five minutes, all the Israeli hostages, with the exception of one elderly woman who had been placed in an Entebbe hospital earlier, were freed and in an aircraft ready for departure. Twenty minutes later the first aircraft departed. The last aircraft took off twenty-five minutes later. All aircraft flew to Nairobi for refueling and medical treatment, and then on to Israel.

KENYAN ASSISTANCE

Kenyan cooperation went beyond offering a secure refueling stop for the "supposed" civilian aircraft flying from Entebbe. Kenya was in fact instrumental in maintaining the Israeli deception plan. Before the arrival of the C-130s:

> [an] unscheduled Boeing 707, El Al charter flight LY 167, landed at 11:26 p.m. local time and taxied to Bay 4, reserved for aircraft requiring security precautions. The 707 was quarantined at once by Kenyan GSU men and El Al staffers. The civil registration number on the tail was 4XBY8, which conflicted with the air control log that recorded this as Flight 169. Almost two hours later another 707 contacted Nairobi control and announced itself as Flight 167 from Tel Aviv.[87]

The collusion continued as Nairobi air controllers did not query the captain's comment that he was late due to engine problems.[88]

The second 707, containing a fully equipped hospital,[89] arrived at 2:06 a.m. Nairobi time and took aboard the wounded brought in by the Israeli rescue aircraft. Kenyan assistance to the operation became more apparent later when people who were badly wounded were rapidly transported to the nearby hospital.[90] As medical assistance was being administered, the rescue aircraft refueled in secure facilities. All the while, released hostages were allowed to deplane and go for food and refreshments. However, they were requested to keep quiet about assistance given and not to "make any fuss" about this hospitality, by officials of the East African Directorate of Civil Aviation who feared retaliation against their colleagues at Entebbe.[91]

As for the Ugandan ground controllers, it was later reported that Ugandan soldiers questioned four radar operators in the wake of the rescue and accused them of not reporting the rescue planes that flew the Israeli commandos into Uganda.[92] The bodies of the four were later found in a wood.

In the post-rescue period, the mood in Nairobi was noticeably varied. Charles Harrison, a correspondent for *The Guardian,* noted:

There's a great deal of jubilation amongst the ordinary people at the humiliation which Uganda has suffered. At the same time there is quite a bit of apprehension because Kenya has been threatened from Uganda for quite a time and the general feeling is that the threats against Kenya will not be made any less by the humiliation which Amin has now suffered.[93]

Although Israeli and Kenyan authorities vehemently denied any Kenyan assistance, it seemed quite clear that Nairobi "provided at least tacit support for the rescue."[94] This became increasingly apparent as:

News agency reports from Nairobi speak of Israeli agents slipping quietly into the Kenyan capital during the week, often staying at private homes rather than hotels to avoid notice. Israeli agents carrying walkie-talkies also patrolled Nairobi Airport before the arrival of the Israeh [*sic*] planes on the return flight from Entebbe.[95]

The response to this publicity was noted in one report from Nairobi:

Kenyans will obviously be very nervous since wrath of Amin will undoubtedly be directed at Kenya which permitted use of Nrobi [Nairobi] military airport at Eastleigh as staging base. In what form this will come is difficult to tell but . . . [the] Kenyan armed forces, particularly air force, is no/no match for Ugandans either in terms of numbers or sophistication of eqpt. [equipment].[96]

Meanwhile Israeli leaders tried to avoid implicating Kenya. Israeli leaders emphasized that they had acted alone and had consulted no outside party before deciding on the rescue mission.[97]

To support Kenya against possible Ugandan reprisals in the post-rescue period, the United States positioned "a P3 Orion long-range reconnaissance aircraft, the first U.S. Air Force [*sic*; U.S. Navy] plane to be based—however temporarily—in Kenya."[98] By 19 July 1976, *Newsweek* reported that Washington had placed:

a Navy P-3 patrol plane at Kenya's service to provide military reconnaissance along the Ugandan border. Washington ordered the frigate U.S.S. Beary to head for the Kenyan port of Mombasa. And a Task Group from the U.S. Seventh Fleet—including the aircraft carrier Ranger—was ordered to steam toward Kenya in a third pointed signal of U.S. support.[99]

These military moves initially were perceived to be a part of America's *new policy of enhancing political relationships* with moderate African states.

Therefore, this large American naval presence off East Africa and the visit of the *USS Beary* were considered, by U.S. Secretary of State Henry Kissinger, as "normal." In reality, it was post-rescue assistance to Kenya and it was intended as "a bold warning to Amin not to let his post-Entebbe lust for revenge lead him into war."[100] Amin, on a more comical note and apparently angered by the Israeli success, argued "that the Israelis would not have been successful at Entebbe except for the fact that their nuclear hand grenades had somehow put [his] . . . soldiers to sleep."[101]

Although international cooperation had been instrumental to the success of the mission, most of it had been indirect. One nation, however, was more intimately involved. A senior officer of the West German Federal Border Police, Lieutenant Colonel Ulrich Wegener[102] was deployed on the ground prior to the rescue. Wegener "was ordered by the federal government to observe what happened because at that time German terrorists were also involved in the actions of the Palestinians."[103] Wegener was well qualified for the task, as he had undergone special military training[104] in both the United States and Israel. Richard Garrett writes that Wegener himself was a highly professional product of international cooperation and "had spent six weeks being tutored by the FBI in the United States, and he had also attended a course at the Israeli paratroop school."[105]

Although West Germany had little experience in counterterrorist operations or special operations in the wake of World War II, Wegener sought out the pertinent information and experience, thereby making it his own. This operational experience would assist him in his subsequent success at Mogadishu.

During the rescue, the Israeli commando force destroyed a number of Soviet-made MIG aircraft belonging to the Ugandan air force.[106] This was not a whimsical act. It had two purposes, one more urgent than the other. The destruction of these aircraft ensured the Israelis of a return flight without fear of a Ugandan aerial intercept. Less urgently, but strategically as important, it diminished the Ugandan military capability to punish Kenya for aiding Israel.

Israeli Post-Operations Brief

Major General Gazit, the director of military intelligence, summoned military attaches to a conference on 4 July 1976. During the briefing, Gazit emphasized three factors that affected the rescue mission: first, until Entebbe, the Israeli authorities had dealt with terrorist hostage incidents only within Israel or inside a friendly country. In such cases Israel acknowledged that the local government authorities were responsible for handling the terrorist activities. This was not the case in Entebbe. Not only did Israel have no diplomatic relations with Uganda, but it became readily apparent, particularly after the initial release of non-Israeli hostages, that there was "no/no chance of co-operation with Amin. In fact all info available indicated that Amin was co-operating fully with [the] terrorists."[107] Second, with the release of all Gentiles, the threat was seen to be directed against Israel. Thirdly, when pressed to release jailed terrorists, Israeli authorities were not concerned so much with the legal or political issues of the hostage-taking as with a situation where Tel Aviv "is being asked to release potential murderers who probably will strike again."[108] The military option was based on these premises. During the course of the briefing, Gazit emphasized that "if the IDF [Israeli Defense Force] had not had very good intelligence of the situation in Uganda, govt [government] would not have authorized [the] operation."[109]

Thunderbolt has been understandably described as "just a routine commando raid that happened to be a bit further in distance."[110] However, in reflection, had it not been for the concerted efforts of a number of countries that forwarded vital intelligence, as the United States and West Germany did, and Kenyan assistance in allowing Israeli aircraft a secure place to refuel and attend to their casualties, this historic rescue operation may not have been attempted. This would have left Israel with no other option but to surrender to the terrorists' demands.

THE MOGADISHU RESCUE

In 1977, West Germany experienced a most difficult year in combating terrorism. It was a year of some dramatic successes, including the capture of many terrorists, some of whom were associated with the Rote Armee Fraktion (Red Army Faction). In this battle against political terrorism, Chancellor Helmut Schmidt was considered by many to be the leading figure, both domestically and internationally. In particular, he directed measures to improve co-operation between the provincial and federal agencies responsible for combating terrorism.

The Mogadishu incident, in connection with the kidnapping of industrialist Hans-Martin Schleyer, was to become a watershed in the history of West Germany's fight against terrorism.[111] Moreover, it underlines the co-operation given to the West German government by friendly countries at critical points during the operation. It is important to understand the context of this drama, one among many of the problems facing West Germany in 1977.

Three major terrorist incidents occurred before the Mogadishu event that persuaded government officials and the West German people that dramatic action was needed to win the battle against terrorism from abroad. These were the murder on 7 April 1977 of Dr. Siegfried Bubeck, the chief public prosecutor, and the murder on 30 July 1977 of Herr Jurgen Ponto, the head of a prominent bank; and the abduction on 5 September 1977 of the well-known industrialist, Dr. Hans-Martin Schleyer.[112] For many, Dr. Schleyer was not only a powerful financial figure but also a symbol of West Germany's capitalist system. Schleyer was ambushed in his car while traveling between his Cologne home and office. Four of his bodyguards were shot. His kidnappers demanded DM 1.1 million, and the release and safe passage of jailed members of the Red Army Faction, including Andreas Baader.

Schmidt and his government initially refused to submit to the demands, but opened a series of negotiations through Denis Payot, a Swiss lawyer. The negotiations saw the passing of a series of ultimata and deadlines. The West German government's strategy was to negotiate to gain time, hoping to locate Schleyer. To ensure that there would be no publicity, a news blackout was instituted, denying the terrorists the media access they sought. This caused the terrorists to mount a support operation[113] to put pressure on Schmidt's government to submit to their demands. The leader assigned to this mission was Zuhair Akkasha, also known as "Martyr Mahmoud."[114] A PFLP radical, and a student of Dr. Hadad, he had, on occasion, assisted the Baader-Meinhof gang. The target for this support mission operation was a Lufthansa Boeing 737 Flight LH 181 which was traveling between Majorca and Frankfurt.[115] On 13 October 1977, four Palestinians, two men and two women,[116] seized this flight and ordered it to fly to Rome. The hostages numbered ninety-two, including five crew members. (It is important to note that the general policy for commercial airlines at this time consisted of avoiding violence, co-operating fully with terrorists, if possible stalling for time and reassuring the passengers so that they would remain calm.)

Italian aviation and police authorities closed the Rome airport to all other traffic, and put military and police units on standby. When Flight 737 arrived, it was parked in a secure area. Martyr Mahmoud then issued his demand that his colleagues jailed in West Germany be released.

Anticipating that a military option, in the form of a rescue operation, might be possible, Werner Maihofer, the West German interior minister, asked the Italian authorities to delay the aircraft. Lt. Colonel Wegener, commander of GSG9,[117] was notified. He placed his unit on alert.[118] As was the case in the Israeli experience, a crisis management team was established and remained generally intact throughout the hijacking and eventual rescue operation. The crisis management team revolved around Chancellor Schmidt and the ministers of Foreign Affairs, of the Interior and of Justice, and was empowered by the Cabinet to make any required emergency decisions. Schmidt began seeking international support and assistance with a telephone call to the prime minister of Great Britain. According to one report, "Schmidt wanted to compare ideas and determine degree of support internationally to various options. Callaghan later in [a] return phone call advised against giving in to hijackers demands."[119] Unbeknownst to Callaghan, Schmidt had no intention of giving in to the terrorists.

Meanwhile, airport authorities in Rome attempted to stall for time as requested, but the hijackers threatened to destroy the aircraft if the Italians refused their demands for fuel. At 5:42 p.m., the Lufthansa 737 departed from Rome destined for Larnaca, Cyprus. Initially, the Cypriot government refused permission to land. However, upon considering the possible implications for the safety of the passengers, the Cypriots allowed the 737 to land. Once in Cyprus, the terrorists requested more fuel and were put in touch with Saharia Abdul Rachmin, a Palestinian Liberation Organization representative.[120] The hijackers then issued a demand in addition to those previously made, calling for the release of two Palestinians imprisoned in Turkey.

West Germany's reaction to this crisis was rapid. Just hours after the first report of the hijacking, an aircraft was dispatched to Cyprus. In the aircraft were the head of the anti-terror department in the Federal Office of Criminal Investigation, a commando element, representatives of the German Federal Criminal Police, foreign office specialists, anti-terrorist experts from the Ministry of the Interior, agents of the German internal and external intelligence services, representatives of Lufthansa and the GSG9 command group.[121] The aircraft conveying the West German officials landed at Akrotiri,[122] a British airbase, fifty miles from Larnaca. For more than an hour, both the hijackers and the German rescue team were on the island. The Cypriot authorities, however, refused a request to attempt a rescue.

Refueled and provided with the latest weather reports, the 737 left Larnaca at approximately 10:50 p.m. and headed to Beirut, where it was refused permission to land. It was later likewise refused permission to land at Damascus, Amman and Kuwait. Desperate, the hijacked 737 pilot received permission to stop temporarily in Bahrain at approximately 1:52 a.m. on 14 October. During this stopover, the link between the Schleyer kidnappers and the hijackers became apparent when the latter forwarded their demands through the office of Denis Payot, the same intermediary employed by the Schleyer abductors. These demands were comparable to those issued for the return of Schleyer. The terrorists told authorities that if by 8:00 a.m. GMT, 16 October their demands were not met, the hostages, along with Dr. Schleyer, would be killed.

The Lufthansa 737 departed from Bahrain at 3:24 a.m. and loitered only to touch down at Dubai in the United Arab Emirates two and a half hours later. Here the hijackers demanded a negotiator, food, and drink. Here, the Defense Minister, Sheik Mohammed bin Rashid al-Maktum,[123] assumed responsibility as chief negotiator. He requested that the hostage-takers release the young and the elderly in exchange for fuel. The hijackers refused. It was at this time that some important tactical intelligence was revealed. Wegener stated that when the Lufthansa plane landed:

we got the first information about the terrorists. We got it from the crew. Some months ago we had worked out a code with Lufthansa personnel which would provide us with some information about the hijackers. In Dubai I got a coded message from the captain of the hijacked aircraft that there were four terrorists aboard, two male and two female.[124]

Photographs were taken of some of the terrorists when the aircraft's doors were open and the terrorists were subsequently identified as members of the PFLP. It was vital for the GSG9 to identify the leader, Captain Mahmoud.[125] As luck would have it a timely breakdown of the power unit provided:

new information on the terrorists. Because of the APU breakdown, the terrorists demanded a ground power unit to get to the aircraft; Lufthansa personnel took it to the aircraft. They tried to get into contact with the crew. When they got close to the aircraft, the terrorists found out that they were not British and not Arabs because of their strong German accent and so Mahmoud fired on them. Thank God nobody was hurt. One of the Lufthansa captains who took the ground power unit to the aircraft was a former military officer and he could tell me after he came back, "Well, they didn't shoot at me with automatic weapons. They used only handguns." That was very important.[126]

One writer, Tony Geraghty, notes that a request for British assistance to GSG9 came soon after the hijack took place. This request was initially of a diplomatic nature and sought political assistance in dealing with the local authorities in Dubai. Geraghty states that: this assistance began when a German minister traveled to London in order to seek British assistance in dealing with the authorities in Dubai, where the hijacked aircraft was destine to land. Dubai has historical close links with Britain and the German aim was to request the British authorities in Whitehall to use their influence with the UAE ambassador in London thereby facilitating diplomatic clearances for GSG9 should they be required to go into action in Dubai.[127]

This Anglo-German diplomatic cooperation in the early stages of the hijacking would rapidly evolve into military assistance as the GSG9 officer accompanying the German minister also requested technical assistance. According to Geraghty, it was thought by the GSG9 representative that the SAS might have access to certain equipment that could assist with forced entry of the aircraft. Moreover, unbeknownst to the German authorities, the SAS had extensive knowledge and connections within the Persian Gulf area and that the presidential guard of Dubai was trained and led by former SAS soldiers. It was during the London meetings that an SAS liaison team would be sent consisting of Major Alastair Morrison, OBE, MC, an experienced SAS squadron commander and Sergeant Barry Davies, BEM, as well as a collection of flash-bangs the liaison team headed for Dubai.[128]

This SAS technical assistance quickly became a diplomatic asset when, on arrival at Dubai, it became apparent that Wegener and two of his personnel were "under escort" by local police authorities while the Lufthansa jet containing the hostages was waiting on the runway. Thanks to Morrison and Davies, this small diplomatic incident was summarily addressed as the bureaucratic issues were quickly resolved and they commenced training the Dubai Royal Guard in the tactics of siege-breaking in order to provide a back-up element for GSG-9.[129]

During this period the West German government was under pressure to succumb to the demands of the terrorists. Schmidt's Cabinet had to weigh the danger posed to the lives of eighty-seven hostages and Dr. Schleyer against the danger in releasing the prisoners as demanded by the terrorists. This situation was the same dilemma that had earlier confronted the Israeli government: release the terrorists with the possibility that they could kill again; or keep the terrorists in captivity, which would probably result in the death of the hostages. In essence Schmidt's decision revolved around the fact that:

> The terrorists held by the West German authorities had been accused of murdering 13 people and attempting to murder 43 more;
> The prisoners released in 1975 in exchange for Peter Lorenz were later charged with murdering four and possibly nine others as well as the attempted killing of a further six.
> The possible effect upon the ability, motivation and willingness of security authorities to risk their lives while arresting or incarcerating such personnel, and,
> The possibility that the hijacked passengers might not be safely released.[130]

Only after careful assessment of the factors in concert with other members of government did Schmidt decide to undertake a rescue operation. As was the case in Israel's operation "Thunderbolt," a two-pronged operational strategy[131] was to be employed. First, all avenues of negotiation were to be employed. If these failed, GSG9 would be assigned to undertake the "final option"—a deliberate assault on the aircraft in order to free the hostages.

By the morning of 14 October the Cabinet had decided not to release the prisoners as demanded by the terrorists. However, the government hoped to mislead the hijackers by seeming to suggest that Bonn would release the imprisoned terrorists in exchange for Schleyer and the hostages. Negotiations continued between the hijackers and the UAE foreign minister. All attempts at releasing the children, women and the sick failed.

The situation within the aircraft was appalling, as the hostages were confined to their seats. The aircraft's sanitation facilities no longer worked and many on board had diarrhea. This, combined with the heat, a degree of psychological tension, and verbal and physical abuse from the terrorists, was almost intolerable. Moreover, the terrorists' requests for sanctuary in South Yemen, Somalia or Vietnam had all been rejected. The situation was further complicated for the West German government when Schleyer's son made an unsuccessful attempt to pay the ransom demanded by his father's kidnappers.

The German crisis management group maintained direct communication with State Minister Hans-JurgenWischnewski in the Dubai control tower. Although the relations between Wischnewski and the representative of the UAE were considered to be "excellent,"[132] they deteriorated somewhat while initial plans for a rescue attempt were being formulated. Sheik Mohammed bin Rashid al-Maktum apparently requested that Wegener instruct his military personnel in the assaulting of an aircraft, so that they could execute the rescue.[133] According to one report, Wegener "observed that this squad was highly inefficient"[134] and that the aircraft they were experimenting with was a Gulf Air 727 jet. During this time Wegener tried to have the UAE military cut the source of power to the hijacked aircraft so that the crew could not start the aircraft. In this initiative the UAE personnel were unwilling to co-operate.[135]

Operational security was broken when a spokesman for the West German government revealed that GSG9 had been sent to Cyprus. When the media broadcasted this information (by which time the GSG9 teams were in Ankara, Turkey), the hijackers ordered that they be returned to West Germany. Bonn immediately acquiesced. However, with the assistance of the West German news media, the terrorists were deceived into believing that the GSG9 had returned to Cologne. Instead, the GSG9 had been forward-based to Crete[136] with the permission of the Greek government. Apparently the "passengers" on this aircraft bearing the GSG9 were described as "technical and health personnel." The German "overflights and stagings were finessed by passing off aircraft as civilian without being too precise on contents and mission."[137] This allowed the Greek government to deny any complicity in the events.

Tensions rose when the power generator on the hijacked plane broke down during the night of 15–16 October blacking out the aircraft and causing the hijackers, who feared a rescue attempt, to fire upon the ground crew who were approaching the aircraft to make repairs. At 5:30 a.m., 16 October, the terrorists demanded that the aircraft be refueled or else the pilot, Captain Juergen Schumann, would be killed. The negotiators complied. Meanwhile the leader of the hijackers, Martyr Mahmoud, had become noticeably jumpy and ordered the pilot to take off an hour before the deadline. Allowing the sudden departure of the Lufthansa flight from Dubai was a political decision made by the government of the UAE.

By this time the SAS were more than just advisors. According to Geraghty, "Morrison and Davies had become de facto members of Wegener's team, and they stayed with him when the hunt moved from Aden to Mogadishu, in Somalia, where the German commander was joined by the main body of his force after a flight from Turkey."[138]

After a short flight the 737 approached Aden and was refused permission to land. The runway was blocked. Short of fuel, Captain Schumann in desperation made a forced landing on a rough strip that paralleled the main runway. The aircraft was immediately surrounded by South Yemeni soldiers, and Schumann was informed that the aircraft was to refuel, then depart. Captain Schumann was allowed to deplane to check for possible damage to the landing gear and while doing so was detained by Yemeni soldiers. Accused of attempting to pass information to the authorities or to escape while he was outside the aircraft, Schumann was summarily executed upon his return.[139] This action prepared the fate of the terrorists.[140]

The co-pilot flew the aircraft to Mogadishu airport in Somalia. Although the Somalis denied permission to land, they did not obstruct the runway. Meanwhile the advance party of German negotiators and the two SAS personnel arrived in the wake of flight 737. Upon landing, Flight 737 was directed to move, for security reasons, to an area approximately 300 meters from the terminal itself. This site was selected to place the aircraft in full view of the control tower. In case of a rescue attempt, it would be easily reached as it was close to sand dunes that would cover an approach. The Somali government was told that if all previous demands were not met, the terrorists would blow up the aircraft. Food and drugs were supplied. In turn, the Somali government asked that women and children be released. This request and a further offer of safe passage out of Somalia were both rejected.

In a subsequent move, Captain Schumann's corpse was dumped unceremoniously on the tarmac. The dumping of a Christian body on Muslim soil had an immediate and dramatic effect on the Somali government in both religious and political terms. This action sparked further diplomatic initiatives aimed at finding a settlement, peaceable or otherwise. Moreover, diplomats from Britain, the United States, France as well as others solicited Middle Eastern and African capitals to back up West German efforts to resolve the hijacking.[141] President Barre of Somalia and Wischnewski met around noon on 17 October to discuss their options, but no decision was made. A major point of contention regarding a rescue operation was the extent of Somali assistance. Wischnewski, Wegener, Bueden and senior Somali security representatives conferred at length. The solution came about after a meeting was arranged with Barre, following a call from Schmidt.

Barre agreed that GSG9 could attempt a rescue. This action would be fully supported by members of the Somali security forces.[142] The aircraft carrying the sixty members of GSG9 received permission to fly to Mogadishu.

Wischnewski maintained close contact with the terrorists throughout the day. This was critical, as it was later discovered that the hijack leader was demonstrating signs of breaking under the prolonged strain. At 2:30 p.m., Martyr Mahmoud contacted Minister Wischnewski and stated that he intended to blow up the aircraft at 3:00 p.m. In preparation, the terrorists kept their hostages in their seats, and began pouring flammable liquids and liquor down the center aisle.[143] By the terrorists doing this, the GSG9 commander ascertained that there were explosives of some type on board.[144]

Wegener believed that, to ensure the greatest probability of success, the approach, assault and rescue had to be conducted under the cover of darkness. Thus it was critical that the rescue forces gain more time. At approximately 3:00, a half-hour delay was given to move the hijacked aircraft away from the area. At 3:30 Wischnewski gambled and radioed the aircraft. He told the terrorist leader that the West German government had acceded to all their demands. The bait was taken; Martyr Mahmoud, believing Wischnewski, gave a seven-hour extension to 1:30 a.m. This desperate deception had worked.[145]

The aircraft containing the rescue force landed in darkness at 7:30 p.m. (local time) in Mogadishu. To assist in the secure landing, Wegener requested Somali assistance: "I talked with the Commander of the Somali Air Force about some supporting measures. I asked him to employ some of their fighters to let them take off and land for the next hours so that we could cover the landing of our own . . . airplane. That worked out very fine. They did very well."[146]

The Lufthansa 727 landed without incident with only two taillights glowing. After it was in position, the landing lights were flashed on and off to signal the control tower of their arrival. Before the main force arrived, Wegener, accompanied by an officer of the Somali Armed Forces, conducted a reconnaissance of the area of operation. From this Wegener made his appreciation, formulated a plan, and briefed his unit upon arrival. In anticipation of any possible crisis before the assault, Wegener deployed some of his personnel so that an immediate rescue could be executed if required. By 11:30 p.m., all preparations were complete. Wischnewski informed Schmidt of the arrival of Wegener's men and the go-ahead was given. This was the last communication with Schmidt until the operation was finished.

The operation was nearly scuttled just after GSG9 arrived in Mogadishu. Radio transmissions from the GSG9 aircraft were apparently overheard by an Israeli journalist,[147] who immediately sent out a report that anti-terrorist police were ready for use in a rescue attempt. The report was transmitted to the Agence France-Presse (AFP) and Reuters.[148]

The Rescue Plan

The responsibility for the operational command of the rescue fell solely upon Wegener. His organization consisted of a main headquarters, a communications center and a first-aid post situated in the airport control tower. A forward, or tactical, communications post would later be positioned near the target aircraft. There were about sixty members of the GSG9 assault unit,[149] of which twenty-eight were to assault the aircraft while another group was to remain as a ready reserve. Somali police and military personnel—consisting of a Somali Ranger battalion equipped with Russian radios—provided airport security and sealed off the area of operations.[150] Later, Somali forces provided a diversion at a critical moment. Surprise was vital.

The target intelligence available for the operation lacked critical detail. Before he was murdered, Captain Schumann had made various attempts to pass vital information, but the intelligence planning staff still needed details, particularly regarding the level of experience and sophistication of the terrorists and where they were located inside the aircraft on a moment by moment basis. It was also critically important for the rescue squad to know if the entrance doors to the aircraft were secured with explosives. At this point, the aim was to continue negotiating in order to garner intelligence, to ascertain the mood of the terrorists and the situation in the aircraft itself.

Orders were issued to the GSG9 troops at about 10:45 p.m. Due to the lack of intelligence regarding the situation within the hijacked aircraft, Wegener wanted to begin an early deployment: "I wanted to put up in a very early stage reconnaissance and sniper teams in the hills around the aircraft. We would know at every minute what is going on in the aircraft."[151]

At approximately 1:00 a.m. the plan was to have the assault team members place themselves in their attack positions beneath the aircraft. The attack was to begin at 2:05.[152] Just after midnight, all sniper and reconnaissance teams were positioned and the first reports were being received as to the whereabouts of the terrorists. Two were sighted in the cockpit and one was walking up and down the aisle.[153] At 1:00 a.m., the assault group, consisting of the operations team, two detachments of three assault teams, a reserve team and a combat engineer team, began to move into their assault areas as planned. These groups got to within 100 meters of the aircraft by 1:30. Then, Wegener went to the aircraft site with all the detachment leaders, to brief them on their assault positions and their areas of responsibility within the aircraft itself.[154] The plan, according to Wegener, was that the first detachment would attack:

the tail [entrance] and doors, the right wing exit and the other three exits. The cockpit doors and the left wing exit were the responsibility of the second unit. Their mission, starting now with the second unit was to penetrate the cockpit, to eliminate the terrorists there, to carry the assault into the first class compartment and to eliminate the terrorists there. The teams at the tail end of the aircraft had to cover and occupy the positions from where we could evacuate the hostages right after we got into the aircraft.[155]

To assist the assault team, deception measures were included. Somali soldiers started a fire in front of the aircraft,[156] and at the same time, the negotiating team began a new stage of negotiations. The reconnaissance party forwarded a second message at 1:59 a.m. reporting that two terrorists, one female, were in the pilot's compartment. With this information Wegener "got the *impression* that the two others were in the back of the aircraft, but here was a situation that was not clear."[157]

During this same period, the GSG9 members checked the cabin pressure conditions within the fuselage and discovered that there was no pressure build-up to assist in opening the doors. As well, the uneven ground made it difficult for the assault members to position the ladders against the aircraft, a small yet crucial problem at this point. On the code words, "Magic Fire," the assault was launched. The six teams went through all entrances, including the emergency exits. At the same time stun grenades were detonated in front of the aircraft. According to Wegener, "We planted three flash bombs, which were given to us by our British friends. But we didn't ignite them inside the aircraft; we just threw them outside the aircraft."[158] This was due to the fact that the grenades themselves were phosphorus and could easily start a fire within the aircraft cabin. Once the aircraft was entered, team leaders ordered the hostages in both English and German, "Down on the ground; heads down." The GSG9 assault teams responsible for the front of the aircraft opened the nose doors and the action was fast and furious, as Wegener recounted:

> we drew fire from the terrorist leader and the female terrorist. We drew fire and returned fire, and one of my men was hit through the neck. (But the GSG9 men can take this, of course. So he is back to duty; he was very fortunate, I have to say that.) The terrorist leader was hit by five .38 bullets, but he could still manage to just jump back into the cockpit and grab a hand grenade. We got him there by a burst of submachine gun fire.[159]

The third hijacker fired upon the teams from the first-class compartment as they were assaulting through the rear section and in the nose area. The terrorist was killed by a shot in the head. A fourth terrorist, another female, was found in one of the front toilets. A team leader shot through the wall of the door, mortally wounding her. By now, all assault teams were occupying their planned responsibility areas. It was at this point that the team leader of the first assault group noticed Russian-type grenades in the vicinity of the cockpit and requested support from the combat engineers.[160] The evacuation was started four minutes after the assault began, using three major exit points: the left and right tail and the emergency exits. Some of the passengers were suffering from mild shock. Two passengers were slightly wounded by grenade fragments when two grenades were rolled under the seats by one of the terrorists. Both grenades went off, but the seats took the blasts. Once out of the aircraft, the hostages were immediately escorted by the reserve assault team, which was under cover about forty meters from the aircraft site. Here they were searched to assure the assault force that they had not missed any of the hijackers. In all, four grenades were found, as were two kilograms of Semtex that had been placed on the doors. The action itself took seven minutes from the start of the assault to the evacuation of the hostages.

At 2:12 a.m., Wegener acknowledged that all terrorists were disabled. At 2:17 the code word "springtime" (end of mission) was sent to State Minister Wischnewski. At 2:18 the GSG9 members were assembled and the hostages were dispatched to the terminal where a medical station was set up. The hijacked Lufthansa aircraft was turned over to German Federal Criminal Police officers and their Somali counterparts. At 5:00 a.m., GSG9 left Somalia.

Wegener points out that the successful operation in Mogadishu demonstrated to all that the GSG9 training and operational concepts were on the right track. There were a number of prerequisites required to ensure the success of this operation and lessons for those in the future. Firstly, the chain of command and control from the decision makers to the tactical commander on scene was in place; there was the noninterference of Mr. Wischnewski, the representative of the Crisis Management Staff concerning tactical matters; and the agreement and co-operation of the Somali government with the tactical planning and proposals of the commanding officer of GSG9.[161]

As far as the British cooperation was concerned:

> Confirmation of the SAS involvement in the Mogadishu operation came immediately after the rescue from Prime Minister Callaghan, then in Bonn with Chancellor Schmidt. In front of television cameras, Callaghan told Schmidt: "It should have been Dubai." But even if the venue was changed, the event added new luster to the SAS reputation, and it was good for Britain's relations with Europe.[162]

In reflection, Mogadishu refined some of the lessons learnt for rescue operations. Practical lessons were to be learnt. As an example, the difficulties experienced in using the GSG9 team radios, due to very high humidity, resulted in the teams reverting to hand signals and the future necessity that radios be capable of operating in differing climates. For Colonel Wegener, Mogadishu demonstrated that the means had to be found to provide better intelligence and to enhance the GSG9 reconnaissance capability. Intelligence officers from West Germany's domestic and foreign intelligence agencies were subsequently seconded to GSG9 to support and facilitate the intelligence requirements of the GSG9, as well as to act as liaison officers. For other nations not already experienced in this type of warfare, they were served notice to take such eventualities seriously, and prepare for them by establishing a counterterrorist option similar to GSG9. Professionally, it is very much to the credit of the West German government and the leadership of GSG9 that they sought and welcomed foreign assistance, in this case acquiring an SAS liaison team and incorporating their knowledge into their operation. As one study noted, "In the war against terrorism, there is no room for false pride and misplaced machismo: those in charge should make use of the best manpower, expertise, equipment and techniques, regardless of origin."[163]

As was the case with Kenya's intimate assistance to the Israelis at Entebbe, the Somalian government should be commended for allowing the GSG9 to operate unimpeded under German command and control. Furthermore, the Greek government must be praised for allowing the GSG9 to be forward-based in Crete during a critical phase of the pursuit operation. As one study underlined, when a well-trained counterterrorist unit is available in the nation involved, the government responsible will likely insist that it be employed. However, should no specialist unit exist or be available and a capable foreign counterterrorist team is available, especially if the hostages are citizens of that foreign country, it is politically and morally responsible for the host nation to set aside sovereignty issues and allow the best counterterrorist unit to deal with the crisis at hand.[164]

The Mogadishu operation was conducted after years of intensive training by highly professional personnel. It drew upon extensive knowledge gleaned from the careful study of previous rescue operations, including Entebbe. Beyond the fundamental requirements of a specially selected and trained hostage-rescue force, it is apparent that a robust and effective governmental crisis decision-making body was readily available in both Entebbe and Mogadishu. Moreover, the value of accurate up-to-the-second intelligence as well as the importance of acquiring a forward-base to either pursue terrorists or project an attack must be emphasized. Further, in both rescues the actual operational leadership rested with the commander on the ground. One of the most salient lessons to be drawn from Mogadishu and Entebbe is the ability of both the West German and Israeli governments to, concurrently, negotiate while preparing to fight.

Rescue missions are daring and sensitive operations that can be easily compromised, as shown by the incident of the reporter monitoring GSG9 air-to-ground transmissions. Any future operations will require a secure and functional means of communications with the appropriate back-up links.[165] The employment of secure means would go a long way in ensuring that any future mission is not compromised.

Beyond the "intimate relationship" which developed before and during the Mogadishu rescue between GSG9 and the SAS, rescue forces must be sensitive to the politics of such operations. The initial reluctance, demonstrated by the authorities in Dubai and Somalia, to allow GSG9 to operate independently on their soil is most significant. In that regard it was apparently an international effort to convince the Somali government to allow the GSG9 the opportunity to free the hostages:

> after uncertainties in or over Dubai, Oman and PDRY, turning point occurred in Mogadishu. Aircraft with GSG-9 was brought forward after Schmidt and other heads of government/state concerned convinced Siad Barre not/not to allow [the] hijacked aircraft to leave and to go along with assault operation. Somalis did not/not take a direct part but played a role in coordinated diversionary actions on runway and airfield. Brits understand that Germans were prepared to let Somalis take direct part if this became sticking point in Somali agreement for GSG-9 operation.[166]

National prestige and political correctness often prevail over common sense. As noted above, the Germans were prepared to allow the Somalis to take part in the rescue. In that regard, counterterrorist teams must be able to accommodate, within their operational planning, suitable roles for foreign police and security forces, if they intend to operate abroad. In short, "Specialist units . . . should build into their procedures and their plans appropriate roles which can be filled at short notice by indigenous personnel, and they must be prepared to give an over-generous share of credit to such participation afterwards."[167]

In the end, the international cooperative assistance was underlined when West German government spokesman Klause Boelling gave the following statement at the successful conclusion of the Mogadishu rescue:

> we weighed the risk [of rescue] as conscientiously as we could. Nevertheless, a high risk remained. Without the consent and aid of the Somali government, we could not have undertaken the rescue operation.
>
> The government of Somalia deserves gratitude, not only from us Germans. Its decision to permit the operation was essential to averting a catastrophe. The moral and political support of many other states for our efforts to liberate the hostages and crew members from the power of dangerous common criminals has materially helped the Federal Republic of Germany.[168]

Another indicator of assistance was noted in a report advising that Helmut Schmidt:

> also sent telegrams of thanks to president Jimmy Carter, premier [*sic*] James Callaghan, president Valery Giscard D'Estaing, Greek premier Konstandinos

[*sic*] Karamanlis and King Kahlid of Saudi Arabia. The chancellor also sent a telegram of thanks to Pope Paul, who had declared his readiness to be exchanged for the hostages if need be.[169]

Both Entebbe and Mogadishu were historically important ventures as they illustrate the determined initiatives of governments to move toward closer co-operative efforts, and proved that such international assistance and co-operation do have a decisive role to play in combating terrorism.

NOTES

1. For an in-depth analysis of the criteria for success in special operations, see Gray, "Handfuls of Heroes on Desperate Ventures: When Do Special Operations Succeed?" 2–24. See also Bayev, "Organizing and Conducting a Special Operation to Free Hostages," 129–140.

2. France's counterterrorist force Groupement d'Intervention de la Gendarmerie Nationale (GIGN) is not covered in this text. It is, however, considered to be a highly professional unit and belongs to the Gendarmerie Nationale. Its most famous action was the February 1976 rescue of thirty children who were being held hostage by members of the Somali Coast Liberation Front (FLCS). As well, on 24 December 1994 GIGN orchestrated the dramatic rescue of 170 passengers and crew from a seized Air France Airbus. Today, the GIGN is based at the Maisons Alfort Barracks near Paris and has four twelve-man teams on standby twenty-four hours a day. In addition to being France's counterterrorist force, the GIGN provides VIP protection and is involved in criminal, prison and terrorist sieges, particularly if the latter is on a sensitive site such as a nuclear power station. See MacKenzie, "GIGN—The French Approach to Counter-Terrorism," 438–439. For further information see Thompson, *The Rescuers: The World's Top Anti-Terrorist Units,* 70–78; Thompson, *Ragged War: The Story of Unconventional Warfare;* and Dobson and Payne, *Terror: The West Fights Back,* 138–148. See also "Save the Hostages!: French Special Forces in Action." This article discusses Operation Farfadet, an exercise to train European nations to locate and liberate hostages held captive in hostile territory. This exercise underlined that only France had the resources and the potential to liberate nationals being held as hostages in a crisis-torn state. Today, special forces have been employed in Bosnia and Herzegovina and in other regions to seize war criminals. According to one report the British Special Air Service has been involved in the apprehension of thirteen of the twenty war crimes suspects in custody. See Smith, "French Military Accused of Blocking Karadzic's Arrest: British SAS Feels it Could Easily 'Snatch' Accused War Criminal." Also, to garner an appreciation of terrorist behavior, see Wilson, "Toward a Model of Terrorist Behavior in Hostage-Taking Incidents."

3. In the wake of the mission, the code name was changed in memory of the leader Lieutenant Colonel Jonathan Netanyahu, who was killed on the rescue mission.

4. Deacon, *The Israeli Secret Service,* 271.

5. Athens had a reputation for having very lax airport security during this period.

6. Deming, et al., "A Daring Rescue in Uganda," 28.

7. Mickolus, *Transnational Terrorism: A Chronology of Events, 1968–1979,* 621. The plane was seized by a total of four terrorists armed with pistols and hand grenades: two members of Baader-Meinhof and two from the Popular Front for the Liberation of Palestine (PFLP).

8. Deming, "A Daring Rescue in Uganda," 29.

9. "When the Commandos Arrived."

10. "53 Names on List." This request consisted of forty held in Israel, six in Germany, five in Kenya, one in Switzerland and one in France.

11. "Uganda Hostage Situation: Israeli Reaction." Report. Canadian Embassy Tel Aviv to Department of External Affairs, Ottawa, Canada (30 June 1976).

12. Ibid.

13. Mickolus, *Transnational Terrorism: A Chronology of Events, 1968–1979,* 622.

14. "Chronology of Hijacking."

15. FBIS 66, "Israeli Government Meeting to Assess Hijack Situation."

16. Smith, "'Hijackers' Orders Challenge Israel."

17. Stevenson, *90 Minutes at Entebbe,* 17.

18. Ibid.

19. Ibid., 7.

20. Mickolus, *Transnational Terrorism: A Chronology of Events, 1968–1979,* 622.

21. See Herzog, *The Arab-Israeli Wars,* 328.

22. During the 1967 Arab-Israeli War, Mordechai Gur commanded the Israeli paratroopers who captured the Old City. He served as Israel's tenth chief of staff from 1974 to 1978, and during this period directed the Israeli rescue of hostages from Entebbe. In 1978, he guided the campaign in Lebanon to drive out the Palestinian guerrillas. In the wake of the 1973 Arab-Israeli War, he oversaw the rebuilding of the Israeli army after the heavy losses and ensuing demoralization. See Greenberg, "Israel Military Leader, 65, Directed Entebbe Rescue."

23. "Rescue at Entebbe: How the Israelis Did It," 46.

24. Ibid.

25. Ben-Porat, et al., *Entebbe Rescue,* 222–223.

26. See Menarchik, "Strike Against Terror! The Entebbe Raid," 70. This initiative has been described as an "unstructured dual-tracked approach."

27. Herzog, *The Arab-Israeli Wars,* 329.

28. Stevenson, *90 Minutes at Entebbe,* 11–13.

29. "Five Facing Secret Trial over Bid to Down Jet."

30. Stevenson, *90 Minutes at Entebbe,* 23.

31. Ibid., 24.

32. "Five Facing Secret Trial over Bid to Down Jet."

33. Stevens and Kubic, "The Odd Couple," 52.

34. Herzog, *The Arab-Israeli Wars,* 329.

35. Stevenson, *90 Minutes at Entebbe,* 32.

36. Ibid.

37. Canadian Broadcasting Corporation, "The Rescue of Hostages Held in Uganda by Israeli Commandos," 2.

38. Stevenson, *90 Minutes at Entebbe,* 32.

39. Herzog, *The Arab-Israeli Wars,* 329.

40. Smith, "Israelis Say Extension of Deadline by the Hijackers Was Crucial to Raid's Success."

41. Ibid.

42. Ibid.

43. See "The McKenzie Affair." Mr. McKenzie was later killed in a mysterious aerial explosion. All aboard the light aircraft were killed. According to Herzog (*The Arab-Israeli Wars,* 336) the subsequent stories of Israeli agents in Uganda and operating on Lake Victoria were complete fabrications. See Stevenson, *90 Minutes at Entebbe,* 33. However, Colonel Wegener was on the ground on orders of the West German government, as was a British diplomat.

44. Garrett, *The Raiders: The Elite Strike Forces That Altered the Course of War and History,* 212–214.

45. Stevenson, *90 Minutes at Entebbe,* 77.

46. Ibid.

47. Ibid.

48. Garrett, *The Raiders: The Elite Strike Forces That Altered the Course of War and History,* 211–212. According to General Wegener, there were seven MIG-19s on the airfield. Discussion with General Ulrich K. Wegener, Royal Military College, Kingston, Canada (5 October 2000).

49. "Raid Reconstructed: Israelis Knew Airport."

50. Stevenson, *90 Minutes at Entebbe,* 89.

51. Discussion with General Ulrich K. Wegener, Ottawa, Canada (3 October 2000).

52. Smith, "Israelis Say Extension of Deadline by the Hijackers Was Crucial to Raid's Success."

53. Stevenson, *90 Minutes at Entebbe,* 41–42. Herzog, *The Arab-Israeli Wars,* 331, notes that, "considerable use was made of the photographs taken by Israeli Air Force personnel some years before, when they were training the Ugandan Air Force."

54. Stevenson, *90 Minutes at Entebbe,* 46.

55. Middleton, "Key to Raid's Success: Analysts Cite Strategic and Tactical Surprise, Achieved Through Deception." Chaim Herzog notes that "In order not to give rise to any suspicion that a military operation was being planned, all the diplomatic negotiations in France and Uganda continued, meanwhile, indicating that Israel would give in to the demands of the terrorists and make the necessary arrangements to meet these demands by Sunday, 4 July." Herzog, *The Arab-Israeli Wars,* 330.

56. Carroll, "How the Israelis Pulled it Off," 43–44. The question of Israeli agents being infiltrated into the Entebbe area is disputed by Herzog.

57. Smith, "Israelis Say Extension of Deadline by the Hijackers Was Crucial to Raid's Success."

58. Discussion with General Ulrich K. Wegener, Ottawa, Canada (3 October 2000).

59. Carroll, "How the Israelis Pulled it Off," 44. Also, discussion with General Ulrich K. Wegener, Royal Military College, Kingston, Canada (4 October 2000).

60. Ibid.

61. Herzog, *The Arab-Israeli Wars,* 331.

62. Ibid., 332.

63. Ibid.

64. Ibid. See also Kolcum, "Israeli Defense Minister Explains Tactics," 25. Peres stated, "From the very first moment it was clear that the operation would not be a calculated military risk but would be a comparative national risk. The comparative national risk [means] what happens if you surrender, what will the consequences be if you surrender." "The cost of surrender always exceeds the cost of a military risk. The food of terrorism is success. The end of terrorism is failure."

65. For an interesting insight into decision-making during a crisis situation, see Maoz, "The Decision to Raid Entebbe: Decision Analysis Applied to Crisis Behavior."

66. For an informative overview of the Sayeret Matkal, see Cohen, "Stealth Warriors." See "The Guys—Israel's Anonymous Heroes." See also Walmer, *An Illustrated Guide To Modern Elite Forces,* 24–33 and Katz, *The Elite: The True Story of Israel's Secret Counter-Terrorist Unit.* The Israeli Army provided some insight into these "commando" units that had been hunting Hezbollah guerrillas in southern Lebanon during the 1994–96 period. This group, code-named Egoy (Hebrew for walnut), was employed solely in Lebanon, and was made up of volunteers from the Golani Brigade, a unit which assisted in the Entebbe raid. Recent events in 1997–98 regarding failures in special operations have come to light, in particular the 4–5 September 1997 of Flotilla 13 operations by the Hezbollah which left twelve of sixteen Israeli operatives dead. See Katz, "Incident at Ansariya," 24–28. The Israeli Army lost three IDF paratroopers, who are claimed by the Hezbollah to be a "Paratrooper Reconnaissance Unit," in an ambush. In this action three IDF para-officers were killed and five soldiers wounded. See O'Sullivan, "IDF Strikes Back at Hizbullah"; and "Israelis Fall Foul of Hizbollah Trap." According to this article, "Israel's intelligence 'eye' in Lebanon has been virtually destroyed, its collaborators arrested or killed, even its own proxy South Lebanon Army militia infiltrated by the Hizbollah." See Blanford, "Hizbullah Attacks Force Israel to Take a Hard Look at Lebanon." It is interesting to note that Israel's former Prime Minister Ehud Barak was with the Sayeret and participated in a wide range of special operations. His election campaign was reportedly organized by 300 former Sayeret men. This indicates some of the political influence that such operatives have within the Israeli democratic process. Rees, "Barak's Special Forces: His Advisers Are Former Soldiers Who Know How to Wage War. But Are They Fit to Fight for Peace?" See also Mahnaimi, "Israelis Risk All in Undercover Missions: Elite Squad Goes Behind Enemy Lines Posing as Arabs." During the Palestinian–Israeli violence in October 2000, Barak ordered Israel's elite Duvdevan (Cherry) brigade to carry out clandestine operations on the West Bank in order to garner information and conduct covert operations in support of the Israeli authorities.

67. Stevenson, *90 Minutes at Entebbe,* 88.

68. Ibid.

69. See Hastings, *YONI: Hero of Entebbe* for a biography of this officer. The only other Israeli military casualty was a soldier shot in the throat, who was unfortunately paralyzed for life.

70. During his time on the ground, Wegener collected pertinent on-site intelligence as to the location of the terrorists and the hostages, as well as defenses in

and around the airport, airfield and facilities. Moreover, on sighting the deployment of Ugandan snipers on the airfield towers, he suggested that this structure be immediately destroyed should a rescue force land, as the tower itself and the Ugandan soldiers posted there could dominate the area in a tactically decisive manner. Unfortunately, this did not occur and Colonel Netanyahu was reportedly killed by one of the snipers situated on the tower. Discussion with General Ulrich K. Wegener, Ottawa, Canada (4 October 2000).

71. Stevenson, *90 Minutes at Entebbe*, 92.

72. For an insight into the background and experiences of an Israeli officer, see Chanoff, *Warrior: The Autobiography of Ariel Sharon.*

73. Deacon, *The Israeli Secret Service*, 277–278. For an interesting study of the Entebbe operation from an *operator*'s viewpoint, see McRaven, *Spec Ops: Case Studies in Special Operations Warfare: Theory and Practice*, 333–380.

74. Ibid., 279.

75. Ibid., 281.

76. Ibid.

77. Stevenson, *90 Minutes at Entebbe*, 103.

78. Ben-Porat, *Entebbe Rescue*, 272. Both 707s were reportedly painted in El Al colors.

79. "Israel Refining Hostage Rescue Tactics," 17. According to this article, "The raiding force experienced a complete breakdown in special communications, and Lt. Gen. Benjamin Peled, the air force commander, was forced to use open radio frequencies for command and control. Each aircraft in the raid was equipped with one VHF and two UHF radios with secure frequencies. All failed to function." The possibility of an operational compromise due to the lack of appropriate and effective secure communications is obvious.

80. Stevenson, *90 Minutes at Entebbe*, 103.

81. Ibid.

82. Brown, (ed.), *Strike from the Sky: Israeli Airborne Troops*, 73.

83. Ibid.

84. For an interesting tactical description of the rescue itself, see the interview of Benjamin Netanyahu, "Operation Jonathan: The Rescue at Entebbe," 2–23. See also Betser and Rosenberg, *Secret Soldier: The True Life Story of Israel's Greatest Commando.*

85. "Uganda Hostages: Israeli Reaction," Report, Canadian Embassy Tel Aviv to Department of External Affairs, Ottawa, Canada (5 July 1976), 4.

86. Ibid.

87. Stevenson, *90 Minutes at Entebbe*, 134. It should be noted that in the post-operation briefing "Gazit Stated That the IDF Aircraft Landed . . . Without Prior Knowledge or Approval of Kenyan Govt." See "Uganda Hostages: Israeli Reaction," Report, 5. This was done probably to pre-empt any hostile action by Ugandan authorities.

88. Ibid.

89. The success of rescue operations is predicated upon not only the successful extraction of the hostages, but also the speedy delivery of any wounded to medical facilities prepared to undertake any emergency requirements. See Olds and Grande, "When Minutes Can Mean a Lifetime: Medical Support of Tactical Operations."

90. Philipp, "Israelis in Nairobi Hospital."

91. Stevenson, *90 Minutes at Entebbe,* 134–135.

92. "Uganda Radar Operators Executed, Sources Say."

93. Canadian Broadcasting Corporation, "Reaction to the Rescue of Hostages by Israeli Commandos," 2.

94. Smith, "Israelis Say Extension of Deadline by the Hijackers Was Crucial to Raid's Success."

95. Ibid.

96. "Israeli Rescue Operation: Kampala," Report, Canadian High Commission, Nairobi, Kenya, to Department of External Affairs, Ottawa, Canada (4 July 1976), 2.

97. "Joy at Rescue of Hostages."

98. Stevenson, *90 Minutes at Entebbe,* 135.

99. Benjamin, "The Fallout from Entebbe," 41.

100. Ibid.

101. Steele and Pringle, "Uganda: Amin vs. the World," 36.

102. "Head of German Raid Is Linked to Entebbe." Wegener became head of West Germany's GSG9 counterterrorist force.

103. Tophoven, *GSG9: German Response to Terrorism,* 76.

104. Livingstone, *The War Against Terrorism,* 179.

105. Garrett, *The Raiders: The Elite Strike Forces That Altered the Course of War and History,* 204.

106. Walmer, *An Illustrated Guide to Modern Elite Forces,* 32. See also "Israeli Commando C-130 Raid Frees 115," 15. This article states that seven MIG-21s and four MIG-17s were destroyed by the Israelis. This differs from information drawn from General Ulrich Wegener, who advised there were only seven MIG-19s in non-operational condition on the airfield. Discussions with General Ulrich K. Wegener, Royal Military College, Kingston, Canada (5 October 2000).

107. "Uganda Hostages: Israeli Reaction," Report, 2. See also Brilliant, "Gur Says Raiders Used 'Several Tricks'" and "Operation Complex, Not Difficult."

108. Ibid., 3.

109. Ibid., 3.

110. Stevenson, *90 Minutes at Entebbe,* 139.

111. For a chronology of events, see *Documentation: on the Events and Decisions Connected with the Kidnapping of Hans Martin Schleyer and the Hijacking of the Lufthansa Jet "Landshut."* For an overview of the 1972 Munich massacre, see Reeve, *One Day in September: The Story of the 1972 Munich Olympics Massacre.*

112. "Remarks by Colonel Ulrich K. Wegener, Commander, 9th Border Guard Group, Special, Federal Republic of Germany," 10. See also Koch and Hermann, *Assault at Mogadishu* and Katz, "GSG-9: Think like a Terrorist, Fight like a Commando."

113. "Hijacking of Jet with 91 to Dubai Linked with German Kidnapping." See also "Hijackers, Holding 92, Back Kidnappers in Schleyer Case."

114. McFadden, "German Troops Free Hostages on Hijacked Plane in Somalia; 3 Terrorists Reported Killed." See also Mickolus, *Transnational Terrorism: A Chronology of Events, 1968–1979,* 739.

115. Authorities speculated, initially, that this operation may have been linked

to the Japanese Red Army (JRA) members who successfully took over a Japanese airliner late in September 1977. In the end, the Japanese government agreed to the JRA demands. This included a six-million-dollar ransom and the release from prison of several of their members. See Benjamin and Martin, "A Detour to Dubai," 62.

116. One of the women, Souhaila Andawes, was sentenced to twenty years in a Somali prison. However, due to poor health she was released after a year and subsequently returned to Beirut, finally settling in Norway in 1992. The German authorities had enough evidence of her participation in the 1977 hijacking that they requested the Norwegian authorities to extradite her to Germany for trial. Andawes was put on trial, found guilty and given twelve years for the hijacking of the Lufthansa jet and the murder of the pilot, Captain Jurgen Schumann. Discussion with General Ulrich K. Wegener, Ottawa, Canada (3 October 2000). See also Boyes, "Germany Jails Palestinian for 1977 Hijack." See also "Mother of All Hijackers."

117. Bundesgrenzschutzgruppe 9 (GSG9) is a specialized counterterrorist commando unit born out of the chaos of the 1972 Munich Olympics. Led, organized and trained by Ulrich K. Wegener, this unit had intimate knowledge of Israeli and British techniques gleaned from exchanges with both countries. See Harnischmacher, "The Federal Border Guard Group 9—Special: The German Response to Terrorism," 1–5. See also Winkhaus, "Munich: The Massacre That Changed the World: Fallouts from Olympics Terror Still Swirls 25 Years Later." The article describes the brutal hostage taking and the failed rescue that killed eleven Israeli athletes, five Arab terrorists and one German policeman as well as the Israeli actions in the wake of this Munich 1972 incident. The reason for naming the German counterterrorist force GSG9 was that the Bundesgrenzschutz already had eight regimental groups, numbered one through eight. Thus, according to Wegener, it seemed logical to make the group the ninth one, the GSG9. It was, however, different in its organization, equipment, training and purpose. The GSG9 is based on the five-man team and each team member has a special role. Selection is based on intellect, physical capability, ability to work in a team, and work under pressure. In 1999, for example, 130 candidates were taken into selection and twenty were finally approved for the unit. Average age is 27 to 28 years of age, and all candidates must be officers or non-commissioned officers. All GSG9 personnel must successfully complete the selection and training process. The GSG9 has conducted more than 1,300 criminal and counterterrorist operations. In 1999 alone, they conducted sixty operations against various criminal enterprises. Discussion with General Ulrich K. Wegener, Royal Military College, Kingston, Canada (5 October 2000). For a contemporary overview of the GSG9, see Katz, "The Embattled Legend of GSG-9: Fighting Terrorism in the New Germany."

118. It should be underlined that, in historical terms, the German military had trained and employed units to conduct special operations in World War II. Two well-known operations were the brilliant seizure of the fort at Eben Emael on 10 May 1940 and the daring rescue of Benito Mussolini on 12 September 1943. For an in-depth account of these two actions, see McRaven, *Spec Ops Case Studies in Special Operations Warfare: Theory and Practice,* and Mrazek, *The Fall of Eben Emael.* According to Ulrich Wegener, when he received his orders to undertake the organization and training of GSG9, he commenced by conducting historical research in the West German archives as to the experiences of German forces in World War II. Discussion with General Ulrich K. Wegener, Ottawa, Canada (3 October 2000).

See also Infield, *Skorzeny: Hitler's Commando*. For an update of this German CT team see Katz, "GSG-9: Think like a Terrorist, Fight like a Commando." For an insightful article on Eben Emael, see Barr Smith, "Silent Blitzkrieg: The Fall of Eben Emael."

119. "Crisis Management in Schleyer Kidnapping/Lufthansa Hijacking Case Summary," Report, Canadian High Commission London to Department of External Affairs, Ottawa, Canada (14 November 1977), 2.

120. University of New Brunswick, Centre for Conflict Studies, *Special Operations: Military Lessons from Six Selected Case Studies*, 99. Apparently Rachmin's attempt to talk to Mahmoud was in vain, underlining a rift between elements of the PLO.

121. "Remarks by Colonel Ulrich K. Wegener, Commander, 9th Border Guard Group, Special, Federal Republic of Germany," 17.

122. Clough, "Perfect Debut for Bonn's Anti-Terror Squad."

123. Mickolus, *Transnational Terrorism: A Chronology of Events, 1968–1979*, 736. See also Howe, "Hijackers Leave Dubai."

124. "Remarks by Colonel Ulrich K. Wegener, Commander, 9th Border Guard Group, Special, Federal Republic of Germany," 13–14. According to General Wegener, GSG9 had trained all Lufthansa aircraft commanders to deal with such eventualities. Discussion with General Ulrich K. Wegener, Ottawa, Canada (3 October 2000).

125. Ibid., 15.

126. Ibid. Shooting at the ground crew using only handguns at 150 meters provided evidence that heavier weapons were not available to the terrorists.

127. Geraghty, *Inside the SAS*, 171. According to a diplomatic report, the British government "offered diplomatic help in demarches to authorities in Dubai, UAE and Somalia in support of German plan for police operation." See "Crisis Management in Schleyer Kidnapping/Lufthansa Hijacking Case Summary." Report, 2. According to General Wegener, British intelligence advised that Captain Mahmoud had shot a Yemeni leader the year before in London, England. Discussion with General Ulrich K. Wegener, Ottawa, Canada (3 October 2000).

128. Ibid. Apparently Schmidt and Callaghan "discussed police operation which led to Brit offer of SAS pers [personnel] and technical help in form of stun grenades. Two SAS men actually participated in assault and threw grenades. (Quote you couldnt [sic] keep them out unquote)." See "Crisis Management in Schleyer Kidnapping/Lufthansa Hijacking Case Summary," Report, 2. For a British participant's view of this operation see Davies, *Assault on LH 181: The True Story of Operation Fire Magic*.

129. Ibid.

130. University of New Brunswick, Centre for Conflict Studies, *Special Operations*, 102.

131. AW 163, Bonn: Associated Press (AP), "Hijack Raid." "West Germany's crisis staff apparently started planning the commando raid that freed all 86 remaining hostages . . . almost instantly after the Boeing 737 was commandeered."

132. University of New Brunswick, Centre for Conflict Studies, *Special Operations*, 105.

133. Koch and Hermann, *Assault at Mogadishu*, 108. Wegener apparently trained twenty UAE paratroops for five hours in aircraft seizure techniques. It also

has been reported that a team of three GSG9, two SAS, three officers of the Dubai Defense Force and two Arabs of the palace guard were also formed. See Davies, *Assault on LH-181,* 109.

134. Canadian Government Memorandum, Canadian Embassy, Bonn, to Ottawa, "Hijacking of Lufthansa Aircraft-13 October 1977," (23 November 1977), 3.

135. Ibid., 4.

136. "Greek Praise for Firm Bonn Stand." This article stated, "Earlier Herr Schmidt had sent a message of thanks to Mr. Karamanlis for his contribution to the success of the rescue operation. The Greek Prime Minister had given consent for the German aircraft carrying the anti-terrorist unit to stand by in Crete." This assistance in allowing the forward-basing of the GSG9 assisted in the overall success of this daring rescue.

137. "Crisis Management in Schleyer Kidnapping/Lufthansa Hijacking Case Summary," Report, 5.

138. Geraghty, *Inside the SAS,* 172.

139. Koch and Hermann, *Assault at Mogadishu,* 121–122.

140. McFadden, "German Troops Free Hostages on Hijacked Plane in Somalia; 3 Terrorists Reported Killed."

141. University of New Brunswick, Centre for Conflict Studies, *Special Operations,* 108.

142. Ibid., 109. It should be noted that in the wake of Mogadishu, "the GSG9 has been providing training assistance for foreign units subject to approval by [the] Ministry of the Interior. The first training assistance . . . was provided to Somalia, as thanks for the cooperation in 1977." Tophoven, *GSG9: German Response to Terrorism,* 81.

143. Ropelewski, "Commandos Thwart Hijackers," 15.

144. Discussion with General Ulrich K. Wegener, Ottawa, Canada (3 October 2000).

145. Tanner, "U.S. Woman Says Ruse Saved the Hostages." According to this report when "the message arrived that the West German terrorists had been freed from jail. . . . The leader of the hijackers ordered the passengers untied and told them: 'It is seven hours flying time from Germany, I give them seven hours.'"

146. "Remarks by Colonel Ulrich K. Wegener, Commander, 9th Border Guard Group, Special, Federal Republic of Germany," 19–20.

147. "Antiguerrilla Squad Reported at Airfield." See also FBIS 09, "Jerusalem Reports FRG Antiterror Unit in Persian Gulf."

148. Ibid. This article incorporated the following statement, "Moments after transmission of this dispatch, Reuters sent a note to editors stating: 'We have just been asked by the West German Government spokesman not to report anything concerning the movements of antiguerrilla squads for use in a possible attempt to storm the hijacked plane.' It added that 'the Government spokesman says that such reports could prejudice the safety of the hostages.' Reuters said later that it had not retracted its earlier report because the news had been released earlier by Agence France-Presse and that it would leave up to its clients the question of how to deal with the report." See also Knipe, "Broadcast 'Put Lives in Danger.'"

149. "Remarks by Colonel Ulrich K. Wegener, Commander, 9th Border Guard Group, Special, Federal Republic of Germany," 20.

150. Ibid.

151. Ibid., 22.

152. Ibid.

153. Ibid.

154. Geraghty, *Inside the SAS,* 16. This author also states that the SAS assisted in composing the plan of attack. See 172.

155. "Remarks by Colonel Ulrich K. Wegener, Commander, 9th Border Guard Group, Special, Federal Republic of Germany," 23.

156. "Airport Fire Started to Aid Rescue Troops." This article is quoted as saying that the "blaze was set some 300 yards in front of the plane in order to entice the hijackers into the cockpit."

157. "Remarks by Colonel Ulrich K. Wegener, Commander, 9th Border Guard Group, Special, Federal Republic of Germany," 23.

158. Ibid., 24.

159. Ibid., 24–25. The female was, as previously noted, Souhaila Andrawes, who was jailed in November 1996 for the 1977 hijacking of this Lufthansa jet and the murder of the pilot. See Boyes, "German Court Jails 1977 Hijacker."

160. Ibid., 26.

161. Ibid., 27–28.

162. Geraghty, *Inside the SAS,* 173, and "Bonn Shows Gratitude to Prime Minister." Herr Schmidt reportedly thanked Mr. Callaghan "for supporting the West Germans' policy of toughness towards the hijackers and terrorists and for his 'active help' in sending two British anti-terrorist specialists to Mogadishu. His support had been 'of enormous value.'" See also "Terror and Triumph at Mogadishu," 28. According to this article, "the British provided the West Germans with 1) special, highly sensitive listening devices for locating the terrorists within the plane and 2) a supply of British 'stun grenades.'" No further information regarding the listening devices has been found in the sources covered in this study.

163. University of New Brunswick, Centre for Conflict Studies, *Special Operations,* 119.

164. Ibid., 119.

165. "Crisis Management in Schleyer Kidnapping/Lufthansa Hijacking Case Summary," Report, 5.

166. Ibid., 6–7.

167. University of New Brunswick, Centre for Conflict Studies, *Special Operations,* 121.

168. FBIS 09, "FRG Spokesman Reads Joint Statement on Hostages Rescue Operation."

169. FBIS 10, "FRG Chancellor Cables Thanks to Somalia's Barre, Others."

4

Malta: Lessons in Unsuccessful Hostage Rescue

In the wake of the success of Entebbe and Mogadishu—and the lessons that can be assimilated—terrorists have recognized that hijacking is not a simple operation. It is, and will remain, a high-risk venture in the terrorist's never-ending search for a bargaining tool, and even more so in the wake of the audacious World Trade Center and Pentagon aerial attacks orchestrated by suicide hijackers. Although hijacking has declined in popularity, it still remains an effective operation that captures the attention of both the media and the nation or nations involved, as witnessed by the Chechen seizure of a Russian airliner and the rescue of the hostages by the Saudis' counterterrorist team in March 2001. Currently, hijacking remains a real day-to-day threat and reality to both passengers and crew. As with any tactical innovation, a hostage rescue must always be evolutionary in tactics, equipment, philosophy and training; otherwise, terrorists will prepare themselves to counter such initiatives. It is notable though that nearly a decade after a number of successful hostage rescues, poor planning and training, and unsophisticated techniques, orchestrated by an ill-led, ill-trained counterterrorist force, resulted in the bloodiest hostage rescue in aviation history.

MALTA RESCUE

On Saturday 23 November 1985, three terrorists well armed with pistols and grenades boarded Egyptair Flight 648 at Athens en route to Cairo. The B737 aircraft carried eighty-six people, including a five-member crew and four Egyptian sky marshals. Today, it is still difficult to comprehend how the terrorists evaded security checks, however, it would seem likely that they were supported by airport ground crew who provided their weapons sometime in the wake of their security check.[1] The leader of the terrorists was reportedly Omar Ali Rezaq, 22.[2] Ali had flown to Athens from Belgrade and was joined by Mohamed Abu-Said Nur-El-Din, 23, and Salem Salab Chakore, 25, both of whom had flown in from Tripoli. It is reported that they claimed to represent the group "Egypt's Revolution"[3] and it is believed that they were under orders of the Abu Nidal group.[4]

Shortly after the aircraft's departure from Athens, the plane was seized. Salem was assigned to move through the aircraft cabin, extracting passports and segregating passengers by nationality. Two of the passengers were Israeli girls traveling independently and they were subsequently separated from the other passengers. According to passengers, when Salem approached another passenger, Medhat Mustafa Kamil, Kamil drew a pistol and shot Salem dead. Kamil, an aircraft sky marshal,[5] and one of the four marshals aboard, was shot seconds later by one of the remaining terrorists and, although gravely wounded, survived. (It is important to note that during a subsequent investigation it was discovered that the three other sky marshals did nothing up until the aircraft was stormed). During the shootout within the cabin, bullets penetrated the fuselage, causing the aircraft to lose pressure. The aircraft captain carried out an emergency descent from 45,000 to 14,000 feet. At that point, Captain Hani Galal requested permission of Malta's Luqa airport to land as the aircraft was in danger of crashing into the sea. The plane arrived at Luqa at approximately 10:30 P.M.. Upon arrival, the hijackers' only demand was to get the aircraft refueled. In turn, the Maltese government agreed, on the condition that the hijackers release all of the passengers. This condition was rejected, and the terrorists threatened to start shooting the hostages. Their words became action when the Maltese authorities had not commenced refueling the aircraft and demonstrated no signs of negotiating. The Maltese police surrounded the aircraft and the authorities refused to supply fuel until the plane's ninety-eight passengers and crew were released. In the airport control tower, the negotiation team was headed by the Maltese Prime Minister, his spokesman, the minister of Foreign Affairs and the Egyptian ambassador. According to reports, the Prime Minister led the negotiations with the hijacked aircraft. Most of the negotiations went through Captain Galal, with minimal contact with the hijackers. Throughout the period the aircraft was on the ground, a hijacker was always present in the cockpit and dictated to the captain the demands to be passed on. Two stewardesses who were wounded were freed before midnight, and a further eleven women shortly thereafter. Fuel was still not forthcoming and the hijackers threatened to kill passengers every ten minutes until the Maltese authorities submitted to their demands. Just after midnight, one Israeli girl was selected and shot, and, ten minutes later, a second Israeli woman was bought forward and shot. One terrorist went through the passports again, selecting the next victims, who were to be Americans. One American hostage was brought forward and shot. The ruthless selection and application of violence was calculated to force both the Maltese and Egyptian authorities to submit to the hijackers' demand for fuel. Instead, what it did was provoke the Egyptians into a hasty and ill-advised assault on the aircraft.

FORCE 777: THE EGYPTIAN RESPONSE

As the aircraft itself was Egyptian, and carrying twenty-two Egyptian nationals as passengers and crew, the Maltese government gave the authority to Egypt to send in its response team Force 777, a formation of sixty-five men. The Egyptian contingent was commanded by Colonel Ismail Abdel-Magwood. The team flew on Sunday afternoon aboard a C-130 transport aircraft escorted by fighters from the U.S. Navy from Egypt to Malta. During the same period, the American government had offered assistance to the Maltese authorities. This offer was refused, likely due to Maltese sovereignty issues. According to one source, the chairman of the U.S. Joint Chiefs of Staff, Admiral William Crowe, was telephoned at midnight on Saturday, Washington time, by General Wiegand, the head of the U.S. Office of Military Cooperation in Cairo. Wiegand advised Admiral Crowe that he and a small team intended to travel with the Egyptian counterterrorist force. The Egyptian force landed innocuously in Malta on Sunday morning at 8:30 A.M. on 24 November 1985, arriving in jeans and t-shirts, and was permitted to go into action. The Americans arrived in their uniforms, to the chagrin of the Maltese authorities, who immediately complained to Washington about what could be perceived as American interference.[6]

It should be noted that Force 777 had been trained by the Americans since 1981 and should have been ideally suited to the task at hand. However, the Egyptian force, according to one analyst, was without the equipment that it needed and had experienced substantial personnel changeover, euphemistically described as "personnel turbulence," which raised numerous doubts about its professional skills and operational capability against a terrorist group. Among the series of initial preparatory mistakes, the Egyptian team had failed to employ any sophisticated listening devices or surveillance equipment to ascertain the number and location of the terrorists within the aircraft, as well as ascertain the evolving situation within the aircraft itself. It was also subsequently reported that there was no serious debriefing of the hostages that had been previously released so as to garner further detailed intelligence related to the hijack. According to one report, members of 777 did not engage in any preparatory activities during the day, other than to look at an Air Malta 737 aircraft and examine both its interior and exterior; however, no rehearsal or training took place in connection with the aircraft. Moreover, the equipment used by the commandos did not include disorientating devices such as the stun grenades used in Mogadishu or any planned deception to miscue and divert the attentions of the hijackers prior to the attack. To make matters worse, half an hour before the assault, the airport lights had been turned off accidentally. This initial incident panicked the terrorists, who believed that it might signal an attack. Indeed, when the lights were turned off the second time, it was felt that the first incident was indeed a rehearsal.

Under substantial political pressure from Egypt, the Maltese government allowed the Egyptians to undertake the assault.[7] The assault team assigned to enter the aircraft first approached the parked airliner, pulling up approximately 100 meters from the rear. Meanwhile, Egyptian 777 snipers positioned themselves behind concrete blocks on both sides of the aircraft from eighty to 100 meters. The Egyptians commenced their assault at 7:10 P.M., when one commando opened the aircraft's rear luggage hold from the outside and placed an explosive charge in order to blast an entry hole through the floor of the aircraft. It appears that the Egyptians did not plan to attack the aircraft through all the emergency and main doors simultaneously, in order to physically flood the aircraft with commandos so as to suppress or kill the terrorists. Rather, they intended to initiate the attack by blasting a hole through the roof of the luggage compartment in the rear of the aircraft. Before the Egyptians attempted to gain access to the aircraft's interior, they unloaded the majority of the cargo and baggage from the aircraft's rear cargo hold and installed an explosive charge at a point right underneath the cabin floor. The detonation of an explosive device in the luggage compartment had a disastrous effect. The cabin floor caved in all the way from the wing section to the rear, together with all the seats. Moreover, the pressure from the detonation shredded all the material covering the cabin. The fire that subsequently broke out completely destroyed everything that was combustible—to the extent that the passenger seats themselves were charred metal frames. Furthermore, the pressure from the explosives punched a number of holes in both the upper and lower sections of the aircraft's outer skin. The ignition of the explosive device was believed to be a signal to the rest of the Egyptian team to launch their assault through the various entry points. To the shock of all involved, the explosion itself was greatly over powered, so much so that six rows of seating were blown from their anchor points. Moreover, the force and pressure of the blast also produced a wall of flame that crushed the seats against the ceiling of the fuselage, killing six passengers instantaneously and setting the interior of the aircraft on fire.[8]

In the wake of the explosion, the rear of the aircraft filled with smoke and flames, feeding upon the burning aircraft insulation. Immediately after the explosion, elements of Force 777 tried to enter through an aircraft door and an emergency exit. The commandos who were on the mobile stairway attempting to enter the main door were held off by a hijacker who threw a hand grenade at them from the cockpit window. As the Egyptian commandos withdrew, some of whom were seriously wounded, it was reported that their hasty retreat was covered by some commandos who fired wildly in all directions. Notwithstanding, two members of the assault team did manage to enter the aircraft through the emergency exit. It was at this point that these two commandos commenced firing their automatic weapons and reportedly sprayed the rear cabin without taking appropriate aim.

Once the Egyptians had entered through the emergency exit, those who survived the explosion—hijackers and hostages alike—attempted to flee the aircraft. Witness reports stated that Egyptian commandos commenced shooting everything that moved outside the aircraft. It was reported that Egyptian commandos, during this period of confusion, also fired on members of the Maltese special forces who were located some distance from the aircraft. As well, the Egyptian commandos initially stopped the well-positioned Maltese fire brigade from approaching the burning aircraft. The result was that the aircraft was badly burned in the rear section. The combination of fire, smoke and poor visibility, along with the terrorists and commandos among a terrified group of passengers and crew, was horrific as passengers attempted to leave a burning plane in a middle of a firefight. The cloak of smoke and flame, as well as the ensuing confusion, gave the commandos no opportunity to sort the terrorists from the hostages. As well, the terrorists were alerted to the attack and met the Egyptian commandos with grenades and a hail of bullets from their pistols.

When the initial explosion happened, one terrorist was located in the cockpit, trying to ascertain what was going to happen. When the terrorist attempted to stand up, he and the captain of the aircraft reportedly struggled. The pilot was wounded by a bullet that grazed his head and the terrorist was subsequently shot by Egyptian soldiers. There is some doubt about the alleged heroism by the pilot, as a follow-up study of events in the aircraft by American and Egyptian investigators noted there was no evidence of the heroic act. The axe supposedly employed by the pilot in the struggle had no blood, hair, or skin tissue on it, according to one published report.

It has been alleged by both witnesses and the hostages themselves that the hostages, some of whom were burned alive in the blazing inferno following the explosion, may have come under fire from commandos within and outside the aircraft as they attempted to escape. It was noted by the

Maltese government that at least one passenger was wounded by the Egyptians, who mistook him for a hijacker. In all sixty-one passengers and two terrorists were killed, one of whom had been killed during the initial seizure of the aircraft. In retrospect, the Malta rescue was an attack that was poorly planned, particularly considering the initial entry point and lack of appreciation that the blast would start a fire fueled by the aircraft insulation, and arguably, an attack that was appallingly executed by a force lacking the critical intelligence, equipment, training and skills to undertake a mission of this importance. Immediately after this rescue attempt, the Egyptian government requested additional assistance and training for Force 777 from the United States. In the wake of this disastrous attack, GSG9 also provided training assistance to the Egyptian counterterrorist team.

POST-OPERATION ASSESSMENT

In reflection, it is important to appreciate that, over the past decades, terrorists have learned many hard learned lessons themselves. Various reports and professional assessments, as well as the state of the aircraft, indicate that the Egyptian counterterrorism response team Force 777 committed grave errors which needlessly cost the lives of a large number of hostages.

Looking back, it is, in general, difficult to understand why Force 777 was not more proactive in using an Air Malta plane of the same model to practice the rescue plan. Considering the conduct of the operation and the Egyptian counterterrorism unit, it would appear they were not well trained on this type of aircraft. As to the extinguishing of lights in the airport thirty minutes prior to the assault, inadvertent or otherwise, this must have alerted the terrorists that an assault was coming. In addition, the lack of any diversionary initiatives immediately prior to the assault made it possible for the terrorists to focus their attention on the approaching Egyptian forces. In that regard, the ongoing negotiations or other measures could have been deployed to distract the hijackers so as to garner the advantage of surprise for the Egyptian assault force. It is also disconcerting that the Egyptian team did not utilize all doors and exits in their assault, which would have maximized their chances of attaining an entrance.

In the initial assault, the Maltese snipers failed to act when one of the hijackers threw the hand grenade out of the cockpit window at the Egyptians approaching the aircraft via the mobile stairway. This could have neutralized one terrorist while facilitating the assaulters in entering the aircraft. This Maltese inaction demonstrated a serious lack of command and control as well as planning and co-ordination in this operation.

From an operator's point of view, the purpose of the explosive charge in the rear cargo hold remains unclear. Moreover, the noise and possible view of the baggage being unloaded would have alerted, if not alarmed, the terrorists themselves. To this day, questions remain. Was the explosive charge meant as a way of initiating the assault or a diversionary tactic or as a way to gain access to the aircraft via the hole caused by the explosion? Did Force 777 misjudge the explosive force produced by the quantity and type of explosive employed and its effect after detonation? Could it have been that the Egyptian intention was to end the hijacking as rapidly as possible without due regard to the price of lives involved? It is certain that most of the hostages in this section were killed instantly by the shock wave set off by the explosion. Those who survived the blast would have likely succumbed to the fumes that were released from the materials covering the seats, floor and interior of the aircraft. Those that survived the fumes were exposed to the shots fired by the two Egyptian commandos who gained access through the emergency exit. As noted previously, witness reports said that Egyptian commandos fired at everything that moved inside or outside the aircraft. Presumably, they also shot some of the fleeing passengers. Lastly, Force 777 stopped the Maltese firefighters from taking prompt action, although it is questionable if they could have acted in any way to save any lives.

No matter how one puts it, the way this hijacking was handled produced tragic results. Of the eighty-six people on board, sixty-one lost their lives with only twenty-five surviving, including both members of the cockpit crew. The hostage rescue operation orchestrated by the Egyptians in Malta seriously lacked a number of key criteria for success, from the overall lack of intelligence as to the location of the terrorists to the failure of ensuring that key operational aspects of hostage rescue operations were followed. The operation itself lacked surprise as the terrorists were alerted to the impending rescue attempt. The Egyptian counterterrorist team failed to utilize all the accessible doors and exits into the aircraft, resulting in a lack of synchronization in the assault when entering the aircraft. A second failure on the part of the Egyptians was that they did not immediately saturate and dominate the interior of the aircraft, which would have neutralized the terrorists. The subsequent failure to safely and effectively evacuate the hostages only further acknowledged the lack of professional capabilities which had thus far been mastered by the Egyptian counterterrorist team. Tragically, this error cost the lives of many and diminished any professional respect that the Egyptians may have previously earned amongst their friends and allies.

Today we face an increasingly sophisticated terrorist threat from terrorists who are ready to sacrifice their own lives as well as those of others, in order to press home their political demands or just to make a statement. Today's terrorist is both physically and mentally fit to employ the threat of or the killing of civilians as a stiletto-like political weapon orchestrated to keep the intelligence, security and counterterrorist forces off guard while concomitantly maintaining pressure on governments, politicians and citizens who have, in the past, experienced terrorism and who will likely be affected by it in the future.

NOTES

1. One article stated that a "caller, who spoke English with an Arabic accent, said the arms used in the hijacking had been smuggled onto the plane at Athens airport by two airport employees who had been paid $12,000 for their help. The Maltese government had no comment on the report." Miller, "Fire, Not Bullets, Reported to Kill Most Victims on Hijacked Plane."

2. Omar Mohammed Ali Rezaq was found guilty in U.S. Federal Court in 1996 for the 1985 hijacking of Egyptair Flight 648. Captured by Egyptian commandos when they stormed the plane, Rezaq was put on trial in Malta in the wake of the hijacking, and found guilty of murder. He was sentenced to twenty-five years in prison. Released in 1993, he traveled to Ghana and Nigeria, where U.S. officials, outraged at his release, secured Rezaq's extradition for trial in the United States. Green, "U.S. Court Convicts Palestinian for 1985 Hijacking."

3. One report noted that the name of the group was also "Egypt Revolutionaries." "Egyptian Jet Hijacked to Malta." The Egyptian Revolutionaries first surfaced in August 1985 with the slaying of the Israeli diplomat Albert Atrakchi, who was killed by machine-gun fire in a Cairo suburb. The attack was claimed in the name of the Egyptian Revolutionaries, who demanded that Egyptian President Hosni Mubarak abrogate the 1979 peace treaty with Israel and furthermore expel all Israeli citizens from Cairo. The group underlined that such attacks would continue until Israel's flag no longer "desecrated" Egypt. Afterward, Egyptian authorities charged that the Egyptian Revolutionaries group was sponsored by Libya. The political complexity escalated when Israel advised that, in the past, Malta had served as a base for Libyan-sponsored terrorist activities, including the 1984 abortive attempt on the life of a Libyan exile living in Egypt. See "An Egyptian Terror Group."

4. Hijazi, "Hijackers Linked to Palestinian Faction." According to this report, the hijackers were pro-Libyan followers of Abu Nidal, a Palestinian known for his strong opposition to Yassar Arafat. The aim was to deal a double blow to Arafat, leader of the PLO, and to President Mubarak of Egypt.

5. Egyptair said that the airlines had four security officers on each flight, supposedly armed with 9mm automatic pistols. There are reasons to suspect that the three remaining sky marshals were not carrying their weapons on their persons, but had them in their hand luggage, which was stowed on the floor. It is possible that they were unable to reach their weapons, because the hijackers, it is believed, had shifted passengers around. It is also possible that they were in a state of shock following the initial hijacking. Passengers and the official version noted the presence of only one security guard. Miller, "From Takeoff to Raid: The 24 Hours of Flight 648." Subsequent research suggests that there were four Egyptian sky marshals. One was apparently dressed in a uniform and was in the cockpit, another occupied a seat on the left side, another on the right side, and a fourth was seated on the left side of the aircraft in the rear. The reason for their inactivity remains unclear.

6. "Hijacking of Egyptian Airliner to Malta; Subsequent Storming of Aircraft by Egyptian Commandos," Keesing Record of World Events, Vol. 32 (April 1986). Moreover, it was later reported that the presence of American military officers may have delayed the Maltese government's approval for the dispatch to Luqa of a special U.S. anti-terrorist team to be composed of members of Delta Force. In any event, the American rescue force was hamstrung due to an inability to get off the ground. According to one source, "the United States offered to send a team from the Joint Special Operations Command, but the Maltese said no"—which was perhaps just as well, given the troubles JSOC had getting airborne. In a letter written by the Pentagon's Noel Koch, it was noted that "the team was to assemble at 2200 [10:00 P.M.] for wheels up. They were there. The plane broke. Three planes broke that night." The team finally got to Sigonella, Sicily, but no farther. With the Maltese firmly opposed to any American presence, the most the United States could do was promise air cover for a transport plane carrying a team of Egyptian commandos to Malta. Martin and Walcott, *Best Laid Plans: The Inside Story of America's War Against Terrorism*, p. 267.

7. Dionne, "Heavy Pressure Pulled Malta Both Ways."

8. During the post mortem of the operation, it was ascertained that the "baggage compartment at the rear section of the plane was close to oxygen tanks and to foam that was used as insulation there and in the over-head racks of the aircraft. When the bomb exploded, an official close to the investigation said, it set fire to the foam insulation, which produced a toxic gas that asphyxiated many of the passengers. 'The first bombs [*sic*] were badly placed and much too powerful,' the official asserted. He said the bomb blew the baggage doors in the cargo hold into bits and pieces, and created an inferno so intense that it scorched the top of the plane. Dr. Psaila, who visited the morgue today, said most of the passengers had died of asphyxiation. 'They had foam coming out of their mouths, ears, and noses,' he said. 'There were not many bodies in bits and pieces; almost all were intact.'" Miller, "Fire, Not Bullets, Reported to Kill Most Victims in Hijacked Plane."

5

Considerations and Conclusions: Final Considerations

HOSTAGE RESCUE OPERATIONS: POLITICAL AND MILITARY CONSIDERATIONS

Entebbe and Mogadishu remain the two most enduring symbols of success-ful hostage rescue operations performed by highly trained military counter-terrorist forces. Within each operation there was the critical element of international cooperation that facilitated the success of the respective res-cue operations. Moreover, hostage rescue operations are unique when they are compared with other military conventional or unconventional opera-tions. The uniqueness is predicated upon who decides to undertake such operations. In that regard the decision to do so rests in the domain of the politicians. Therefore, it must be understood that such undertakings are embarked upon as a result of a political decision and, in the end, for solely *political* motives.[1]

Contrary to wartime conditions, the decision to undertake high-risk res-cue operations is within the domain and, therefore, the responsibility of the political leadership in charge at that time. This is predicated upon two is-sues; firstly that hostage rescue operations are essentially political in na-ture. Secondly, there are high military and political stakes involved as indeed prestige and international reputations ride on such serious and difficult operations. This situation further separates such rescue initiatives from the mainstream of conventional and for that matter unconventional operations.[2]

This uniqueness of hostage rescue operations resides in the demanding nature of these missions, as their overall success is measured by the international political and military communities through the utilization of a number of now standard but nevertheless stringent set of criteria that have evolved through a sociology of previous operations, both successful and not. Firstly, the hostages involved must be swiftly rescued without harm and there must not be any casualties among the hostage rescue force. Secondly, the terrorists/hostage-takers must be the only casualties. Lastly, the rescue operation must not create any further military or political problems in its wake.[3]

It has been argued by one observer that rescue operations must be considered "the climax of a war which must be resolved in a single military act. The diplomatic, psychological, and military struggles to free the victims—all bear a remarkable microcosmic resemblance to war. And the success or failure of such an operation means the victory or defeat in that war."[4] This perception is most poignant when one recalls the recriminations that followed in the wake of the highly sensitive, but ill-fated, 1980 American rescue attempt in Iran and the doomed Malta rescue attempt conducted by Egyptian commandos who stormed an Egyptair Boeing 737 on 23 November 1985, which killed sixty-one of the eighty-six people on board.

The perception of many laymen is that counterterrorist operations, including hostage rescue actions, are conducted, for the most part, unilaterally. The reality is that many of these operations are successfully conducted assimilating varying degrees of international cooperation and assistance both offered and requested. This has provided both policy makers, analysts and operators a growing sociology of counterterrorism activity based on or influenced by international cooperation. In this regard it is important to underline the politically sensitive character of hostage rescue operations. This study has attempted to illustrate a number of areas where international cooperation has been effective in recent history and where it will probably assist in the future. These initiatives revolve upon four separate, but interrelated, areas. These are firstly, the acquisition and relay of timely, accurate, strategic and tactical intelligence that is germane to the operation(s) at hand. Secondly, the timely access to forward bases in allied or friendly countries in anticipation of, or during, a rescue mission. Thirdly, effective, secure and rapid communications for all parties involved. Lastly, cooperation between counterterrorist forces, particularly exchanges, attachments, and training, and sometimes during CT operations themselves.

There are four principal areas of international cooperation that allied/friendly governments may wish to enhance or expand to their respective and mutual advantage.

THE IMPORTANCE OF INTELLIGENCE
IN HOSTAGE RESCUE

There is no doubt that timely, accurate intelligence is critical for success in all military operations, including low-intensity warfare and modern counterterrorism missions.[5] Even beyond the Western experience, intelligence is the sine qua non of victory, particularly in the famous hostage rescue operations in Entebbe (1976), Mogadishu (1977) and, more recently, Lima, Peru (1997). In some countries, such as Great Britain, historical imperial experiences and geographical range have innately underscored the vital importance of intelligence.[6] It is understated yet remains a reality that colonial regimes could be maintained only if the imperial power and security forces fully appreciated and understood what was occurring among the local inhabitants. The failure to garner such accurate intelligence often witnessed the colonial rulers' inability to effectively deal with major internal security difficulties if and when they happened.

The Israeli and German experiences, as has been shown, demonstrate the pre-eminent role of intelligence in counterterrorist operations. Both Tel Aviv and Berlin give considerable priority to the importance of effective intelligence-gathering and-disseminating functions, even if the application of this priority varies from situation to situation and government to government. The 1998 bombings of American embassies in Kenya and Tanzania, the 2000 attack on the USS Cole in Aden, as well as the suicide hijackers in the United States in September 2001—although American in context—only go to underscore the importance of this intelligence requirement.

History has demonstrated that terrorism, even in its rudimentary yet effective nineteenth-century and twentieth-century manifestations, posed dramatic and substantive difficulties for security forces. Particularly as security forces were confronted by effective small groups of highly dedicated and ruthless individuals who were comfortable in operating in a populated, industrialized environment within ever-evolving complex societies. Today, international terrorism, especially in its most modern and effective forms, incorporates the vast dimension of a worldwide communication network in a highly permeable, interdependent and interrelated global society to the basic difficulties of counterterrorist work. As well, when one considers the dramatic and extremely effective attacks in Washington and New York City, there is a new dimension of high-concept, low-tech attacks against prestigious targets by a segment of highly determined Islamic extremists who had led the life of sleepers in America.

In the wake of World War II the world reflected not only nationalistic but also irredentist, ethnic, minority rights, tribal, religious, criminal and ideologically based stimuli for the growth of terrorism. Today, a pervasive media, known to some as the CNN factor, can describe terrorist activities to an audience of millions of viewers within minutes, if not in seconds. Terrorist activities and their ensuing publicity, combined with the increasing vulnerabilities of modern societies, guarantee the continuance and evolution of the terrorist phenomenon. The CNN factor was demonstrated in the dramatic visuals of a commercial airliner flying "live" directly into the World Trade Center, and in the wake of the fears of a nation, this was compounded by the anthrax scare, fear of smallpox, and as well the potential of nuclear and radiological weapons. These issues were a constant fuel for the media and manifested within the North American population an unsettled sense of safety.

Reflecting upon the national terrorist movements in the nineteenth and twentieth centuries, it was understandably difficult to counter terrorism due to the problems that security forces faced in the field of intelligence gathering. In today's more complicated and far-reaching terrorist activity, this situation continues, particularly when one takes into account the determination, capabilities, access and the level of sophistication of the terrorist groups themselves.

Some countries with or without experience in the field of terrorism are sometimes stymied in gathering the information needed to effectively deal with terrorist groups and their activities. In some cases terrorist groups can easily outstrip their own national counterterrorist resources. This has been witnessed, for example, by the inabilities of the Yemen security and intelligence authorities in the wake of the attack on the USS Cole. For most it is readily apparent that today's terrorism has no respect for national borders, and the concept itself. This will continue and be more acute as globalization further obscures the notion of nationhood and independent states.

Intelligence remains the core of any successfully conducted counterterrorist operation. In order to effectively counter modern terrorism, nations concerned must be able to mount a coordinated international intelligence response, as exemplified by the continuing attempts of the Moscow-dominated Commonwealth of Independent States to create a joint Anti-Terrorist Center.[7] This reality has not been lost on security, intelligence and military apparats, which, in all countries noted in this book, continue to enhance their intelligence capabilities and access. In tandem they have emphasized that their elite military units be able to make effective use of such intelligence. In both cases examined, there were, and continue to be, established and informal links between the Israeli and the German military, intelligence and counterterrorist forces through which timely intelligence can rapidly be passed and, if need be, transformed into a plan. The well-coordinated February 1999 anti-Turkish demonstrations around the world underlined the need for accurate and timely intelligence. In fact, one Western counterterrorist team did not receive any intelligence about the violent anti-Turkish activities for up to eleven hours after the commencement of the demonstrations. This dearth of intelligence underlined an overall lack of liaison and communications that in at least one case must not be allowed to occur.

The German and Israeli experiences in hostage rescue confirm the need for an effective intelligence apparat and specialized forces, capable of translating vital, current intelligence into successful operations. Considering the international character of contemporary terrorism, the acquisition of timely, accurate intelligence demands international cooperation, and with it all the related political complexities that are implied by such cooperation. This situation was exemplified in the U.N.-sponsored operations in Bosnia (UNPROFOR) when the U.N., consisting of 183 sovereign states, was forbidden to undertake normal conventional intelligence operations. Moreover, Great Britain, Canada, and France were concerned about sharing certain sensitive information, particularly with their Russian and Ukrainian counterparts, who were undertaking significant roles with UNPROFOR. Today, Russia and former states of the Soviet empire are critical allies in the war against al-Qaeda and Osama bin Laden.

In some countries intelligence trends of a more technical nature have underlined certain concerns and international cooperation may assist in providing a partial solution. The United States has the most ambitious and aggressive national intelligence-gathering service, and has from time to time moved toward accessing intelligence that may prove to be far from optimal.[8] Today many Americans lean toward what has been called "high-tech" intelligence—that information which is drawn from communication intercepts, satellite imagery, electronic monitoring, and other formidable technical means. And from time to time there has been a significant downplaying of the critical importance of acquiring and developing human intelligence sources,[9] or "humint," to aid in the provision of tactical and strategic information. This situation is well known and is openly debated in American intelligence circles, with ensuing foreign policy implications.[10] This continuing discourse surfaced again in the summer of 1998, when George Tenet, the director of the CIA, created two new positions to manage both the collection and analysis of both technical and human intelligence sources.[11]

The United States in the 1960s became more and more dependent upon "high-tech" gathering at the expense of covert intelligence operations, which were allowed, to some extent, to wither during this period. This was a result of several factors, from budget cuts to the overt distrust of covert operations. There are some sources that have argued that the number of covert operatives has fallen dramatically since the 1950s.[12] The reality is that the intelligence required for counterterrorist operations and hostage rescue missions demands the type of information that *human intelligence* alone can provide. As former CIA director and president George Bush noted, the lack of human source information pre-empted the American leadership from conducting any rescue of American citizens held hostage in Beirut, Lebanon.[13] Today, it is critical in finding bin Laden and his terrorist network.

The issue at hand resides not in the area of resource allocation but in the requirement to minimize the risk of political embarrassment that can arise from the failure or compromise of covert operations. Fully accepting that the potential for such political embarrassment exists, recent experience, especially that of the British against the IRA, suggests that effective management of covert operations can yield substantial results to the dispatching state. Again, this situation must be measured against the costs caused by the occasional discovery or compromise of a government-sanctioned covert activity.

The success of a hostage rescue mission will depend much on the quantity and quality of timely intelligence. Such intelligence will likely be drawn from human sources on the ground, who have "their eyes on the sparrow (target)." Considering that rescue operations are politically strategic in character and tactical by nature, they demand finely detailed information. With that in mind, the following checklists illustrate the nature and detail of information[14] required in a rescue mission.

The Terrorists Involved

- How many terrorists are involved in the operation?
- What weapons are they armed with? Types, ammunition?
- What is their motivation (political/monetary/religious, etc.), and psychological and physical condition?
- What are their initial demands?
- What is their deployment/position within the aircraft, building?
- What nationalities are the terrorists?
- Ages, sex, description and background of the terrorists?
- Names, nicknames employed in conversation?
- What terrorist group do they represent and what is their operational history?
- What languages are spoken?
- What is the intelligence level and vigilance of the terrorists?
- What outside support can they access?

The Hostages Involved

- How many hostages are involved?
- Where are the hostages exactly located?

- What is the physical and psychological condition of the hostages?
- Are any hostages/nationalities of particular interest to the terrorists?
- What are their names and particulars?
- What are their ages, sex, description, and any details as to careers, expertise, etc.?

The Aircraft Involved

- Airline, handling agent.
- Type of aircraft and exact internal layout to include all modifications.
- Condition of aircraft.
- Information regarding fuel, range, speed, and flight duration.
- State of aircrew, names, ages, description.
- Aircraft call sign and frequencies employed.
- Situation inside aircraft.
- Flight manifest.
- Food and water situation on board.

The Building Involved

- Detailed street map, with the exact position of building and all pertinent structures surrounding the site.
- Engineer plans of building, including all modifications, electrical, structural, mechanical.
- Telephone numbers and where telephones are located.
- List of all persons occupying building and their exact locations.
- List of all key holders.
- Details on all alternative exit/entry sites.
- A comprehensive list of electrical, gas, oil, entrances and water points with all possible detail.
- Air conditioning/heating plant and duct work.
- Details and plans to all adjacent buildings.
- Sewer outlets nearby.

As one can appreciate, the data necessary for the planning of a hostage rescue can be provided only by human sources such as released hostages, witnesses and agents, although some technical means will be used.

The United States' lack of success in a series of covert operations in the late 1980s, particularly in the Middle East[15] and Latin America, should underline to observers that human intelligence is becoming more important, especially in all aspects of counterterrorism.

With that in mind international cooperation may improve this situation in several ways. First, more experience in working with foreign security, intelligence agencies and military forces may assist in an overall improvement of national intelligence services. Moreover, international cooperation would provide many of the more powerful nations such as the United States and its key allies with a clearer perception of the many advantages of human intelligence, perhaps encouraging them to return or enhance their capabilities in the area.

One important consideration is that less economically robust countries, which can rarely afford "high-tech" assets to acquire intelligence, are much more likely to be able to afford human intelligence assets. These poorer nations may well find that cooperation with wealthier states could lead to valuable and otherwise inaccessible information being provided to them from otherwise unaffordable high-tech assets. In return, modern first-tier countries, such as the United States, Canada and Germany, could discover that, on occasion, some smaller nations can have access to important human intelligence sources, and therefore these states can be attractive partners in intelligence-gathering initiatives abroad.[16] In the specific case of hostage rescue missions, as seen in the review of the three operations previously reviewed, Third World countries appear, somehow, to be involved in one way or another. Therefore, the building of international intelligence links with Third World countries should provide real benefits.

THE IMPORTANCE OF FORWARD-BASING IN HOSTAGE RESCUE OPERATIONS

As previously noted, hostage rescue operations are by their very nature politically sensitive. To be effective, a counterterrorist force must be able to move rapidly to the site of the incident, or close to it, in order to rescue the hostages.[17] For a spectrum of reasons—be they geographic, historic, or political—getting into "range" is often far from easy. For example, the United States' Delta Force, based at Fort Bragg, North Carolina, would normally take about sixteen hours to arrive at the scene of a Middle East hostage taking, while the SAS near Hereford would take seven to eight hours. Such delays could very well limit, or even preclude, the execution of proper on-site reconnaissance, as well as the time for planning and intelligence gathering, all of which are critical for success. Although counterterrorist teams must be readily available for rapid deployment, the time and distance factors can reduce the time available to thoroughly plan the operation and, thereby, could seriously further hamstring any rescue attempt.

American counterterrorist forces could use a prepared special operations base in Great Britain, Germany, or Cyprus where facilities could permit a long-term basing of specialist counterterrorist forces that would respond to terrorist actions in Europe, Africa and the Middle East. Such an arrangement would also guarantee access, at short notice, to key allied counterterrorist forces and agencies, which could be of immediate operational, technical, or moral support.

The lack of a forward base has already contributed to the failure of one counter-terrorist mission. Delays in supporting Egyptian commandos in their disastrous 1985 assault on an aircraft in Malta contributed to the failure of this mission.[18] A closer support base and better cooperation and assistance in the form of a joint effort would possibly have reduced the confusion, poor planning and unprofessional execution that resulted in the deaths of sixty-one passengers.

For example, in 1989 the United States deployed the MH-53J Pave Low III (Enhanced) helicopter[19] to the Special Operations Squadron, based at Woodbridge in Suffolk. The aim was to support America's special forces and ensure that an effective special operations and counterterrorist aviation capability would be available should they be required in Europe or Great Britain.

To be fully successful, forward-basing requires allies in or near the region to be prepared to permit the local positioning of not only special operations units but also small numbers of highly trained personnel and their supporting organizations. Further to speeding up the response capability of counterterrorist forces, local police, paramilitary and military forces, tasked to conduct counterterrorist operations, would be provided an opportunity for joint training.[20] Russia, for example, as well as others, has taken advantage of joint training opportunities, particularly in the wake of the daring Russian-orchestrated seizure of a top Chechen field commander, Salmon Raduyev, east of Grozny on 11 March 2000. The operation was reportedly undertaken under the noses of his 100 security guards.[21] Such experiences would benefit countries whose national capabilities for counterterrorism are slight and would be of value even in states, such as Great Britain and Germany, where exchange training and other cooperative initiatives are daily events. Forward-basing also provides the forces of the dispatching state to garner exposure to general conditions outside their homeland. More dramatic still might be the overall benefits for countries, such as the United States, in developing pools of selected, skilled personnel who have a demonstrated capacity to operate efficiently and effectively with foreign forces.[22] Similar to the intelligence issue, the political constraints, particularly for potential receiving states, have delayed or sometimes halted such deployments.

THE CRITICALITY OF EFFECTIVE AND SECURE COMMUNICATIONS

The foundation for success in the increasingly fast and complex military operations characteristic of the late twentieth century and the twenty-first is flexible, secure and rapid communications. Counterterrorist operations, and in particular hostage rescue tasks, are no exception from this vital requirement of contemporary warfare. Communication security remains of paramount importance. One of the most potentially dangerous events during the Entebbe operation occurred when an Israeli reporter monitored the radio communications. Such incidents could have led to dire results. Although the reporter's actions were not considered to have compromised the mission, the fact that an "outsider" monitored these activities is a shortcoming that cannot be permitted in future operations. Hostage taking and hijacking are, by their nature, politically sensitive and highly volatile acts. The discovery of counterterrorist units either in the act of preparing or in the execution stages of an operation can easily force the terrorist's hand. Moreover, when one realizes the widespread availability of sophisticated, off-the-shelf equipment for secure communications and monitoring capabilities, and given the particularly vital requirement to maintain the principle of surprise, counterterrorist missions must have rapid and secure communication by voice, paper and digital readout. Another problem with communications arose for GSG9 at Mogadishu, when they experienced serious communication difficulties due to the high humidity. This forced them to employ traditional hand signals.

Secure communications must link all elements of a CT force conducting hostage rescue or other counterterrorist activities. Terrorists appreciate both the vulnerability and centrality of communications,[23] and it is very likely that at some point they will be able to not only monitor rescue force communications but possibly have the capability to disrupt or jam them. In order to frustrate this eventuality, counterterrorist units must possess the best secure communications equipment available, as the very success of an operation will depend on it. International cooperation could help in this regard by ensuring compatibility of equipment types. As well, the provision of modern, efficient and compatible communications equipment to the counterterrorist forces of poorer states could be a sound investment. Overall, communications considerations are perhaps the least subject to political concerns and, in certain circumstances, international cooperation in this area would normally carry few risks.

TRAINING ASSISTANCE, ATTACHMENTS AND EXCHANGES

After the study of German, Israeli and Egyptian operations in counterterrorism, there can be little doubt that cooperation is essential among the various governments concerned about terrorism and in their respective national special forces. In that light, cooperation in training, attachments and exchanges, as well as in the actual counterterrorist operations[24] themselves, will do much to improve the professional skills of special forces and enhance the coordination of more effective responses at a national level. This book has shown, through two operations, a spectrum of international cooperative efforts and the benefits that they have produced, particularly in hostage rescue operations. Current emphasis should be on the potential for further development and improvement in these areas of joint activity, particularly with the pending expansion of NATO and with countries such as Poland. Since 1990, Poland has created its own counterterrorist force— Grupa Reagowonia Operacyjno Mobilego (Operational Mobile Response Group), known in Polish as GROM (Thunder). This unit has operated overtly and covertly in Haiti and the former Yugoslavia. Through its sheer professional capability and experience, GROM has garnered the respect of Western special operations forces, and is considered the only Polish military element capable of undertaking a NATO operational assignment under the present treaty framework. GROM has profited from training with GSG9, the SAS and Special Forces Operational Detachment (Delta).[25]

The benefits that accrue from international cooperation in the area of training, both individually and collectively, are evident for countries all over the world, from Canada to South Africa, from Dubai to Egypt.[26] It should be understood that attachments and exchanges have vastly broadened the experiences of key personnel in national counterterrorist forces. Such attachments greatly enhanced the professional development of both Wegener and Colonel Charlie Beckwith, founders of their countries' counterterrorist units, and, more recently, Colonel Petelicki of the Polish GROM. Nowhere has international cooperation been more obvious than in the counterterrorist operations themselves,[27] and most emphatically in hostage rescue missions.

In the two cases reviewed, the assistance provided to individual national forces by the presence, advice, operational and technical support, and moral reinforcement of other countries has been seen repeatedly. The questions that remain are: What fields of endeavor might allow for the further development of training, attachment, exchange, and operational cooperation, and in what manner could such development be facilitated?

In exchanges and attachments it seems clear that while special forces responsible for counterterrorism are generally small in numbers, their specialized skills appear to lend great scope for attachments, perhaps even more for exchanges as a means of improving the international response to terrorism. Saudi Arabia is one country that has reaped the benefit of Germany's skills in counterterrorist operations through the secondment of Wegener and a number of his officers who organized, equipped and trained Saudi CT forces.[28] More recently, this assistance enabled the Saudi CT team to rescue the passengers of a hijacked Russian airliner orchestrated by the Chechen rebels in March 2001.[29] The American 3d Special Forces Group has taken the lead in training African troops under the program African Crisis Response Initiative (ACRI). The aim of the ACRI is to develop rapidly deployable, interoperable battalions and companies from stable democratic countries that can operate together to maintain peace in Africa. Since 1997, ACRI has provided training to Uganda, Senegal, Mali, Malawi, Ghana, Benin and the Ivory Coast. Another example is the 1st Special Forces Group participation in Cobra Gold 99, an annual conventional and special ops exercise between the United States and Thailand. Also, in 1999 the 7th Special Forces Group conducted counternarcotics training for Ecuadorian and Colombian military personnel, as well as instruction in airborne and waterborne operations, weapons and small-unit tactics.[30] In general terms, exchanges are likely more acceptable to lesser powers, while attachments can be seen as useful at all levels, as underlined throughout this study.

Enhanced training also appears to need greater improvement. The allocation and deployment of small numbers of specialists is far less costly than conventional military units such as air force squadrons and army battalions. Such training has been, and could continue to be, done without great fanfare and, if necessary, far from the public limelight. Such opportunities provide exposure to other countries, their forces, to the personalities involved, and to their respective operational procedures and their equipment can hardly fail to provide the stimulus for more effective cooperation when required. Moreover, such training[31] opportunities could lead to greater understanding among the allied and friendly forces and the individuals who constitute them. In the case of more sophisticated allied forces, such training could also be an incentive to modify and enhance the structure, capabilities, and doctrine of counterterrorist forces, as well as the means to compare the advantages of various types of weapons, tactics, organization and equipment. The benefits are evident in the numerous training attachments and exchanges between the American special forces and the SAS, particularly as Delta's first commander Charlie Beckwith closely followed SAS training methodology and organization when he commanded Delta Force. Australia is known to have one of the world's most complete counterterrorist training grounds, which was built by the Australian SAS. These facilities have been used by counterterrorist units from all over the world. This site has been visited by 22 SAS, Delta, SEALs, Japanese police, Special Weapons and Tactics (SWAT) teams, and other units.[32] It must be realized that the nature of terrorism demands that CT units are able to cooperate. Such training opportunities allow teams to work closely together, to familiarize themselves with each other's methods, equipment and training, which can be important in cooperative CT efforts. The importance has been noted in one hijack operation, which was orchestrated by Abu Nidal.

The seized aircraft landed in Cyprus before carrying on to Algeria. Throughout this operation, both the SAS and GIGN coordinated their operations and intelligence. One analyst noted, "While the plane was in Cyprus, the responsibility for a rescue operation was with the SAS and when it flew on to Algeria . . . it switched over to the GIGN."[33] Intelligence was vital and the British gathered the necessary intelligence on the plane, passengers, crew and the terrorists. Both the French and British CT teams set up a computer link to provide each other with information and intelligence. This amply demonstrates that joint training adds enormously to facilitating international cooperation "on the day,"[34] if and when increasingly sophisticated international terrorism demands an increasingly sophisticated and coordinated international military response.

The foregoing discussion is not intended to minimize the various and serious obstacles that enhanced cooperation would likely surface, which are largely a result of political factors. However, the reality is that the most fundamental constraints to international cooperative efforts among national special forces combating terrorism are political considerations, to which this chapter will now turn.

POLITICAL CONSIDERATIONS IN INTERNATIONAL COOPERATION

In democratic nations, armed forces serve political masters who have issues and concerns that go beyond those that are strictly related to the employment and use of military force. The preparations to fight terrorism do not happen against the background of a *tabula rasa,* but rather in the context of a highly complex national and international backdrop. That environment, in turn, limits the responses available to governments that have the initiative to take up the international terrorist challenge.

As underlined in this study, terrorism is a political act with political objectives in mind, even if the exact nature of those goals is, from time to time, unclear. Therefore, it is not surprising that many of the factors that affect the responses to terrorist activity are of a political stripe.

Contemporary terrorist acts are generally spectacular, short-lived, and aimed at quite specific objectives. These acts are aimed to attract considerable attention when they occur, after which national political life returns to normal. During such terrorist incidents, initially governments are forced to focus inordinate interest on the event and its issues, but are, generally, only too pleased to be able to return to more mundane concerns of government once the crisis is over.

Additionally, national governments have differing perceptions of what terrorism is and what constitutes terrorist activity. Some governments have openly supported some terrorist organizations. Most nations, however, denounce the terrorism phenomenon, and many of these are, have been, or might well become the targets of terrorists. A successfully coordinated international approach to terrorism depends on these states agreeing to a concerted response to the phenomenon. States, however, are very divergent, predicated on the extent to which they themselves feel threatened, and therefore will reflect varying degrees of zeal in attempting to defeat terrorism.

In the 1970s and 1980s, the United States was clearly more concerned than the former Soviet Union on how to deal with terrorism; however, the situation has evolved.[35] Likewise, middle powers such as Great Britain, France, Germany and Spain perceive the problem quite differently from those of virtually untargeted states such as China or Costa Rica. The spectrum of urgency felt by other states in the world community range from the deep concern of countries exposed to terrorism, such as Israel or Spain, to the unruffled calm of countries such as Finland or New Zealand.

There are a number of political obstacles to obtaining a cooperative effort on the issue of terrorism, particularly in an international setting as complex and varied as it is today. An enhanced threat perception usually will bring strident requests from one capital for a greater and more effective international response to terrorism. Yet, another capital with no perceived threat will have little or no interest in the issue and likely will be occupied with quite different priorities. Into this already complex situation comes the further obstacle that the Western and, sometimes, often the former colonial powers are frequently the major targets of terrorism. Any international coordinated response involving Third World countries could likely involve certain delicate issues of sovereignty with recently independent countries or those in a neocolonial relationship with a developed nation. Moreover, the differing levels of national power, even among allied or friendly countries, may cause governments to be extremely wary and sensitive to unequal relationships that can become, or already are, domestic political issues. This potential reality lies silently ready to undermine decisive international cooperation in combating terrorism.

Another available, but more difficult, option in dealing with terrorism involves a dramatically different route from the reactive, frequently military, and international courses so far discussed. Instead of dealing with the symptoms, individual states, as well as the international community, should concentrate harder on solving the deep and serious underlying causes of terrorism. Such an initiative would undermine the *raison d'être* of terrorist organizations and acts. Sadly, however, the present problems giving rise to international terrorism are extremely deep-rooted and generally unresponsive to either a general panacea or rapid ad hoc solutions, such as the Fatwa (religious ruling) against Americans that was issued by Osama Bin Laden. The Fatwa reportedly stated that "to kill the Americans and their allies—civilian and military—is an individual duty for every Muslim who can do it in any country in which it is possible to do it."[36] Such problems resist attempts at easy fixes. The Palestinian situation as it exists today bears dramatic witness to this state of affairs on the international scene; however, recent events indicate a glimmer of hope.[37] The national terrorism phenomena in places such as the United States, France, Northern Ireland, Spain, India and elsewhere offer continuous proof that the conditions from which terrorism thrives are not easily remedied. It seems clear that the international community, as well as individual states, will continue to place emphasis on dealing with the manifestations of terrorism rather than root causes. Many Third World states, often guarding their newly won sovereignty, will in all likelihood remain reluctant to enter into long-term agreements aimed at combating terrorism, particularly where such initiatives could place them in easily criticized public postures alongside Western powers. The hostage-taking incidents as noted have elicited in their wake some cooperation among both Western and Third World states. Although such efforts have resulted in quite close and longer lasting cooperation among Western and Western-leaning countries in some respect, they have spurred little follow-up in concrete, long-term agreements between the Western powers and the Third World states.

This is not to say, however, that no Western–Third World cooperation is possible. Terrorism now affects many Third World states, most recently Kenya and Tanzania, a situation that may require these Third World nationals to deploy much-needed resources in order to increase their own security and intelligence capabilities, as well as to create or enhance counterterrorist forces by themselves. Some states already involved in this rather painful process appreciate that the costs in terms of lost development opportunities may have a negative political spin-off. This is due to the reallocation of funds from economic or social development to security and intelligence agencies in response to a terrorist threat. However, the success of cooperative efforts elsewhere may stimulate Third World governments to greater interest in international cooperation, as may their own domestic, political situations. Cooperation and training with highly respected elite military forces from other, even Western countries may provide a much-needed deterrent against terrorism and outweigh the political costs incurred through such cooperation. It is important that international cooperation remain a critical element in America's counterterrorism strategy. The Secretary of State, Colin Powell, stated that cooperation was increasing and starting to pay dividends against the terrorist threat. He noted that "terrorism shows the dark side [of globalization] as it exploits the easing of travel restrictions, the improvements of communications, or the internationalization of banking and finance, making it easier for terrorists to do their work." According to State Department data, Western Europe witnessed the largest decrease in terrorist activity from eighty-five to thirty incidents. As well, there were fewer attacks in Germany, Greece and Italy, with none in Turkey.[38]

Terrorist operations, like most military operations, seek objectives that are the weak points in the "enemy" structure. Such "soft targets" are less likely to be found in states whose special forces are assisted by, or include, members of internationally reputed, elite counterterrorist forces from abroad. It is clear that the level of terrorism has lessened in those countries whose troops have received training from the SAS, for example. Be that as it may, it is clear that political factors have a direct impact on the potential for military cooperation on an international level for countering terrorism.

THE CRITICALITY OF INTELLIGENCE

One could argue from the Western perspective, there are two tiers where cooperation in intelligence is possible. The first is inter-allied cooperation, a long-standing arrangement generally functioning smoothly and on an often routine basis. The second, much more problematical perspective involves Western relationships in the intelligence area with Third World countries. The difference between these two tiers is, naturally enough, based on two factors, the perception of the threat and Western assessments of the degree of professionalism and capability present in many Third World intelligence services.

It should be appreciated that the two-tiered system is not a straightforward one. Western powers have varying levels of links with different parts of the world, the United States being particularly strong in Latin America, while Great Britain benefits from strong links with many Commonwealth and Middle East countries. Even within the Western alliances there are somewhat different perceptions of threats emanating from various quarters. This is, of course, particularly true between NATO members, on the one hand, and developing countries, on the other; however, this situation has seen some dramatic changes as Arab nations have now called for a concerted effort to fight terrorism.[39]

In alliances such as NATO, intelligence cooperation with many Third World countries is often questioned because of their poor human rights records. The resulting criticism from influential Western groups may affect both the level of cooperation from Western intelligence services and the kind of assistance that those services may be willing to provide Third World states.

Even among friendly, but not necessarily allied, countries, there are often political difficulties in the area of counterterrorism intelligence cooperation. Intelligence gathering in the Western world has long been perceived as an unseemly, if not actually sordid, activity. Espionage, in particular, has had negative media coverage, although the need for it has, in this century, usually been understood by governments. Western capitals remain highly sensitive to the potential political costs of flawed covert intelligence-gathering operations. They are reluctant to enter such activities without assurances that such embarrassments will be unlikely. Information exchanges, even between allies in war as well as peace, have been beset with problems that reflect the intensely sensitive nature of intelligence gathering and use. In peacetime, it is an even more sensitive activity. A shared perception of a threat in an alliance can aid immensely in furthering cooperation. Major powers, active in intelligence gathering, while reluctant to share their information, are still anxious to have alliance cooperation in dealing with terrorism. Smaller powers, which are less likely to be active in intelligence gathering, are also eager to have access to information, the only source for which may be a major allied state. Hence cooperation may develop, in part, as a result of the confidence gained through the exchange of intelligence, even though this is largely provided by the greater state.

The extremely delicate nature of various responses to terrorism further complicates this already complex and shifting relationship among allies. States sharing a roughly similar view of the balance of power requirements in Europe may differ greatly on matters relating to international terrorism. Compromise of sources and information, fear of third-party links, and the general frustration of highly threatened governments with what they perceive as insufficient activity of generally allied, but less threatened, states, all lead to lesser cooperation in counterterrorism than in other spheres.

Highly threatened countries, even when they are not formally allied to one another, may still be able and willing to forge close links in their counterterrorist operations. A good example is provided by Germany and Italy, which while far from being close security allies, like Great Britain and the United States, nonetheless cooperate effectively in this field. Allied and friendly states that lack a common threat perception may have great difficulty in mounting cooperative counterterrorist efforts. Italy and the United States, for example, differ on the seriousness and nature and degree of the challenge, which cripples their efforts to cooperate.

THE IMPORTANCE OF FORWARD-BASING

As noted in our case studies, the timely arrival of counterterrorist forces is vital for success in hostage rescue missions. Home-based special forces may need lengthy periods of time to deploy to the site of a terrorist activity; this threatens lives as well as the potential for success. In such cases, the threatened government will obviously try to gain the use of a deployment site as close as is safely possible to the terrorist activity. Unfortunately, political and military considerations make such arrangements highly difficult to bring about. Western European allies of the United States, for example, feel that a visible American antiterrorist presence or the basing of such units in their national territory will more likely result in being targeted themselves by terrorist organizations.

Considering the high level of terrorist activity related to Middle Eastern concerns, countries in that region, although generally favorable to the

United States, nonetheless believe that the political disadvantages of allowing the stationing of American military forces, particularly counterterrorist forces, far outweigh any political advantages that they might bring. This is true in other parts of the world as well. It should be noted that counterterrorist operations are not the only type of military activity similarly stymied at an international level. The antidrug struggle in Colombia, Bolivia, Turkey and other parts of the world has experienced similar obstacles. These obstacles exist because of the commonly held view that such deployments, involving states of power, are related to the issue of national sovereignty. All countries are jealous of their sovereignty because their status as independent states could be jeopardized. Raymond Aron suggests that no country can be sovereign unless it has population, territory and government control over that population and territory.[40] If any of these three elements are missing, the state is not considered sovereign. This is due to the fact that should the state not have the power to make its writ run throughout its territory, the country in question does not have the right to claim equality with other sovereign states making up the international system. Since international recognition is an essential attribute of statehood, its lack can lead to questions of the gravest kind. Nowhere is this concern more telling than in countries either newly independent from colonial rule or those that find themselves in relationships with superpowers or great powers that threaten their claim to sovereign state status.

The inability to defend oneself against internal and external threats is a prime example of the sort of issue that threatens countries' attempts to assert their sovereignty. A country that must appeal to others for help opens itself to question. While developed nations with long histories have little reason to worry over such matters, the Third World abounds with states whose sovereignty is shaky and whose regimes are likewise. The insecurity of such governments prevents them from entertaining requests for forward-basing arrangements from major powers. If one adds to this other political factors, such as the possible accusation of being the pawn of a greater power, it becomes clear that only great benefits, in other areas of national concern, can make such agreements palatable. Since such a government probably would not perceive the terrorist threat with the same concern as does the threatened country seeking the forward-basing arrangement, the potential for such arrangements is limited.

In contrast, alliances or other arrangements such as the Commonwealth may aid in reducing the problem greatly. If defense agreements already exist or if a greater power has forces already stationed in a Third World country, the addition of small groups of specialist troops, especially where their deployment avoids public exposure, may well cause little difficulty for a receiving government. Formal alliances have long included agreements on stationing of forces that could facilitate special deployments. Nonetheless, the negative experiences of some governments caused by lack of consultation, separate decision making and flawed operations have led to the reluctance of even close allies to accept such deployments in their territory.

A number of technical, administrative and operational problems exist and, therefore, complicate the political dimension. They include the status of specialist forces, rotation of personnel, subunits, or units and the security of personnel. The greatest risk, however, remains a political one. While the U.S. success in deploying special forces' assets to Great Britain demonstrates that such arrangements are possible, Washington's difficulties in the Middle East and elsewhere,[41] even in the wake of the Gulf War, underscore the political difficulties involved. The Great Britain–United States accord reflects the similarity of these two countries' perception of the terrorist threat, as well as their shared ideological views. Hence, their close struggle against bin Laden and al-Qaeda.

Notwithstanding the foregoing, it is conceivable that, in a number of ways, a more subtle and flexible type of arrangement might bear some fruit. In countries where the dispatching state already has facilities, as mentioned before, the stationing of a small force might not raise undue alarm. Both states party to the agreement may have to remain flexible and may even have to turn a blind eye to certain sensitive aspects of such a stationing arrangement. Generally though, there is no reason that, in some states at least, such teams could not be deployed under some sort of "cover" arrangements such as a mobile training team. An additional benefit of such arrangements for the forward-based personnel would be the enhanced security provided by an appropriate cover story that purports to explain their presence.

CONCLUSIONS

Terrorism as we witness it today is the logical continuation of a long historical experience that can be traced back for centuries. It is, however, more complex, certainly more global, and infinitely more dangerous than any historical previous example.[42] It has seen a greater impetus in the wake of the post–Cold War era and the subsequent devolution of the countries in the former Warsaw Pact, Africa and elsewhere. Also, the issues with a pre-disposition to cause fanaticism have rarely existed in greater numbers than in the present era. Moreover, the increasing ease of communications has added to the special nature of the post–Cold War world and has resulted in the internationalization[43] of the objectives and the activities of terrorists.

The responses of national governments to terrorism were historically national and involved resources common to the state apparatus of most countries. Today, the nature of terrorist activities has called for a growing level of cooperation among nations facing this threat, as witnessed in the wake of September 2001. Special forces, whose historical lineage grew largely out of the World War II and postwar experiences, were in place when modern international terrorism evolved. Such forces appeared to many governments as the most likely and flexible instrument to take on the sometimes delicate role needed in modern counterterrorist operations. There are many historical and recent operations, such as the hostage rescue in Peru in 1997, that have provided substantial and dramatic evidence of both the utility of these forces and the difficulties that surround their employment.

The aim of this study was to offer some insights into the past, present and possible future uses to which these forces might be employed in a counterterrorist context. In doing so, it has focused on the experiences of Israel and Germany. The British have continuously emphasized the human element in counterterrorist operations. In contrast, the American tendency appears to have favored high technology and sophisticated equipment as the means to success, as witnessed in their campaign in Afghanistan. This situation was underlined in its ill-fated 3 October 1993 operation in Mogadishu, where a group of determined, but ill-equipped, Somalis willing to sacrifice themselves in their cause were encountered by a highly professional and well-trained American force equipped with the latest "high-tech" equipment.[44] In both political and military terms, the American forces were predisposed to employ firepower rather than manpower.[45] This value and emphasis on human life is and remains America's true "center of gravity."[46] This was dramatically demonstrated in the suicide bombing of the USS Cole and the ensuing media coverage over the loss of American servicemen, and remains of concern with the military action in Afghanistan.

The highly successful Entebbe and Mogadishu operations, as well as the lessons learned from British and American counterterrorist operations, have repeatedly emphasized both the real and potential advantages to be gained through cooperative international efforts. An analysis of these experiences points to areas where international cooperation can assist counterterrorist forces and can be especially advantageous during hostage rescue missions. It is therefore concluded that intelligence, forward-basing, secure communications, and attachment and training assistance[47] can provide significant, and sometimes critical, advantages when terrorist operations demand an effective counterterrorist response. This was demonstrated in the 2001 to 2002 Afghanistan campaign when British, Canadian, German, New Zealand, Australian, and American special forces operated successfully in concert.[48]

Unfortunately, more difficult than the technical considerations will be the political ones. International cooperation, while vital in many cases, has in some respect remained limited in both scope and effectiveness. In turn, cooperation has come about in the face of considerable pressures, with the most significant pressures against international cooperative efforts being political. From this study, one thing has become evident: the greatest advances in international cooperation have occurred between countries with similar views of the threat posed by international terrorism.

It is therefore important to appreciate that threat perception is critical to an understanding of the likelihood of future intergovernmental cooperation so as to combat global terrorism. Governments' views as to the extent to which they should be concerned by the terrorist problem may vary, and those nations least likely to be targets tend to be the least anxious to assist.

As has been noted, well-established intelligence networks exist to acquire, analyze and share intelligence, and there is always scope for employing and expanding these in the context of counterterrorism. At present, there are a number of allied and friendly governments that are presently involved in forward-basing, and there could be some further scope for expansion of such links. This study also presented the advantages of attached and exchanged personnel,[49] which, if implemented, could assist with the task. Equally important, communication problems are far from insurmountable given the impetus to overcome them.

However, the likelihood of considerably enhanced cooperation runs afoul of political constraints as well as present and future realities. International cooperation in the surgical employment of counterterrorist forces is not and cannot be the complete and final answer to the international terrorist dilemma. It has, however, already given indications of its efficiency under certain circumstances in providing timely interventions to combat terrorist activities. It is far from clear whether the political will exists in a sufficient number of important countries to overcome the constraints that act against international cooperation. If such a will would become manifest, this study has suggested that there is much that could be done. Moreover, in the wake of the 11 September 2001 attacks, these considerations become true imperatives in the global war against extremist terrorists who seek to wage a conflict of mass casualties. It is the hope of all peaceable nations that we may vanquish this threat and learn from its manifestations so that governments may pre-empt future initiatives as witnessed on the morning of 11 September 2001.

NOTES

At the suggestion of several reviewers, this final chapter of considerations and conclusions has been based on the final chapter in *The Evolution of Special Forces in Counter-Terrorism: The British and American Experiences*. It has been updated and revised to reflect the new developments since the publishing of *The Evolution of Special Forces in Counter-Terrorism*, especially the events of 11 September 2001.

1. For an excellent overview of hostage rescue operations and what they represent, see Gazit, "Risk, Glory, and the Rescue Operation," 112; for an overview

of special operations see Gray, "Handfuls of Heroes on Desperate Ventures: When Do Special Operations Succeed?," 2–24. The importance of special forces in countering terrorism was emphasized in an article by Edward Luttwak. It is his contention that the employment of effective airpower in concert with elite ground troops is an unbeatable combination. Luttwak, "How to Win: Bombs Plus Brawn."

2. In a roundabout way, the preparations for rescue operations have continued within the former Yugoslavia, as well as "snatch operations" aimed at capturing war criminals such as Radovan Karadzic. See Smith, "Secret Meetings Killed Karadzic Capture Plan: U.S. Blames French in Foiled Mission." According to this article, a French leak pre-empted U.S. and allied plans to seize Karadzic, the former Bosnia Serb president indicted for war crimes. It was noted that in the past few months, "British and Dutch special forces have arrested five war criminals and slain another in the British sector, and U.S. special forces have captured one of the indictees known to reside in the U.S. sector." In December 1999 it was reported that General Stanislav Galic, 56, who commanded the Sarajevo-Romanija Corps responsible for keeping Sarajevo under siege, was seized by twenty British soldiers believed to be the SAS. The subject of a sealed indictment as a suspected war criminal, General Galic was subsequently moved to the United Nations International Criminal Tribunal for the Former Yugoslavia in the Hague, where he was charged with crimes of war and crimes against humanity. See Evans, "Former Bosnian General Arrested: Special British Unit Nabs Man behind Sarajevo Siege"; Strauss, "British Arrest Ex-Commander of Bosnian Camp." On 14 October 2000, a Bosnian Serb war crimes suspect who had been indicted for rape and torture took his own life as NATO soldiers attempted to seize him. Janko Janjic blew himself up with a grenade, wounding four German soldiers. This indicates that possible arrests in the future will likely be more problematic. See Strauss, "War Crimes Suspect Blows Himself Up." One report underlines that due to the continuing problems in the Balkans there has been an increase in cooperation. The Czech Republic's Police Anti-Terrorism Unit (UNRA) has been advised by the U.S. Army's Delta Force and subsequently has made contacts with the British Special Air Service. Apparently, British specialists conducted a number of visits in the spring of 1999 to the Czech capital teaching the defusing of bombs and working on joint snatch ops exercises. See "Spy in Hack's Clothing." In the case of the arrests of fifteen Fatah men suspected of planning and carrying out numerous attacks, the arrests were coordinated between members of the Shin Bet and a number of elite commando units. See Harel, "15 Fatah Men Held for Role in Shooting Barak: 'The IDF Will Strike at Anyone Who Harms Israelis.'"

3. Gazit, "Risk, Glory, and the Rescue Operation," 112.

4. Ibid., 113.

5. This fact has been repeatedly affirmed by the highly successful operations conducted against terrorists, for example the 16 February 1992 ambush sprung on the IRA that killed four terrorists after they attacked a local police station in Coalisland. See "Who Is the IRA insider?" See also the SAS operation on 8 May 1987 in Loughgall in Northern Ireland. The ambush killed eight terrorists and one passerby. This operation stunned the IRA as it lost two active service cells in this engagement. Believing that there was a mole, the IRA began a period of self-examination and assessment. See Davies, *SAS Rescue,* 137–139.

6. For an interesting insight into British intelligence operations in Northern Ireland, see Rennie, *The Operators: Inside 14 Intelligence Company: The Army's Top Secret Elite;* Lewis, *Fishers of Men,* which provides insights into the Force Research Unit. See also Clarke, "Army Foiled Plot to Murder Adams." The Force Research Unit (FRU), a highly secret corps of army intelligence officers who handled agents in terrorist groups, accessed the assassination plans, saving Gerry Adams while capturing the loyalists and maintaining their agent in place. For further information regarding Northern Ireland intelligence operators, see Clarke, "MI5 'operated network of Garda agents'"; "The British Spy at heart of IRA"; Bamber, "Police Foil Plot to Poison England's Water Supply: Irish Terrorists Threaten to Conduct 'Campaign of Chemical Warfare.'"

7. In ideal circumstances, countries should be able to count on assistance from foreign sources as a matter of course. Recently, Spanish police claimed to have eliminated a unit of the Basque separatist organization ETA, when six members were arrested in Madrid on 7 November 2000. The Madrid arrests followed a tip-off from the Cuban embassy when two women asked Cuba for political asylum. See Wilkinson, "Police Claim Destruction of ETA Cell with Help of Cubans." In the August 2001 insertion of NATO forces in Macedonia, SAS personnel had been deployed to the area of operations weeks in advance in order to protect NATO peacekeepers. See Clark, "SAS Unit on Secret Recce in Balkans." When counter-terrorist operations fail, nations are known to continue to provide support, as exemplified by American support to the Egyptian government in the wake of the devastating and ill-fated rescue attempt on 23 November 1985. A more recent, and indeed dramatic, rescue occurred in Sierra Leone, using a force of 110 soldiers from the 1st Battalion Parachute Regiment, men of D Squadron 22 SAS and the Royal Marines' Special Boat Service. Operation Barras was a two-pronged attack to take the village of Magheni controlled by the well-armed West Side Royal boys, a renegade militia. Six British soldiers of the Irish Regiment were rescued. The coordinated rescue took a total of two hours and was predicated on the information garnered by D Squadron observation posts that had monitored the area from covert observation posts for two weeks. By the end of the fighting, twenty-five West Side Boys were dead and their leader "Brigadier" Foday Kally had been taken prisoner. The cost was one SAS man killed and twelve wounded. This operation was assisted by the media when journalists were called in to the Ministry of Defence more than a week prior to the operation and were advised that certain units were put on standby for Sierra Leone. The journalists were requested not to divulge this information or to speculate on a possible rescue. See Evans, "SAS Emerged from Swamp to Launch Deadly Attack"; and Hall, "Army Magazine Gagged over SAS Jungle Raid." In October 2000, the Philippine Army also conducted a reportedly successful rescue operation of three Malaysian hostages held by Muslim rebels on a southern Philippine island. See "Philippine Military Rescues Three Hostages Held by Muslim Rebels." See also "Ex-Soviet Leaders to Discuss Security at Summit." The Moscow-dominated CIS is attempting to create a joint Anti-Terrorist Center, to orchestrate joint intelligence and joint counterterrorist operations.

8. The American military decided in 1993 on a plan to capture Mohammed Farah Aidid, a Somali warlord. After one raid that went awry and the capture of a prominent member of a United Nations relief mission, subsequent attempts at seizing the Somali leader were aborted due to a lack of timely, accurate intelligence.

According to one analyst, "One of the problems was that the CIA team was relying on electronic eavesdropping to find Aidid, and had brought with it a mass of the latest technology from America. Aidid's troops were, however, using very low-tech walkie-talkies and talking drums to signal each other, and the CIA's equipment was incapable of dealing with either. The technology gap had started to work against the Americans." Adams, *The Next World War: Computers Are the Weapons and the Front Line Is Everywhere,* 67. The issue of garnering allies capable of assisting the United States may be hindered by America's tendency to be over dependent on high-tech weapons; this could leave them with allies incapable of interoperability. Mirlinger, "Force Divider."

9. Debusmann, "Poor Intelligence Cripples U.S. Military Might, Experts Say."

10. Ibid.

11. See "Intelligence Monitor, U.S.A. Today."

12. Cory et al., "Where Spies Really Matter," 24.

13. Worsnip, "Shortage of Spies in Lebanon Hampers Efforts to Find Hostages."

14. For an overview of intelligence requirements, see Bolz, "Police Works: Intelligence Requirements in Hostage Situations."

15. Ottaway and Oberdorfer, "Administration Alters Assassination Ban; In Interview, Webster Reveals Interpretation."

16. In respect to this situation, one article noted, "Considering that the CIA and other intelligence organizations have routinely failed to significantly penetrate any terrorist cells, and their human intelligence sources have been notoriously poor at ferreting out information or terrorist plans." See Andrade, *Counterterrorism and Security Report.* For an insightful article regarding the effectiveness of American intelligence see Betts, "Fixing Intelligence" and Deutch and Smith, "Smarter Intelligence." See also Greenaway, "U.S. Offers Antiterror Assistance to Israel." The issue of terrorism as it relates to the December 1999 arrest of Ahmed Ressam has underlined further implications. Experts agreed that if Algerian operatives are in Canada and the U.S., they are likely working for a worldwide Islamic revolution and not the specific objectives of Algeria's Armed Islamic Group. See Vanpraet, "New Breed of Terrorism Has Investigators Guessing: Is Montreal Man Tied to Terrorist Bin Laden? Proof Is Elusive." Ressam is expected to go on trial in March 2001 in Los Angeles. See "Group Helped Ressam Get Canadian Passport for Terrorist Activities."

17. In early 1998 the British SAS had forward-based some of its personnel to the Gulf so as to prepare for rescue operations, albeit for allied aircrew who might be shot down during military action against Iraq. The little-known operation in which the SAS was involved came when a small SAS party rescued Britons caught in the fighting in Afghanistan in the spring of 1998. See "British Commandos Head to Gulf." In September 2001, the British conducted a joint Omani-British exercise in Oman and, in the wake of the exercise, dispatched the SAS and other special troops to Afghanistan.

18. Smith et al., "Massacre in Malta," 26.

19. "USAF Special Mission Aircraft in Close-Up," 306. This forward-basing issue became relevant during the operations in Afghanistan when U.S. defense secretary Donald Rumsfeld visited Azerbaijan, Armenia, and Georgia. These nations offered use of their respective airspace to the American military; Rumsfeld's visit

was to discuss this as well as other venues of military co-operation. "Rumsfeld Seeks Help in Caucasus."

20. Russian counterterrorist units have conducted joint training operations with other countries. According to one article, the Russian Federal Security Service (FSB) counterterrorist team known as the ALPHA unit held a joint exercise with the South Korean Army Unit 47 in Russia. This training reportedly encompassed joint hostage release and assault training for railway car, aircraft, bus and building. The article quoted Lieutenant General Aleksandr Gusev that "anti-terrorist squads should learn from one another as long as the world situation required this." See "Russia: Border Units Hold Anti-Terrorist Drills with South Koreans." In October 2000, Turkey and Russia, who suspected each other of assisting hostile guerrilla groups, resolved to cooperate in the war against terrorism. Russia had suspected Muslim Turkey of fostering or at the very least tolerating Chechen terrorists on its soil. See Unal, "Russia and Turkey Co-operate on 'Terrorism.'"

21. Whittell, "Chechen Leader Snared by Russia: Undercover Operation Surprises Rebel Surrounded by Bodyguards."

22. The U.S. Army Special Forces have continually been providing military aid to both allied and friendly nations. The training and joint operational assistance provides an excellent vehicle for future expansion. See "U.S. Trains Sri Lanka in Counter-Terrorism." This report notes that a special forces team had arrived in Sri Lanka to train government military personnel in counterterrorism techniques. This U.S. assistance was limited to training Sri Lankan officers under Washington's International Military and Exchange program. According to reports, this assistance has been advising not only foreign military and police forces but also the Federal Bureau of Investigation (FBI). In one article a former CIA officer stated that "a secret U.S. Army unit played an active role in helping the FBI in the final assault on the Branch Davidian compound in Waco, Texas in 1993." Former CIA agent Gene Cullen stated that three or four Delta Force personnel were "present, up-front and close" during the operation. If this is so, they could have been seen as contravening American federal laws that prohibit the military from direct involvement in domestic law enforcement unless a presidential waiver is granted. Department of Defense sources advised that these personnel were in an advisory capacity only. A Pentagon officer advised that three military observers were special forces officers with expertise in hostage rescue and terrorism and were under strict instructions not to participate or even give advice. "U.S. Army Linked to Waco Assault: Military Says It Merely Sent Observers, Advisers." See also Shenon, "Military at Compound Earlier than Thought: Declassified Papers—'The Department of Defense Played No Operational Role,' FBI Says." According to this article, the Clinton administration's officials stated that the "military's role in the siege was purely advisory to law-enforcement agencies." It should be noted that the Office of Special Counsel investigated allegations that American military personnel had violated the law. The findings of the Danforth Waco Report noted that the armed forces of the United States provided extensive support for law enforcement agencies, including reconnaissance, equipment, training, advice and medical assistance, and they were careful in their conduct and were well-advised legally as to exactly what support they—as American military personnel—were able to provide. In short, the armed services conducted themselves in a proper and commendable manner at Waco. Http://www.osc-waco.org.

23. This situation has long been appreciated, particularly since the 1991 Gulf War, where the extent of this technology gap was dramatically emphasized. Allies suddenly realized their own deficiencies vis-à-vis the Americans, particularly in the fields of communications, transport, logistics, intelligence and surveillance capabilities. See Landay, "U.S. Military Outpaces Its NATO Peers." Such deficiencies may require financial assistance to purchase this equipment so as to keep their friends and allies *operationally compatible.*

24. Such counterterrorist assistance has expanded to include those nations fighting drug barons. See Krushelnycky, "SAS in Secret War on Cocaine." In a speech made six months after the 11 September 2001 attacks, U.S. president George W. Bush expanded the American commitment to train and provide military aid to those nations joining America in the fight against terrorism. He also noted that against terrorism there is no immunity and there can be no neutrality. Bumiller, "Bush Vows to Aid Other Countries in War on Terrorism." The training assistance noted by the President was in fact well underway in the Philippines where American special forces were training Philippine troops in order to improve their capability to counter the terrorist group Abu Sayyaf which is believed to be linked to the al-Qaeda network. "Future Terror Havens Target of Philippine Exercise."

25. See Katz, "GROM: The Advent of Polish Thunder."

26. Australian SAS training exchanges or assistance with the British and New Zealand SAS, GSG9 and Delta. Canada: training exchanges with the British SAS, GSG9, GIGN and Delta. Japan: training exchanges with the British SAS, GSG9 and Israel. Singapore: training exchanges with the British SAS, GSG9, Israel and India. Hong Kong: training exchanges with the British SAS, SBS, GIGN, GSG9 and Royal Dutch Marines. Indonesia: training exchanges with the GSG9 and British SAS. Philippines: training exchanges with the British and Australian SAS, U.S. and Israel. Pakistan: training exchanges with the British SAS. Sri Lanka: training exchanges with the British SAS. Malaysia: training exchanges with the British SAS. Honduras: training exchanges with the U.S. Ecuador: training exchanges with Israel. Chile: training exchanges with the GSG9, Israel and South Africa. Saudi Arabia: training exchanges with the GIGN, GSG9 and U.S. Bahrain: training exchanges with the British SAS and GSG9. Jordan: training exchanges with the British SAS. Oman: training exchanges with the British SAS and GSG9. Tunisia: training exchanges with the GIGN and U.S. Morocco: training exchanges with the GIGN and British SAS. Sudan: training exchanges with the British SAS, Egypt and U.S. Egypt: training exchanges or assistance with the GSG9, GIGN and U.S. See Thompson, *The Rescuers: The World's Top Anti-Terrorist Units.* It has been recently reported that the SAS are recruiting men from the GSG9 and Kommandos Specialkräfte (KSK) to serve with them for up to two years. It was noted that German soldiers have been on operations with the SAS in the Balkans. This secondment was due to the lack of suitable candidates for the SAS, predicated on what one officer called the "softening of society." Clark, "SAS to Recruit Troops from German Army." It was reported in late August 2001 that Israeli intelligence had several teams in Kashmir instructing Indian counterinsurgency personnel. No specifics were given; however, it was understood that Israel was "heavily involved" in assisting the Indian authorities combat Islamic militants. See Rajghatta, "Israeli Teams Training Forces in Kashmir."

27. The CIA has provided training for both Palestinian police and intelligence service personnel. The aim of this effort is to increase the professionalism of the Palestinian security authorities so they may identify, track and arrest suspected terrorists. Second, the intention is to increase the Israeli government's confidence in the professional abilities of the Palestinian security authorities. This training took place under the umbrella of a larger program of cooperation that includes both the Palestinian and Israeli security and intelligence authorities. See Weiner, "C.I.A. Teaching Palestinian Police the Tricks of the Trade."

28. "German Experts to Establish Saudi CT Unit." This article states that Wegener and five other officers will be spending three years assisting the Saudis to organize a CT unit similar to the GSG9. See also "UN Considers Its Own Army to Intervene Early in World Crises." According to this article, there is a little-known provision in the U.N. Charter, Article 43, which describes a standing army under U.N. command. This could arguably incorporate an international CT force should the need arise.

29. See LaGuardia, "Three Dead as Saudis Storm Hijacked Jet"; York, "Hijackers down Russian Plane," and Malik, "Three Killed as Saudis Storm Hijacked Russian Jet."

30. Gourley, "Boosting the Optempo," 25–28. This article notes that in fiscal year (FY) 1998 SOF carried out 2,178 missions outside of the continental U.S. across 152 countries. In relation to Colombian assistance, see Marks, "Slip, Stumble, and Fall: U.S. Gears-Up for War in Colombia," 54–57.

31. Although not germane to the CT field, indicative of the type of assistance that can be garnered, Canada's Prime Minister Jean Chrétien offered assistance to President Andres Pastrana to train Colombian peacekeepers. O'Neill, "PM Offers Canadian Training for Colombian Peacekeepers."

32. Arostequi, "Counter-Hijacking and the Killing Village."

33. Ibid.

34. Multinational commando forces have for some time been tasked to undertake special operations in Bosnia. British, French, and American forces have been deployed to Bosnia to seize Radovan Karadzic. See Stephen, "NATO Plans Karadzic Swoop." According to one media report, a squadron of SAS personnel conducted reconnaissance and intelligence operations during the NATO Kosovo Force (KFOR) advance into Kosovo. Once KFOR has established a troop presence, the SAS will begin tracking war criminals with the Serbian army and with the Kosovo Liberation Army. Although recognized for their hostage rescue skills, the SAS "snatch operations" against war criminals are presently in demand, and the planning is painstaking, requiring both detailed intelligence and a highly skilled team of professionals. McManners, "'Snatch Squad' Enters Kosovo: Undercover Unit Begins Hunting War Criminals." The continuing turmoil in some African nations has also caused the planning of rescue operations by some nations in order to extract their nationals. See "British Hostages in Sierra Leone All Free"; Farrell and Evans, "Hostages Wait as Rebels Stick to Demands." This article states, "A team of SAS and police negotiators is in Sierra Leone and is anxious to avoid any hasty attack . . . fearing a repetition of rescue attempts in Yemen and Chechnya, in which hostages were killed."

35. Lardner, "Cold War Adversaries Discuss Co-operation; International

Terrorism Said to Be Most Likely Target of Any CIA-KGB Joint Operation." See also "Cloak and Flowers." This latter article notes that the CIA and the KGB "could team up to combat terrorism."

36. Cooperman, "Terror Strikes Again," 12.

37. Hepburn, "Mideast Peace Deal Still Far Off, Baker Says." See also Friedman, "Diplomacy by Other Means."

38. Mackenzie, "Terrorism Strategy Paying Off."

39. Due to an increase in terrorist violence in Algeria and Egypt, Arab interior ministers have agreed to step up cooperation against political violence. This agreement was aimed at militant terrorism. This agreement called upon Arab states not to provide terrorists with safe haven or funding for groups that are provided to destabilize other Arab states. See Blanche, "Arab Nations Intensify Plans to Fight Terrorism." Egypt itself seems to have pushed the issue of combating terrorist activity. The Egyptian Interior Minister Hassan Alfy was known to urge "his fellow ministers to move aggressively against religious extremism." The agenda for Arab interior ministers was cooperation in the apprehension of terrorists, better cooperation between police forces, fostering exchanges of information and agreeing to a set of unified rules for extradition. See "Arab Nations Urged to Combat Terrorism."

40. See Aron, *Paix et guerre entre les nations.*

41. There continue to be numerous reports of American special forces positioned near the Afghan border and prepared to capture Osama bin Laden, particularly in the wake of the USS Cole attack. See "Bin Ladin Endorses Attack on the USS Cole, Denies Kuwaiti Daily's Report" and "FBI's Inquiry in Cole Attack Nearing a Halt." According to the reports, only the lack of intelligence regarding his whereabouts preempts this action. Such an operation would appear to be an excellent opportunity for a cooperative "snatch operation," particularly considering the 23 February 1998 Islamic proclamation, which stated "to kill Americans and their allies, both civil and military, is an individual duty of every Muslim who is able, in any country where it is possible, until American armies, shattered and broken-winged, depart from all the lands of Islam." See Weiner, "Commandos Hope to Pounce on Bin Laden: They're Counting on His Afghan Protectors Betraying Him, American Officials Say"; and "Bin Ladin Quarters in Afghanistan Fearful of U.S. Military Strike." What is disturbing is that a former member of the U.S. Army, Ali Mohamed, pleaded guilty in the planning of the American embassy bombings in Nairobi, Kenya in 1998. According to his testimony, he conducted surveillance at the embassy. See Hosenball and Nordland, "Pointing a Finger at bin Laden." It was reported that the Afghan Taliban leadership have selected Osama bin Laden as the general supervisor of military operations. "Bin Laden Oversees Taleban's Military Operations." As the war against the Taliban progressed in Afghanistan, it became apparent that even if Osama bin Laden were to be killed, his al-Qaeda network of terrorist operators is now scattered throughout the world, with cells uncovered in Germany, France, Spain and the United States. These lower-level operators will undoubtedly pose a threat to nations in the years to come. See "Al-Qaeda Won't Cease If Bin Laden Is Killed." For a view as to the importance of intelligence in special forces' operations, see Scarborough, "U.S. Special Forces Troops Calling the Shots in Afghanistan." With the subsequent "victory" over the Taliban, it was vital for American intelligence to "max out on the intelligence windfall." Informa-

tion gleaned from the Afghan war pre-empted planned attacks on American interests in Singapore and Yemen. The prisoners taken in the Afghan conflict represent "raw data" and it is the duty of American intelligence and security authorities to exploit these assets. Krauthammer, "The Moral High Ground is a Slippery Slope." It was subsequently reported that the American government missed three opportunities to capture Osama bin Laden. Woodward, "CIA After bin Laden for 4 Years, Report Says."

42. See Cetron, with Davies, "The Future Face of Terrorism"; Handelman, "Security Chiefs Prepare for New Terrorist Tactics."

43. Terrorist links can develop from seemingly the most innocuous situations. The University of South Florida (USF) in Tampa reportedly had ties to a front for Islamic terrorism in 1996. According to one article, a USF committee had ties with Ramadan Abdullah Shallah and the institute called the World of Islam Studies Enterprise (WISE). Apparently, Dr. Shallah, a doctoral graduate from Durham University in the United Kingdom who had taught for two semesters at the USF, was named as the leader of the Islamic Jihad, one of the most violent terrorist groups operating in the Middle East. Shallah replaced the assassinated leader of the Islamic Jihad, Fathi Shikaki. The Islamic Jihad's objective is to replace Israel with an Islamic state and it has carried out numerous suicide bombings as well as various other assaults upon Israeli soldiers and citizens. Reports noted that WISE had a three-year relationship with the USF, sharing library facilities, cosponsoring conferences, training graduate students and exchanging staff. Dr. Shallah represented WISE and reportedly signed for the research institute. Federal authorities believe WISE was used for fund-raising for the Islamic Jihad. In discussions with USF faculty, it was readily apparent that this link with Dr. Shallah had garnered much embarrassment, which was only compounded when USF was given the nickname of "Jihad U." On 29 April 1996, USF was the target of terrorist threats to set off a bomb. Authorities had received a letter threatening to bomb a campus building and kill a female professor. The threat forced the university to hold final exams a week early and saw the imposition of tight security requirements upon the campus. McGonigle, "Florida College Grapples with Islamic Jihad Ties; Group's New Leader Taught at University; Professor Has Denied Running Terrorist Front."

44. Some of the modern technology employed by American special forces was underlined in an article by Dane, "America's Secret Commandos," 25–32, 116.

45. According to a senior U.S. Special Forces staff officer at Special Operations Command at MacDill AFB, Florida, the SF community was most interested in "getting a part of the real action," and after a number of successful ops had become somewhat careless and believed the Somali opposition as not being a particularly capable threat. For an exceptional view of what occurred, see Bowden, *Black Hawk Down: A Story of Modern War.*

46. For an insightful description of the American events leading up to this October 1993 encounter which left eighteen Americans dead and more than seventy badly wounded, and reportedly over 500 Somalis dead and 1,000 wounded, see Bowden, *Black Hawk Down: A Story of Modern War.* See also Fritz Heingen, "The Future of Raids," in Southworth, *Great Raids in History: From Drake to Desert One,* 311–328.

47. It has been reported that the successful Peruvian operation received assistance from the British SAS, and police negotiators from Scotland Yard were also

on-site as well. The latter contribution was confirmed by the British Foreign Office, according to Macko, "Peru Hostage Crisis Comes to a Violent End." One source noted that "the U.S. CIA, British SAS and other advisors contributed input, during which the terrorists were lulled into complacency." See O'Ballance, "A Salutary Terrorist Saga in Peru"; Chu, "Rescue in Lima: A Bold Assault Sends a Message to Terrorists." This article states that some of the technical gadgetry used during the siege was a "part of $40 million worth of sophisticated intelligence equipment that the military bought from the United States shortly after the crisis began." Apparently, some of this listening equipment was hidden in a chess piece, crutches and a Bible provided to the hostages, which subsequently provided vital intelligence. It has also been reported that the Peruvians had trained in the United States. See Knox, "Guerrilla Handed Fujimori Reason to Attack." Although there have been some announcements that the British SAS was not involved, a number of media reports assert that there were British SAS officers on-site advising their Peruvian colleagues. See Lewis, "Hostages Freed in Bloody Raid." The fact that an SAS team had been sent to Lima appears to have been confirmed by the British ambassador to Peru, John Illman, who reportedly advised that "there was no direct British involvement in the rescue." See "Careful Planning of 40-minute Raid." American assistance to the rescue came from a report that the CIA operated an Air Force RG-8A aircraft equipped with "forward-looking infrared photos at night, spotting mines and booby-traps. An RU-38A Twin Condor surveillance plane was also used." See Mickolus, "Peru." In contrast, during the Indian Airlines hijacking in December 1999, the Taliban militia advised that "special commando troops were prepared to storm the Indian Airlines aircraft if the hijackers carried out their threat to kill any more passengers." See Stock, "Commandos Set to Storm Hijacked Jet."

48. "German Troops See Action in War on Terrorism." The article notes that German special forces are fighting alongside their American counterparts in Afghanistan.

49. GROM, the Polish special forces, has had its instructors trained at both Fort Bragg and Hereford. GROM personnel are screened through an arduous selection mirroring the SAS selection program. Apparently, those who passed were then sent to St. Augustin, near Bonn, for advanced training under GSG9.

Bibliography

BOOKS

Adams, James. *The Next World War: Computers Are the Weapons and the Front Line Is Everywhere.* New York: Simon and Schuster, 1998.

———. *Secret Armies.* London: Hutchinson, 1988.

Allon, Yigal. *The Making of Israel's Army.* New York: Bantam Books, 1971.

Aron, Raymond. *Paix et guerre entre les nations.* Paris: Colmann, 1968.

Asprey, Robert B. *War in the Shadows: The Guerrilla in History.* 2 vols. New York: Doubleday, 1975.

Baylis, John, Ken Booth, John Garnett and Phil Williams. *Contemporary Strategy: Theories and Policies.* London: Croom Helm, 1975.

Beals, Carleton. *Great Guerrilla Warriors.* Englewood Cliffs, New Jersey: Prentice-Hall, 1970.

Beckett, Ian F. W., and John Pimlott (eds.). *Armed Forces and Modern Counter-Insurgency.* New York: St. Martin's Press, 1985.

Bell, J. Bowyer. *Assassin, the Theory and Practice of Political Violence.* New York: St. Martin's Press, 1979.

Ben-Porat, Yeshayahu, Eiton Haber and Zeev Schiff. *Entebbe Rescue.* New York: Delacorte Press, 1977.

Betser, Miki, and Robert Rosenberg. *Secret Soldier: The True Life Story of Israel's Greatest Commando.* New York: Atlantic Monthly Press, 1996.

Bodansky, Yossef. *Bin Laden: the Man Who Declared War on America.* Roseville, CA: Prima Publishing, 2001.

Bowden, Mark. *Black Hawk Down: A Story of Modern War.* New York: Atlantic Monthly Press, 1999.

Braver, Richard F., Jr. *Critical Examination of Planning Imperatives Applicable to Hostage Rescue Operations.* Carlisle Barracks, Pennsylvania: U.S. Army War College, 16 April 1984.

Brown, Ashley (ed.). *Strike from the Sky: Israeli Airborne Troops.* New York: Villard Books, 1986.

Burton, Anthony. *Revolutionary Violence.* London: Leo Cooper, 1977.

———. *Urban Terrorism.* London: Leo Cooper, 1975.

Burton, Bob. *Top Secret: A Clandestine Operator's Glossary of Terms.* Boulder, Colorado: Paladin Press, 1986.

Callwell, C. E. *Small Wars: Their Principles and Practice.* Abingdon, England: Purnell Book Service, 1976.

Campbell, Arthur. *Guerillas: A History and Analysis.* London: Arthur Barker, 1967.

Canada. Minister of Supply and Services. *The Report of the Senate Special Committee on Terrorism and the Public Safety,* 1987.

Carver, Michael. *War since 1945.* New York: G. P. Putnam's Sons, 1981.

Charters, David, and Maurice Tugwell. *Armies in Low-Intensity Conflict: A Comparative Study of Institutional Adaptation to New Forms of Warfare.* Ottawa: Department of National Defense Operational Analysis Establishment, Extra-Mural Paper no. 38, December 1985.

Cline, Ray S., and Yonah Alexander. *Terrorism: As State-Sponsored Covert Warfare.* Fairfax, Virginia: Hero Books, 1986.

Clutterbuck, Richard. *The Future of Political Violence, Destabilization, Disorder and Terrorism.* London: Macmillan, 1986.

———. *Guerrillas and Terrorists.* London: Faber and Faber, 1977.

———. *Kidnap, Hijack and Extortion: The Response.* London: Macmillan, 1987.

———. *Living with Terrorism.* London: Faber and Faber, 1975.

Combs, Cindy C. *Terrorism in the Twenty-First Century.* Upper Saddle River, NJ: Prentice Hall, 1997.

Dareff, Hal. *The Story of Vietnam.* New York: Avon Books, 1966.

Davies, Barry. *Assault on LH181: The True Story of Operation Fire Magic.* Rochester, Kent, England: 22 Books, 1994.

———. *SAS Rescue.* London: Sidgwick and Jackson, 1996.

de B. Taillon, J. Paul. *The Evolution of Special Forces in Counter-Terrorism.* Westport, CT: Praeger, 2001.

Deacon, Richard. *The Israeli Secret Service.* London: Hamish Hamilton, 1977.

Debray, Régis. *A Critique of Arms.* Vol. 1. London: Penguin Books, 1977.

Depuy, Trevor N., Curt Johnson, and Grace Hayes. *Dictionary of Military Terms: A Guide to the Language of Warfare and Military Institutions.* New York: H.W. Wilson, 1986.

Dobson, Christopher, and Ronald Payne. *The Dictionary of Espionage.* London: Harrap, 1984.

———. *Terror! The West Fights Back.* London: Papermac, 1982.

Dupuy, Trevor N., Curt Johnson, and Grace P. Hayes. *Dictionary of Military Terms: A Guide to the Language of Warfare and Military Institutions.* New York: H. W. Wilson, 1986.

Elliot-Bateman, Michael (ed.). *The Fourth Dimension of Warfare Volume I: Intelligence, Subversion, Resistance.* New York: Praeger, 1970.

Falkenrath, Richard A., Robert D. Newman, and Bradley A. Thayer. *America's Achilles' Heel: Nuclear, Biological, and Chemical Terrorism and Covert Attack.* Cambridge, MA: MIT Press, 1998.

Foot, M.R.D. *SOE in France: An Account of the Work of the British Special Operations Executive in France 1940–1944.* London: Her Majesty's Stationary Office, 1966.

———. *SOE: An Outline History of the Special Operations Executive, 1940–46.* London: BBC, 1984.

Freedman, Lawrence, Christopher Hill, Adam Roberts, R. J. Vincent, Paul Wilkinson and Philip Windsor. *Terrorism and International Order.* London: Routledge and Kegan Paul, 1986.

Gabriel, Richard. *Operation Peace for Galilee.* New York: Hill and Wang, 1984.

Gal-or, Noemi. *International Cooperation to Suppress Terrorism.* New York: St. Martin's Press, 1985.

Garrett, Richard. *The Raiders: The Elite Strike Forces That Altered the Course of War and History.* New York: Van Nostrand Reinhold, 1980.

Gearty, Conor. *The Future of Terrorism.* London: Phoenix Paperback, 1997.

Geraghty, Tony. *Inside the SAS.* Agincourt, Ontario: Methuen, 1980.

———. *This Is the SAS: A Pictorial History of the Special Air Service Regiment.* London: Arms and Armour Press, 1982.

———. *Who Dares Wins: The Special Air Service, 1950 to the Gulf War.* London: Little, Brown, 1992.

Giap, Vo Nguyen. *People's War, People's Army.* New York: Bantam Books, 1968.

Gutteridge, William (ed.). *The New Terrorism.* London: Mansell, 1986.

Halperin, Morton H. *Contemporary Military Strategy.* London: Faber and Faber, 1972.

Hastings, Max. *YONI: Hero of Entebbe.* New York: Dial Press/James Wade, 1979.

Haycock, Ronald (ed.). *Regular Armies and Insurgency.* London: Croom Helm, 1979.

Herzog, Chaim. *The Arab-Israeli Wars.* Toronto: Methuen, 1982.

Hoffman, Bruce. *Commando Raids: 1946-1983.* The Office of the Undersecretary of Defense for Policy, Rand Note, N-2316-USDP, October 1985.

Infield, Glenn B. *Skorzeny: Hitler's Commando.* New York: Military Heritage Press, 1981.

Jenkins, Brian Michael. *New Modes of Conflict.* Santa Monica, California: Rand Corporation, June 1983.

Joint Special Operations Command. *Special Operations Dominican Republic–Mayaguez–Mogadishu–Kolwezi–Kabul–Iranian Embassy, London.* Centre for Conflict Studies, University of New Brunswick, 1982.

Jonas, George. *Vengeance.* London: William Collins Sons, 1984.

Katz, Samuel M. *The Elite: The True Story Of Israel's Secret Counterterrorist Unit.* Toronto: Simon and Schuster, 1992.

Keegan, John, and Andrew Wheatcroft. *Who's Who in Military History.* London: Weidenfeld and Nicolson, 1976.

Klare, Michael T., and Peter Kornbluh (eds.). *Low-Intensity Warfare.* New York: Pantheon Books, 1988.

Koch, Peter, and Kai Hermann. *Assault at Mogadishu.* London: Corgi Books, 1978.

Kupperman, Robert H., and Darrell M. Trent. *Terrorism: Threat, Reality, Response.* Stanford, California: Hoover Institution Press, 1979.

Ladd, James. *SAS Operations.* London: Robert Hale, 1986.

Lake, Anthony. *6 Nightmares: Real Threats in a Dangerous World and How America Can Meet Them.* Boston: Little, Brown and Co., 2000.

Lang, Walter N. *The World's Elite Forces.* New York: Military Press, 1987.

Laqueur, Walter. *Guerrilla: A Historical and Critical Study.* London: Weidenfeld and Nicolson, 1977.

———. *Terrorism.* London: Abacus-Sphere Books, 1978.

Leonhard, Robert R. *The Principles of War for the Information Age.* Novato, California: Presidio Press, 1998.

Liddell-Hart, B. H. *Strategy.* New York: Signet Books, 1974.

Livingston, Marius H., et al. (eds.). *International Terrorism in the Contemporary World.* Westport, Connecticut: Greenwood Press, 1978.

Livingstone, Neil C. *The War against Terrorism.* Lexington, Massachusetts: Lexington Books, 1982.

Livingstone, Neil C., and Terrell E. Arnold (eds.). *Fighting Back: Winning the War against Terrorism.* Lexington, Massachusetts: Lexington Books, 1986.

Mao Tse-tung. Trans. Samuel B. Griffith. *On Guerrilla Warfare.* New York: Anchor Press/Doubleday, 1978.

Mao Tse-tung, and Che Guevara. *Guerrilla Warfare.* London: Cassell, 1969.

Martin, David C., and John Walcott. *Best Laid Plans: The Inside Story of America's War Against Terrorism.* New York: Harper and Row, 1988.

McFadden, Robert D., Joseph B. Treaster, Maurice Carroll, et al. *No Hiding Place.* New York: Times Books, 1981.

McKnight, Gerald. *The Mind of the Terrorist.* London: Michael Joseph, 1974.

McRaven, William H. *Spec Ops: Case Studies in Special Operations Warfare: Theory and Practices.* Novato, California: Presidio Press, 1995.

Mickolus, Edward F. *Transnational Terrorism: A Chronology of Events, 1968–1979.* Westport, Connecticut: Greenwood Press, 1980.

Morris, James. *Sultan in Oman.* London: Faber and Faber, 1957.

Morris, Jim. *War Story.* New York: Dell Publishing, 1985.

Mountfield, David. *The Partisans: Secret Armies of World War II.* London: Hamlyn, 1979.

Mrazek, James E. *The Fall of Eben Emael.* Novato, California: Presidio Press, 1991.

Netanyahu, Benjamin (ed.). *International Terrorism: Challenge and Response.* Jerusalem, Israel: Jonathan Institute, 1981.

———. *Terrorism: How the West Can Win.* New York: Avon Books, 1986.

Operational Research and Analysis Establishment Report No. R100. *Contemporary International Terrorism and Its Impact on Canada.* Ottawa, 1988.

Osgood, Robert E. *Limited War Revisited.* Boulder, Colorado: Westview Press, 1979.

Osmanczyk, Edmund Jan. *The Encyclopedia of the United Nations and International Agreements.* Philadelphia and London: Taylor and Francis, 1985.

Paget, Julian. *Counter-Insurgency Campaigning.* London: Faber and Faber, 1967.

———. *Last Post: Aden 1964–1967.* London: Faber and Faber, 1969.

Pimlott, John (ed.). *British Military Operations: 1945–1984*. London: Bison Books, 1984.

———. *Guerrilla Warfare*. New York: Military Press, 1985.

Quarrie, Bruce. *The World's Elite Forces*. London: Octopus Books, 1985.

Rapoport, David C. *Assassination & Terrorism*. Toronto: Canadian Broadcasting Corporation, 1971.

Reeve, Simon. *One Day in September: The Story of the 1972 Munich Olympics Massacre*. London: Faber and Faber, 2000.

Ropp, Theodore. *War in the Modern World*. New York: Collier Books, 1973.

Royal College of Defence Studies. *An Examination of the Characteristics of International Terrorism and the Case for an Improved Response*. 1986 Course.

Royle, Trevor. *Orde Wingate: Irregular Soldier*. London: Weidenfeld and Nicolson, 1995.

Schackley, Theodore. *The Third Option*. New York: Reader's Digest Press, McGraw-Hill Books, 1981.

Schiff, Zeev. *A History of the Israeli Army (1870–1974)*. San Francisco, California: Straight Arrow Books, 1974.

Shafritz, Jay M., Todd J. A. Shafriz and David B. Robertson. *The Facts on File Dictionary of Military Science*. New York: Facts on File, 1985.

Sharon, Ariel, with David Chanoff. *Warrior: The Autobiography of Ariel Sharon*. New York: Simon and Schuster, 1990.

Southworth, Samuel A. *Great Raids in History: From Drake to Desert One*. New York: Sarpedon, 1997.

Sterling, Claire. *The Terror Network: The Secret War of International Terrorism*. New York: Holt, Rinehart, and Winston, Reader's Digest Press, 1981.

Stetler, Russell (ed.). *The Military Art of People's War: Selected Writings of General Vo Nguyen Giap*. New York: Monthly Review Press, 1970.

Stevenson, William. *90 Minutes at Entebbe*. New York: Bantam Books, 1976.

Sully, François. *Age of the Guerrilla*. New York: Avon, 1970.

Taber, Robert. *The War of the Flea: Guerrilla Warfare Theory and Practice*. St. Albans, Frogmore, Herts, Great Britain: Paladin, 1977.

Thayer, Charles W. *Guerrilla*. Toronto: New American Library of Canada, 1965.

Thompson, Leroy. *The Illustrated History of the U.S. Army Special Forces*. Secaucus, New Jersey: Citadel Press, 1988.

———. *Ragged War: The Story of Unconventional Warfare*. London: Arms and Armour, 1994.

———. *The Rescuers: The World's Top Anti-Terrorist Units*. Boulder, Colorado: Paladin Press, 1986.

Tompkins, Thomas C. *Military Countermeasures to Terrorism in the 1980's*. Rand Corporation, August 1984.

Tophoven, Rolf. *GSG9: German Response to Terrorism*. Koblenz, Germany: Bernard and Graefe Verlag, 1984.

United States. Army Command and General Staff College. *Terrorism Counteraction*. FC 100-37. Fort Leavenworth, 1984.

United States. Defense Intelligence Agency. Symposium on International Terrorism. Washington, D.C., 1985.

United States. Defense Nuclear Agency. *Proceedings of the 10th Annual Symposium* on the Role of Behavorial Science in Physical Security; *Outhinking the Ter-rorist: An International Challenge, 23 and 24 April 1985 Springfield, Vir-ginia.* Washington D.C., 1985.

United States. Department of Army. *Counterguerrilla Operations.* FM90-8. Wash-ington, D.C., 1986.

———. Counterintelligence Production Division. *Intelligence: Its Role in Counter-terrorism (U).* U.S. Army Intelligence and Threat Analysis Centre, CISR-07-81, October 1981.

United States. Department of Defense. *Dictionary of Military and Associated Terms.* Joint Chiefs of Staff, Washington, D.C., 1 June 1967.

United States. Department of State. *Patterns of Global Terrorism: 1987.* August 1988.

———. *Patterns of Global Terrorism: 1990.* April 1991.

———. *Patterns of Global Terrorism: 1998.* April 1999.

———. *Patterns of Global Terrorism: 1999.* April 2000.

———. *Patterns of Global Terrorism: 2000.* April 2001.

———. "U.S. Deposits Ratification of Hijacking Convention." *Department of State Bulletin 65,* no. 1684 (4 October 1971).

United States. Vice President's Task Force on Combating Terrorism. *Public Report of the Vice President's Task Force on Combatting Terrorism.* Washington, D.C., February 1986.

University of New Brunswick, Center for Conflict Studies. *Special Operations: Military Lessons from Six Selected Case Studies.* Fredericton, New Brunswick: Center for Conflict Studies, 1982.

von der Heydte, Friedrich August. *Modern Irregular Warfare: In Defense Policy and as a Military Phenomenon.* New York: New Benjamin Franklin House, 1986.

Walmer, Max. *An Illustrated Guide to Modern Elite Forces.* London: Salamander Books, 1984.

Wardlaw, Grant. *Political Terrorism: Theory, Tactics, and Counter-Measures.* Cambridge: Cambridge University Press, 1982.

Warner, Philip. *The Secret Forces of World War II.* London: Granada, 1985.

Wilkinson, Paul. *Political Terrorism.* London: Macmillan, 1974.

———. *Terrorism and the Liberal State.* (1st ed.). London: Macmillan, 1979.

——— (ed.). *British Perspectives on Terrorism.* London: George Allen and Unwin, 1981.

Wilkinson, Paul, and Alasdair M. Stewart (eds.). *Contemporary Research on Ter-rorism.* Aberdeen: University Press, 1987.

PERIODICALS

"A Culture of Hate." *Jerusalem Post* (19 August 2001).

"Air Transport: IFALPA Mounts Anti-Hijack Drive." *Aviation Week and Space Technology* (8 September 1969), 22–24.

"Airlines, Government Accelerate Efforts at Hijacking Prevention." *Aviation Week and Space Technology* (27 January 1969), 33.

"Airlines vs. Skyjackers." *Newsweek* (22 July 1968), 13.

Alexander, David. "The Force Options: Using an Often Overlooked Weapon in the Counterterrorism Arsenal." *Counterterrorism and Security* (Summer 1995).

"Algeria: Skyway Robbery." *Time* (2 August 1968), 52.

Alvey, Ruth. "Russian Hackers for Hire: The Rise of the E-mercenary." *Jane's Intelligence Review* (July 2001), 52–53.

Anderson, R. N. "Search Operations in Palestine: The Problem of the Soldier." *The Army Quarterly* 55 (October 1947/January 1948), 201–208.

Andrade, Dale. *Counterterrorism and Security Report*. 5, no. 3.

"Anti-terrorist Expert Signs Saudi Contract." *Jane's Defence Weekly* (9 April 1988), 658.

"The Anti-Terrorist Intervention Role in the U.K." *Intersec* (January 1999).

Arostequi, Martin C. "Counter-Hijacking and the Killing Village." *Journal of Counterterrorism and Security Intelligence* (Summer 1997).

Arquilla, John and David Ronfeldt, "Fighting the Network War." *Wired* (December 2001), 148–151.

"Aviation: The Skyjackers." *Time* (26 July 1968), 29–30.

Babievsky, Kirill K. "Chemical and Biological Terrorism." *Low Intensity Conflict and Law Enforcement* (Autumn 1997), 167–184.

Barr Smith, Robert. "Silent Blitzkrieg: The Fall of Eben Email." *WWII History* (March 2002), 72–90.

Bayev, A. A. "Organizing and Conducting a Special Operation to Free Hostages." *Low Intensity Conflict and Law Enforcement* (Autumn 1997), 129–140.

Benjamin, Milton R. "The Fallout from Entebbe." *Newsweek* (19 July 1976), 41.

Benjamin, Milton R., and Paul Martin. "A Detour to Dubai." *Newsweek* (24 October 1977), 62.

Bergen, Peter. "Terrorism's Dark Master." *Vanity Fair* (December 2001), 251–328.

Betts, Richard K. "Fixing Intelligence." *Foreign Affairs* (January/February 2002), 43–59.

"Bio-Terrorism Vaccine." *Jane's Intelligence Review* (October 2000), 3.

"Biothreats: Just the Facts: II." *Scientific American,* 285, no. 6 (December 2001), 23.

Blanche, Ed. "Arabs Likely to Aid U.S. Efforts to Track Down Terrorists." *Jane's Intelligence Review* (October 2001), 3.

———. "Arab Nations Intensify Plans to Fight Terrorism." *Jane's Defence Review* (14 January 1998).

———. "Israeli Intelligence Agencies under Fire." *Jane's Intelligence Review* (January 1998).

Blanford, Nicholas. "Hizbullah Attacks Force Israel to Take a Hard Look at Lebanon." *Jane's Intelligence Review* (April 1999).

Bolz, F.A. "Police Works: Intelligence Requirements in Hostage Situations." *Counterterrorism and Security* (Summer 1995).

Bremer, L. Paul. "Counterterrorism Strategies and Programs." *Terrorism* 10, no. 4 (1987), 337–344.

Burgess, William H. "Special Operations Forces and the Challenge of Transnational Terrorism." *Military Intelligence* (April–June 1986), 8–15.

Calabresi, Massimo, and Romesh Ratnesar. "Can We Stop the Next Attack?" *Time* (11 March 2002), 16–26.

Carr, Caleb. "Terrorism as Warfare: The Lessons of Military History." *World Policy Journal* (Winter 1996).

Carroll, Raymond. "How the Israelis Pulled it Off." *Newsweek* (19 July 1976), 42–46.

"Cash for Carnage: Funding the Modern Terrorist." *Jane's Intelligence Review* (May 1995).

Cetron, Marvin J., with Owen Davies. "The Future Face of Terrorism." *The Futurist* (November–December 1994).

Chapman, Robert D. "Reflections on Terrorism: A Sideline View." *International Journal of Intelligence and Counterintelligence* (Summer 1999).

Charters, David A. "Eyes of the Underground: Jewish Insurgent Intelligence in Palestine, 1945–47." *Intelligence and National Security* (Winter 1998), 163–177.

———. "Special Operations in Counter-Insurgency: The Farran Case, Palestine 1947." *RUSI Journal* (June 1979), 56–61.

Chalk, Peter. "U.S. Environmental Groups and 'Leaderless Resistance.'" *Jane's Intelligence Review* (July 2001), 12–15.

Chaze, William L., et al. "What Price for the Hostages?" *U.S. News and World Report* (8 July 1985), 20–23.

"Chemical, Biological, Radiological and Nuclear (CBRN) Terrorism." *Report 2000/02* (18 December 1999).

Chu, Showwei. "Rescue in Lima: A Bold Assault Sends a Message to Terrorists." *Maclean's* (5 May 1997).

Church, George J. "Targeting Gaddafi." *Time* (21 April 1986), 22–31.

Chyba, Christopher F. "Biological Terrorism and Public Health." *Survival* 43, no. 1 (Spring 2001), 93–106.

Cohen, Rich. "Stealth Warriors." *Vanity Fair* (December 2001), 284–314.

"Command Posts Manned by Key Braniff Officials During Hijack." *Aviation Week and Space Technology* (12 July 1971), 20.

"Conference Exchanges Anti-Hijacking Data." *Aviation Week and Space Technology* (18 January 1971), 19.

"The Consequences of Selective Killing." *Economist* (4 August 2001).

Cooperman, Alan. "Terror Strikes Again." *U.S. News and World Report* (17 August 1998), 12.

Cory, Peter, Brian Duffy, Kenneth T. Walsh and Charles Fenyvesi. "Where Spies Really Matter." *U.S. News and World Report* (28 August–4 September 1989), 24–25.

"Costa Rica: Terrorizing Terrorists." *Time* (27 December 1971), 23–24.

Dane, Abe. "America's Secret Commandos." *Popular Mechanics* (September 1992), 25–32, 116.

Davis, Anthony. "Riding the Wave of Illegal Immigrants." *Jane's Intelligence Review* (January 2001), 54–55.

"Death to Hijackers." *Newsweek* (22 December 1969), 50.

Dening, B. C. "Modern Problems of Guerilla Warfare." *Army Quarterly*, 13 (October 1926 and January 1927), 347–354.

Deutch, John, and Jeffrey H. Smith. "Smarter Intelligence." *Foreign Policy* (January/February 2002), 64–69.

Devotie, Michael W. "Unconventional Warfare: A Viable Option for the Future." *Special Warfare* (Spring 1997), 30–32.

De Zengotita, Thomas. "The Numbing of the American Mind." *Harper's* (April 2002), 33–40.

Doran, Michael Scott. "Somebody Else's Civil War." *Foreign Affairs* (January/February 2002), 22–42.

Doty, Laurence. "Air Crimes Convention Supported Heavily." *Aviation Week and Space Technology* (18 November 1968), 60.

"The Early History of Contagion." *Scientific American,* 285, no. 6 (December 2001), 21.

"El Al Stresses Terrorist Security, Advises Other Airlines in Tel Aviv." *Aviation Week and Space Technology* (13 September 1971), 26.

Eshel, David. "Israel Reviews Profile of Suicide Bombers." *Jane's Intelligence Review* (November 2001), 20–21.

Fox, C. William Jr. "Phantom Warriors: Disease as a Threat to U.S. National Security." *Parameters* (Winter 1997–1998), 121–136.

Garrett, Laurie. "The Nightmare of Bioterrorism." *Foreign Affairs* 80, no. 1 (January/February 2001), 76–89.

———. "Unprepared for the Worst." *Vanity Fair* (December 2001), 194–214.

Gazit, Shlomo. "Risk, Glory, and the Rescue Operation." *International Security* 6, no. 1 (Summer 1981), 111–135.

Gelman, David, and Rich Thomas. "Banality and Terror." *Newsweek* (6 January 1986), 60.

Gerecht, Reuel Marc. "The Counterterrorist Myth." *Atlantic Monthly* (July/August 2001).

Gerecht, Reuel Marc. "The Gospel According to Osama bin Laden." *Atlantic Monthly* (January 2002), 46–48.

Goldberg, Jeffrey. "The Martyr Strategy." *New Yorker* (9 July 2001), 34–39.

Gotowicki, Stephen H. "Confronting Terrorism: New War Form or Mission Impossible?" *Military Review* (May–June 1997).

Gourley, Scott R. "Boosting the Optempo." *Jane's Defence Weekly* (14 July 1999), 25–28.

Gray, Colin S. "Handfuls of Heroes on Desperate Ventures: When Do Special Operations Succeed?" *Parameters* (Spring 1999), 2–24.

Gunaratna, Rohan. "Blowback." *Jane's Intelligence Review* (August 2001), 42–45.

———. "Terror from the Sky." *Jane's Intelligence Review* (October 2001), 6–9.

———. "Terrorist Trends Suggest Shift of Focus to National Activities." *Jane's Intelligence Review* (June 2001), 47–49.

———. "Transnational Threats in the Post-Cold War Era." *Jane's Intelligence Review* (January 2001), 46–50.

Hassan, Nasra. "An Arsenal of Believers." *New Yorker* (19 November 2001), 36–41.

"Hijack Detector Tested by FAA." *Aviation Week and Space Technology* (22 September 1969), 53.

"The Hijack War." *Newsweek* (21 September 1970), 20–21.

Hirschkorn, Phil. "Convictions Mark First Step in Breaking up Al-Qaeda Network." *Jane's Intelligence Review* (August 2001), 46–51.

"A History of Assassination." *Maclean's* (13 October 1997).

Hoffman, Bruce. "Creatures of the Cold War: The JRA." *Jane's Intelligence Review* (2 February 1997).

———. "Intelligence and Terrorism: Emerging Threats and New Security Challenges in the Post-Cold War Era." *Intelligence and National Security* (April 1996), 207–223.

Homer-Dixon, Thomas. "The Rise of Complex Terrorism." *Foreign Policy* (January/February 2002), 52–62.

Hotz, Robert. "More on Hijacking." *Aviation Week and Space Technology* (10 November 1969), 11.

Hunter, Thomas. "Bomb School: International Terrorist Training Camps." *Jane's Intelligence Review* (March 1997).

———. "Manportable SAMs: The Airline Anathema." *Jane's Intelligence Review* (October 1996).

Hutchinson, M. C. "The Concept of Revolutionary Terrorism." *Journal of Conflict Resolution* 6, no. 3, (1973), 383–96.

"IFALPA Mounts Anti-Hijack Drive." *Aviation Week and Space Technology* (8 September 1969), 22–24.

"In the Mind of the Terrorist." *Economist* (2 March 1996).

"INLA: The Deadly Hand of Irish Republicanism." *Jane's Intelligence Review* (2 February 1997).

"Intelligence Briefs." *Intersec* (March 1999).

"Intelligence Monitor, U.S.A. Today." *Jane's Intelligence Review* (August 1998).

Isby, David C. "Special Operations Forces Response." *Military Intelligence* (January–March 1985), 24–27.

"Israel Refining Hostage Rescue Tactics." *Aviation Week and Space Technology* (27 September 1976), 17.

"Israeli Commando C-130 Raid Frees 115." *Aviation Week and Space Technology* (12 July 1976), 15–16.

Jacobs, Stanley S. "The Nuclear Threat as a Terrorist Option." *Terrorism and Political Violence* (Winter 1998), 149–163.

Kaplan, David E. "Terrorism's Next Move: Nerve Gas and Germs Are the New Weapons of Choice." *U.S. News and World Report* (17 November 1997).

Kaplan, Robert D. "Looking the World in the Eye." *Atlantic Monthly* (December 2001), 68–82.

Karon, Tony. "Bin Laden Rides Again: Myth vs. Reality." *Time Magazine* (20 June 2001).

Katz, Samuel M. "The Embattled Legend of GSG-9: Fighting Terrorism in the New Germany." *Special Ops: Journal of the Elite Force and Swat Units* 14 (2001), 3–18.

———. "GSG-9: Think like a Terrorist, Fight like a Commando." *Soldier of Fortune* (December 1997).

———. "GROM: The Advent of Polish Thunder." *Jane's Intelligence Review* (August 1998).

———. "Incident at Ansariya." *Jane's Intelligence Review* (January 1998), 24–28.

Kelly, Robert J. "Curses and Dreams: Ernesto 'Che' Guevara, the Implacable Revolutionary." *Low Intensity Conflict and Law Enforcement* (Autumn 1997), 1–14.

Klepak, H. P. "Colombia: Why Doesn't the War End?" *Jane's Intelligence Review* (June 2000), 41–45.

Kolcum, Edward H. "Israeli Defense Minister Explains Tactics." *Aviation Week and Space Technology* (2 August 1976), 25.

Krause, Lincoln B. "Insurgent Intelligence: The Guerrilla Grapevine." *International Journal of Intelligence and Counterintelligence* (Fall 1996), 291–311.

Krauthammer, Charles. "The Case for Profiling." *Time* (18 March 2002), 60.

Krauthammer, Charles. "In Defense of 'Assassination.'" *Time* (27 August 2001), 20.

Latter, Richard. "After 11 September, CBW Threat Looms." *Jane's Intelligence Review* (November 2001), 30–31.

Leader, Stefan. "Osama bin Laden and the Terrorist Search for WMD." *Jane's Intelligence Review* (June 1999).

Lelyveld, Joseph. "All Suicide Bombers Are Not Alike." *New York Times Magazine* (28 October 2001), 48–53, 62, 78–79.

Livingstone, Neil C. "Fighting Terrorism and Dirty Little Wars." *Air University Review* 35, no. 3 (March-April 1984), 4–16.

Lungu, Angela Maria. "Irregular Warfare and the Internet: The Case of the Zapatista Revolution." *Strategic Review* (Spring 2001), 49–52.

MacKenzie, Alastair. "GIGN—The French Approach to Counter-Terrorism." *Intersec* 5, no. 11/12 (November–December 1995), 438–439.

Maguire, Keith. "The Intelligence War in Northern Ireland." *International Journal of Intelligence and Counterintelligence* 4, no. 2 (Summer 1990), 145–165.

Manwaring, Max G. "Italian Terrorism, 1968–1982: Strategic Lessons That Should Have Been Learned." *Low Intensity Conflict and Law Enforcement* (Summer 1998), 121–135.

Maoz, "The Decision to Raid Entebbe: Decision Analysis Applied to Crisis Behavior." *Journal of Conflict Resolution*, 25, no. 4 (December 1981), 677–707.

Marks, Tom. "Slip, Stumble, and Fall: U.S. Gears-Up for War in Colombia." *Soldier of Fortune* (April 2000), 54–57.

McAllister, J.F.O. "Should He Just Be Killed? As Tempting as It May Be, Assassination Is a Bad Idea." *Time* (24 November 1997).

McGeorge, Harvey J. "Plan Carefully, Rehearse Thoroughly, Execute Violently: The Tactical Response to Hostage Situations." *World Affairs*. 146, no. 1 (Summer 1983), 59–63.

"The McKenzie Affair." *Africa Magazine* (July 1978).

Meilinger, Phillip S. "Force Divider." *Foreign Policy* (January/February 2002), 76–77.

Meys, Eitan. "Counter-Terrorist Intervention Units." *Intersec* (August 1998).

Mickolus, Edward F. "Peru." *Iterate* (17 December 1996).

"Mideast: Coup in the Sky." *Newsweek* (5 August 1968), 41–42.

Musser, George. "Better Killing Through Chemistry." *Scientific American*, 285, no. 6 (December 2001), 20–21.

Nordland, Rod, et al., "A Sneak Attack." *Newsweek* (23 October 2000), 27–29.

———. "Were the Deals Worth It?" *Newsweek* (16 December 1991), 38.

O'Ballance, Edgar. "Osama Bin Laden and His al-Qaida Organization." *Intersec* (February 1999).

————. "A Salutary Terrorist Saga in Peru." *Intersec* (May 1997).

————. "Terrorism & Intelligence." *Intersec* (12 November 1996).

Ofri, Arie. "Intelligence and Counterterrorism." *Orbis: A Journal of World Affairs* 28, no. 1 (Spring 1984), 41–52.

Olds, Michael A., and Christopher M. Grande. "When Minutes Can Mean a Lifetime: Medical Support of Tactical Operations." *Counterterrorism and Security* (Summer 1995).

"Overseas: Guards, Detectors, Searches." *U.S. News and World Report* (21 September 1970), 19.

Perl, Raphael F. "Terrorism, the Media, and the Twenty-first Century: Perspectives, Trends, and Options for Policy Makers." *Low Intensity Conflict and Law Enforcement* (Autumn 1997), 93–102.

Perry, William J. "Preparing for the Next Attack." *Foreign Affairs* (November/December 2001), 31–45.

"Pilots Spur Anti-Hijacking Drive." *Aviation Week and Space Technology* (18 January 1971), 19.

Powell, Stewart M., et al. "If Fanatics Strike the U.S." *U.S. News and World Report* (8 July 1985), 28–29.

"The Problems with Retaliation: Four ex-CIA Chiefs Weigh the Options for Countering Terrorism." *Time* (8 July 1985).

"Profile of a Terrorist." *Newsweek* (13 January 1997).

"Progress in War on Skyjackers." *U.S. News and World Report* (9 August 1971), 25.

"Protecting Diplomats Increasingly Risky, Complex." *USA Today* (20 December 1996).

Prunckun, Henry W., Jr., and Philip B. Mohr. "Military Deterrence of International Terrorism: An Evaluation of Operation El Dorado Canyon." *Studies in Conflict and Terrorism* 20, no. 3 (1997), 267–280.

Purver, Ron. "The Threat of Chemical/Biological Terrorism." *Commentary,* no. 60 (August 1995).

Ratnessar, Romesh. "Sneak Attack: a Terrorist Bombing in Yemen 17 U.S. Sailors and Raises Questions about America's Vulnerability." *Time* (23 October 2000).

Rauf, Tariq. "Future Trends in CBRN Terrorism to 2010." *Roundtable on the 'New Face' of Terrorism.* DFAIT, Ottawa (26 October 2001).

Rees, Matt. "Barak's Special Forces: His Advisers Are Former Soldiers Who Know How to Wage War. But Are They Fit to Fight for Peace?" *Newsweek* (16 August 1999).

"Remarks by Colonel Ulrich K. Wegener, Commander, 9th Border Guard Group, Special, Federal Republic of Germany." *Proceedings of FBI International Symposium on Terrorism* (6–8 July 1978).

"Rescue at Entebbe: How the Israelis Did It." *Reader's Digest* (October 1976), 44–50.

Rhee, Will. "Comparing U.S. Operations Kingpin (1970) and Eagle Claw (1980)." *International Journal of Intelligence and Counterintelligence* 6, no. 4 (Winter 1993), 489–506.

"The Rise of World Terrorism." *U.S. News and World Report* (8 July 1985), 27.

Ropelewski, Robert R. "Commandos Thwart Hijackers." *Aviation Week and Space Technology* (24 October 1977), 14–16.

Rosenau, William. "Aum Shinrikyo's Biological Weapons Program: Why Did it Fail?" *Studies in Conflict and Terrorism* 24 (July/August 2001), 289–301.

Roule, Trifin J., Jeremy Kinsell, and Brian Joyce, "Investigators Seek to Break up Al-Qaeda's Financial Structure." *Jane's Intelligence Review* (November 2001), 8–11.

"Russia: Border Units Hold Anti-Terrorist Drills with South Koreans." *FBIS Report 138046* (30 June 1997).

Salisburg, Steve. "Guatemalan Human-Rights Report Opens Old Wounds." *Jane's Intelligence Review* (May 1999).

"Saudi to Set up Elite Anti-Terrorist Squad." *Jane's Defence Weekly* (29 November 1986), 1255.

"Save the Hostages!: French Special Forces in Action." *Raids* (October 1992).

"The Search for a Way to Stop 'Skyjacking.'" *U.S. News and World Report* (30 December 1968), 34.

"Second Wind for Moscow's Enemies." *Intelligence Newsletter,* no. 387 (27 July 2000).

"Security and Civilian Airports." *Intersec* 6 (9 September 1996).

"Skyjacking: 'A Calculated Risk.'" *Newsweek* (2 August 1971), 24.

"Skyjacking: The Deadly Dilemma." *Newsweek* (1 November 1971), 21.

"Skyjacking: Death at the Terminal." *Time* (2 August 1971), 18.

"Skyjacking: Holding Pattern." *Newsweek* (17 February 1969), 34–39.

"Skyjacking: Take Me Along." *Newsweek* (8 November 1971), 47–48.

Slone, Michelle. "Responses to Media Coverage of Terrorism." *Journal of Conflict Resolution* 44, no. 4 (August 2000), 508–522.

Smith, G. Davidson (Tim). "Single Issue Terrorism." *Commentary,* no. 74 (Winter 1998).

Smith. "The Terrorists and Crime Bosses Behind the Fake Passport Trade." *Jane's Intelligence Review* (July 2001), 42–44.

Smith, William E., et al. "Massacre in Malta." *Time* (9 December 1985), 24–26.

Sprinzak, Ehud. "The Lone Gunmen." *Foreign Policy* (November/December 2001), 72–73.

———. "Rational Fanatics." *Foreign Policy* (September/October 2000), 66–73.

"Spy in Hack's Clothing." *Intelligence Newsletter* (24 June 1999).

St. John, Peter. "Analysis and Response of a Decade of Terrorism." *International Perspectives* (September/October 1981), 2–5.

"State of Insecurity: Sri Lanka and the War That Lost Its Way." *Jane's Intelligence Review* (May 1999).

Steele, Richard and James Pringle. "Uganda: Amin vs. the World." *Newsweek* (9 August 1976), 35–36.

Stevens, Mark and Milan J. Kubic. "The Odd Couple." *Newsweek* (26 July 1976), 52.

Summers, Harry G., Jr. "A Review Essay, 'Delta Force: America's Counterterrorist Unit and the Mission to Rescue the Hostages in Iran.'" *Military Review* (November 1983), 21–27.

Suter, Keith. "What Is Terrorism?" *British Army Review,* no. 57 (December 1977), 66–72.

Tanner, Henry. "U.S. Woman Says Ruse Saved the Hostages." *New York Times* (20 October 1977).

"Terror and Triumph at Mogadishu." *Time* (31 October 1977), 28–30.

"Terror Attacks on Air Travel—What Can Be Done." *U.S. News and World Report* (21 September 1970), 17–19.

"Terrorism: Fewer Incidents, Higher Casualties." *Jane's Defence Review* (7 May 1997).

"'Terrorists Stepping up Operations,' Says U.S. Report." *Jane's Defence Weekly* (13 May 1998).

"This Week: Special Delivery: Does This Package Contain Anthrax?" *Saturday Night* (5 May 2001) 21.

Tremayne, Penelope. "Guevara through the Looking Glass: A View of the Dhofar War." *RUSI Journal* (September 1974), 39–43.

"Trends in Terrorism." *Perspectives.* Report, no. 2000/01 (18 December 1999).

"USAF Special Mission Aircraft in Close-Up." *Jane's Defence Weekly* (19 August 1989), 306.

Venter, Al J. "Biological Warfare: The Poor Man's Atomic Bomb." *Jane's Intelligence Review* (March 1999), 42–47.

———. "Spectre of Biowar Remains: Al J. Venter Analyses the Frightening Facts Revealed by Ken Alibek, the Most Senior Defector from the Former USSR's Biological Warfare Programme." *Jane's Defence Weekly* (28 April 1999), 22–23.

Vest, Jason. "Fourth-Generation Warfare." *Atlantic Monthly* (December 2001), 48–50.

Wallace, Bruce. "The Fear Factor, Governments Grapple with a New Anonymous Style of Terror." *Maclean's* (12 August 1996), 27.

"Washington Whispers." *U.S. News and World Report* (28 September 1970), 8.

Watanabe, Manabu. "Religion and Violence in Japan Today: A Chronological and Doctrinal Analysis of the Aum Shinrikyo." *Terrorism and Political Violence* (Winter 1998), 80–100.

Watkins, Harold D. "Air Transport: Federal Action in Hijackings Urged." *Aviation Week and Space Technology* (2 December 1968), 24–25.

Wedgwood, Ruth, "The Law at War: How Osama Slipped Away." *The National Interest,* no. 66 (Winter 2001/2002), 69–75.

Weinberger, Casper W. "When Can We Target the Leaders?" *Strategic Review* (Spring 2001), 21–24.

"What Can Be Done About Skyjacking." *Time* (31 January 1969), 19–20.

"When Armed Guards Ride Your Plane." *U.S. News and World Report* (28 September 1970), 22–23.

Whitaker, Mark. et al. "Ten Ways to Fight Terrorism." *Newsweek* (1 July 1985), 26–29.

"White House Panel Warns of Infowarfare Threats, Computer Terrorism." *National Security Institute* (December 1997).

White, Jeffrey B. "Irregular Warfare: A Different Kind of Threat." *American Intelligence Journal* 17 (1996), 57–63.

Whitelaw, Kevin. "Terrorists on the Web: Electronic 'Safe Haven.'" *U.S. News and World Report* (22 June 1998).

Wilkinson, Paul. "The Role of the Military in Combatting Terrorism." *Terrorism and Political Violence* 8, no. 3 (Autumn 1996), 7–8.

———. "Terrorism: Motivations and Causes." *Commentary,* no. 43 (January 1995).

Willenson, Kim, with Nicholas Proffitt. "The Tan Berets." *Newsweek* (24 May 1976), 47.

Wilson. "Toward a Model of Terrorist Behavior in Hostage-Taking Incidents." *Journal of Conflict Resolution* 44, no. 4 (August 2000), 403–424.

Wilson, Jim. "Electromagnetic Pulse Bomb: It's Called the E-Bomb." *Popular Mechanics* (September 2001), 51–53.

NEWS

Abd-al-Salam, Mahmud. "Sources Cited on Bin-Ladin's Possession of 'A Biological or Chemical Weapon.'" *London Al-Majallah* (5–11 August 2001). Translated in FBIS.

Abraham, Carolyn. "The 'Poor Man's Nukes.'" *Globe and Mail* (22 September 2001).

Abreu, Elinor. "Tech-Security Survey—Insiders Are Main Computer Security Threat." *Reuters* (19 June 2001).

Adams, David, and Damian Whitworth, "Clinton Exhorts Colombia to Join War on Drugs." *London Times* (31 July 2000).

Adams, James."Anti-terror Squads Face Tough Challenge." *Montreal Gazette* (20 April 1988).

Adams, Paul. "Young, Keen and Ripe for Recruitment." *Globe and Mail* (29 December 2001).

"AFP Reports Japanese Sect Aum Conducted 'Trial Run of Anthrax Weapon.'" *Hong Kong Agence France Presse* (29 August 2001). In FBIS.

"Airlines Begin Installing Steel Bars, Locks on Doors to Restrict Access to Cockpit." *National Post* (3 October 2001).

Akin, David. "Canada's Computer Security Loopholes Called Threat to U.S.: Branch Office 'Back Door:' Teens, Foreign States Represent Threat Conference Told." *National Post* (30 October 2000).

Aldinger, Charles. "Anti-terrorism Training Recommended for U.S. Troops." *Reuters* (9 January 2001).

al-Khatib, Majid. "German Intelligence: Fundamentalists Are Preparing New Terror Campaign in the West." *Al-Sharq al-Awsat* (31 May 1999). Translated in FBIS.

"Al-Qaeda Won't Cease If Bin Laden Is Killed." *Ottawa Citizen* (19 November 2001).

Amr, Wafa. "Militants Say Israeli Wrongs Drive Suicide Bombers." *Reuters* (21 August 2001).

Anderson, Bruce. "Is This the Way bin Laden Escaped?" *National Post* (16 February 2002).

"Antiguerrilla Squad Reported at Airfield." *New York Times* (18 October 1977).

"Anti-Tank Projectile Hit London Spy HQ." *Toronto Star* (23 September 2000).

"Anti-Terrorist Teams at Philippine Airports on Red Alert." *Philippine Star* (18 August 1999).

Apple, R. W., Jr. "Bush Says Act of Terrorism Won't Change U.S. Policies." *New York Times* (27 October 1983).

Appleson, Gail. "Bin Laden Supporter Tells of Order on Americans." *Reuters* (6 February 2001).

"Arab Nations Urged to Combat Terrorism." *Globe and Mail* (30 July 1996).

"Arafat Warns of Strife: PLO Chief Invokes Spectre of Hijacking." *Globe and Mail* (28 May 1991).

"Arens Says Syrians Bombed Marines' Building in Lebanon." *New York Times* (31 October 1983).

"Armed Mounties Now on Many Flights." *Ottawa Citizen* (29 January 2002).

"Army Set to Join Battle on Crime." *Sunday Times* (2 September 1997).

"Australians Warn of Computer Terrorism." *Ottawa Citizen* (17 February 1998).

"Axworthy Says 'Give In' If It Saves Lives." *National Post* (29 December 1999).

Azulay-Katz, Orly and Amit Eytan. "Russian Missiles Sold to Iran Might Reach Hizballah, Endanger IDF Planes 'Know-How' to Iran to Continue." *FBIS* (24 November 2000).

Bailey, Ian. "Hunt for Air India Bombs Has Cost about $26 Million." *Canadian Press* (CP) (11 March 1999).

———. "British SAS Soldier Reported Lost in Kosovo." *Reuters* (5 May 1999).

———. "Two B.C. Men Charged in Bombing that Killed 329." *National Post* (28 October 2000).

Bamber, David. "British Troops Bid Farewell to Belfast." *Telegraph* (13 September 1998).

———. "Police Foil Plot to Poison England's Water Supply: Irish Terrorists Threaten to Conduct 'Campaign of Chemical Warfare.'" *Ottawa Citizen* (11 July 1999).

Bamber, David and Mike Blanchfield, "Bin Laden Takes Credit for Sept. 11." *Ottawa Citizen* (11 November 2001).

Barr, Cameron W. "The World of a Suicide Bomber." *Edmonton Journal* (18 August 2001).

Baxter, James. "Canada to Comply with U.S. in New Airline Security Act." *Ottawa Citizen* (5 January 2002).

Beaudin, Monique. "Terrorists Could Try to Poison Our Food: Sabotage Gets Easier Symposium Is Told to Be Set for Attacks." *Montreal Gazette* (11 August 1999).

Beeston, Richard. "Israel on Alert for More Female Suicide Bombers." *Ottawa Citizen* (29 January 2002).

Bell, Stewart. "Better Spies Needed Overseas—Senator: Law Agency Called For: Canada Now Relies on Allies for Foreign Intelligence." *National Post* (14 June 1999).

———. "CSIS Works with 'Unsavoury' Foreign Agencies: Watchdog." *National Post* (27 December 1999).

———. "Mideast Terrorists Run Toronto Web Site." *National Post* (14 August 2001).

———. "Passport Office Did Little Checking, Ressam Trial Told." *National Post* (15 March 2001).

———. "Ressam Convicted of Terrorism." *National Post* (7 April 2001).

———. "Sri Lankan Terrorist Group Agrees to Peace." *National Post* (23 February 2002).

———. "Web Site Used to Recruit Terrorists Moves to U.S." *National Post* (24 August 2001).

Bell, Stewart, and Adrian Humphreys. "Terrorists' Supermarket: Canada Has Everything for the Discriminating 'Freedom Fighter.'" *National Post* (21 October 2000).

Bell, Stewart, and Marina Jimenz. "Al-Qaeda Operatives in Canada." *National Post* (15 December 2001).

Bell, Stewart, and Marina Jimenz. "Canada On Al-Qaeda Hit List, Officials Say." *National Post* (15 December 2001).

Bellavance, Joël-Denis. "FLQ Killing Was Used to Promote Unity in 1970." *Globe and Mail* (24 April 2001).

Bellavance, Joël-Denis and Bell, Stewart. "Canada Soft on Terrorism, Alliance MP Charges: Jewish Congress Urges Ottawa to Step up the Fight." *National Post* (23 February 2001).

Belluck, Pam. "Airport Inquiry Faulted Security before Explosion." *New York Times* (27 July 1996).

Beltrane, Julian. "'Let's Kill Saddam,' Frustrated Americans Ponder Murderous Tactics." *Ottawa Citizen* (13 November 1997).

———. "U.S. Bombs Terrorist Outposts." *Ottawa Citizen* (21 August 1998).

Benzie, Robert. "Anti-Poverty Activists Vow Sabotage." *Ottawa Citizen* (20 August 1999).

Bindman, Stephen. "Mock Terrorist Attack Set to Roll near Border." *Ottawa Citizen* (7 June 1989).

"Bin Laden Oversees Taleban's Military Operations." *Khabar Name* (15 August 2001). Translated in FBIS.

"Bin Laden Said Sending More Fighters to Chechnya, but Facing Curbs in Afghanistan." *Associated Press* (29 August 2000).

"Bin Laden Vows to Continue Holy War Against the United States." *Ottawa Citizen* (11 June 1999).

"Bin Laden's Long Tentacles of Terror." *Globe and Mail* (21 August 1998).

"Bin Ladin Endorses Attack on the USS Cole, Denies Kuwaiti Daily's Report." *The News: Islamabad* (14 November 2000). In FBIS.

"Bin Ladin Quarters in Afghanistan Fearful of U.S. Military Strike." *Doha Al-Jazirah Satellite Channel Television* (15 November 2000). Translated in FBIS.

"Bin Ladin Said to Fund Terrorism 'School' in Chechnya." *RIA News Agency* (24 August 1999). Translated in FBIS.

Binyon, Michael. "Saddam's Foes Draw Line at Assassination." *London Times* (18 February 1998).

———. "Terrorist Profile Identifies New Threat." *Calgary Herald* (6 May 1999).

Blair, Edmund. "Investigators Probe Yemen Blast Site." *Globe and Mail* (16 October 2000).

Blatchford, Christie. "Canada and Terrorism." National Post (24 November 2001).

Bohn, Glenn. "Vancouver, Seattle Targets in a Mock Anthrax Attack." *Vancouver Sun* (20 February 2002).

Bone, James. "Gas Mask Sales Skyrocket in Wake of Terrorist Attacks." *Ottawa Citizen* (24 September 2001).

Bone, James, Zahid Hussein, Michael Binyon, Michael Theodoulou and Michael Evans. "The Hunt for Osama bin Laden; Russia and American Have Become Allies Against the Muslim Pimpernel." *London Times* (25 November 2000).

"Bonn Shows Gratitude to Prime Minister." *New York Times* (19 October 1977).

Bowers, Faye. "Ground Personnel: Gap in Airport Security System." *Christian Science Monitor* (7 August 1996).

Bowers, Faye, and Jonathan S. Landay. "Terrorist Threat Spurs New Debate on 'Human' Spies." *Christian Science Monitor* (2 August 1996).

Boyes, Roger. "German Court Jails 1977 Hijacker." *London Times* (20 November 1996).

———. "Germans Urged to Resist Neo-Nazis." *Calgary Herald* (29 November 2001).

———. "We Do Not Need Any More Foreigners: Germany's Right Whips up Public Support for 'Culture' Rules Designed for Immigrants." *Ottawa Citizen* (6 November 2000).

Bremner, Charles. "Paris Trio Accused of Nuclear Smuggling." *London Times* (24 July 2001).

"Britain Draws Weapon Against Terrorism." (13 February 2001).

"British Commandos Head to Gulf." *Ottawa Citizen* (11 February 1998).

"British Hostages in Sierra Leone All Free." *London Times* (10 August 1999).

"British Security Foils Plot to Bomb London: Report." *Ottawa Citizen* (12 November 2000).

"The British Spy at Heart of IRA." *London Times* (8 August 1999).

"British Spy Cameras Can Identify Terrorists." *Ottawa Citizen* (11 February 1999).

"British Troops Storm Ship." *Ottawa Citizen* (2 January 2002).

Brodie, Ian. "U.S. Navy Changes its Story on Cole: Terrorists Not Part of Mooring Operation." *Ottawa Citizen* (23 October 2000).

Bronskill, Jim. "Canada Becoming More Vulnerable to Hackers: CSIS." *National Post* (25 June 1999).

———. "Canada Faces Cyber-threat, DND Warns: Forces must Develop Ability to Counter New Forms of Attack." *Ottawa Citizen* (11 March 2001).

———. "Canada Not Ready for Terrorism: Ottawa." *National Post* (21 September 2001).

———. "Canada Won't Outlaw Terror Groups: Liberals Stop Short of Ban for Fear of Alienating Ethnic Communities." *Ottawa Citizen* (6 March 2001).

———. "CSIS Targeting Anti-Racists, Annual Report Reveals: 'Potential for Violence': Foreign Conflicts Could Bring Trouble Home to Canada Spy Agency Adds." *National Post* (3 June 1999).

———. "'Hactivists' and Cyber-Outlaws Growing Threat: CSIS." *National Post* (26 June 1999).

———. "Pre-APEC Anti-Terrorist Drill Sparked Friction, Report Says." *Ottawa Citizen* (17 May 1999).

———. "Protests over Modified Crops to Escalate: CSIS Confidential Report Spy Agency Warns over Bio-Engineering." *National Post* (12 February 2001).

———. "Ressam Makes Deal, Agrees to Talk." *Ottawa Citizen* (25 June 2001).

Bronskill, Jim, Rick Mofina, and Kathryn May. "Bio-Terrorism Risk Hits Home." *Ottawa Citizen* (1 February 2001).

Brouwer, Andrew. "Don't Slam the Door." Globe and Mail (8 January 2001).

Brown, Drew. "Al-Qaeda Cache of Low-Grade Uranium, Cyanide Found Near Kandahar Airport." *Ottawa Citizen* (22 December 2001).

Browne, Malcolm. "Security Experts Turn to Computers to Keep One Step Ahead of Terrorists." *Vancouver Sun* (4 June 1988).

Bruce, Harry. "Internet Is an Open Door to Crime and Terrorism." *Calgary Herald* (25 October 1996).

Bugge, Axel. "Drugs, Colombia Preoccupy America's Defense Chiefs." *Reuters* (19 October 2000).

"'Bullets Will Fly' in Terrorist Hunt." *Toronto Sun* (22 October 2001).

Bumiller, Elisabeth. "Bush Vows to Aid Other Countries in War on Terror." *New York Times* (12 March 2002).

Burns, Robert. "Attack Alert Ignored, Spy Says Congress Told Officials at Pentagon Failed to Heed Warning of Terrorism Expert: Senators." *Globe and Mail* (26 October 2000).

———. "U.S. Forces on High Alert in Gulf: New Indications of Terrorist Threats." *Ottawa Citizen* (1 November 2000).

"Bush Worried About Terrorist Attacks on U.S. Food Supply." *Canadian Press* (14 March 2002).

Butler, Katherine. "War Crimes Suspect Blows Himself Up." *Independent* (14 October 2000).

Calamai, Peter. "Terrorism in a Test Tube." *Toronto Star* (21 September 2001).

Campbell, Matthew. "Russian Hackers Steal U.S. Weapons Secret." *London Times* (25 July 1999).

Campbell, Murray. "Oklahoma Bombing Saga Nears an End." *Globe and Mail* (20 February 2001).

"Canada Deemed Ill-Prepared for Chemical, Biological War." *Saskatoon Star Phoenix* (21 September 2001).

"Canada Likely to Follow U.S. Air Security Process." *Ottawa Citizen* (25 October 2001).

"Canada–U.S. Borderless." *Canadian Press* (28 July 2001).

"Careful Planning of 40-Minute Raid." *Weekly Telegraph,* no. 301.

"Chechen Plans to Put Domestic Chemicals to Test." *Moscow TV RTR* (15 August 2001). Translated in FBIS.

"Chemical Bomb Attack Thwarted, Italians Say." *Globe and Mail* (25 February 2002).

"China 'Bombs' White House Web Site in Hacker War." *National Post* (1 May 2001).

Chivers, C. J., and David Rhode. "Afghan Camps Turn Out Holy War Guerillas and Terrorists." *New York Times* (18 March 2002).

Christie, Michael. "Australia Stands its Ground on Migrants: Man-Eating Shark Video Has Deterred Boat People, Government Says." *National Post* (22 February 2001).

"Chronology of Hijacking." *New York Times* (5 July 1976).

"A Chronology of Terror." *Ottawa Citizen* (19 April 1986).

"CIA Chief Takes Responsibility for Chinese Embassy Bombing." *Associated Press (AP)* (22 July 1999).

"C.I.A. Picked a Bombing Target Only Once: The Chinese Embassy." *New York Times* (23 July 1999).

Clark, James. "SAS to Recruit Troops from German Army." *Sunday Times* (2 July 2000).

———. "SAS Unit on Secret Recce in Balkans." *London Times* (19 August 2001).

Clark, James, and Adam Nathan. "SAS Men Seek Help to Stem Wave of Suicides." *Sunday Times* (5 August 2001).

Clarke, Liam. "Army Foiled Plot to Murder Adams." *Sunday Times* (1 August 1999).

———. "MI5 'Operated Network of Garda Agents.'" *London Times* (8 August 1999).

Clarke, Liam and Nick Rufford. "IRA Team Testing 'Napalm' Bomb." *Sunday Times* (19 August 2001).

"Clash Between bin Ladin's Men, 'U.S. Commandos' Feared." *Ausaf* (12 May 1999). Translated in FBIS.

"Cloak and Flowers." *New York Times* (6 October 1992).

Clough, Patricia. "Perfect Debut for Bonn's Anti-Terror Squad." *New York Times* (19 October 1977).

"Cold War Legacy: U.S. Ban on Assassination." *Reuters* (22 April 1999).

"Confident They Had Defeated Guerrillas, Security Forces Let Guard Down." *Vancouver Sun* (21 December 1996).

Conradi, Peter. "Stasi Plot Lies Behind Neo-Nazi Revival: Report." *Ottawa Citizen* (13 August 2000).

Conyers, Tony. "Thatcher Gives Pledge to Iran Government." *Telegraph* (2 May 1980).

Cowley, "Republican Renegades Blamed for N. Irish Attacks." *Reuters* (13 August 2000).

Craig, John, and Mark Hosenball. "U.S. Agents to Patrol Airports in Britain." *London Times* (14 May 1989).

Cramb, Auslan. "Lockerbie Bomb 'Was Put on at Heathrow.'" *Telegraph* (17 January 2001).

"Crop-Dusting Firm Raises Alarm." *Winnipeg Free Press* (26 September 2001).

"The Danger of Spotlights." *International Herald Tribune* (7 May 1980).

de Bruxelles, Simon. "Moor Farmers Brace for 'Doomsday.'" *Ottawa Citizen* (6 March 2001).

"Defense Grills Terror Witness on bin Laden." *New York Times* (14 February 2001).

Deiller, Jean-Hervé. "Europe's Last Marxist Army Dismantled: Seven Spanish Arrests." *Ottawa Citizen* (11 November 2000).

Delacourt, Susan. "Terror Is, after All, Psychological." *Ottawa Citizen* (29 September 2001).

Diamond, John. "Serb Letters Make Threats to Kill in U.S." *National Post* (15 April 1999).

Diebel, Linda. "Disputed Legacy of a Revolutionary." *Toronto Star* (8 October 1995).

———. "Guerrilla Leader Captivates the World." *Toronto Star* (23 December 1996).

Dionne, E. J., Jr. "Heavy Pressure Pulled Malta Both Ways." *New York Times* (28 November 1985).

Doran, James. "CIA on the Trail of Terrorist Cash." *Edmonton Journal* (20 September 2001).

Drohan, Madelaine. "Tougher Air-Travel Security Likely, G7 Ministers Expected to Agree Today to Beef up Anti-Terrorism Measures." *Globe and Mail* (30 July 1996).

Drozdiak, William. "Ex-East Germans on Trial for Helping Terrorists: Security Officers Say They Reduced Violence." *Washington Post* (20 February 1997).

Duffy, Andrew. "Ressam Came Perilously Close to a Terrible Success." *Ottawa Citizen* (7 April 2001).

Dutter, Barbie, and Ben Fenton. "Uranium and Cyanide Found at bin Laden Base." *Weekly Telegraph* (26 December 2001/1 January 2002).

Dyer, Gwynne. "Bombing Attacks Just Spitting in the Wind." *Toronto Star* (22 August 1998).

Edwardes, Charlotte. "Hezbollah's Islamic Revolution Goes Online: Terrorist Group Takes Lesson from West to Promote its Cause." *Calgary Herald* (12 September 1999).

Edwards, Steven. "Islamic States Reject Terror Definition." *National Post* (22 November 2001).

"Egyptian Jet Hijacked to Malta." *New York Times* (24 November 1985).

"Egyptian Terror Group." *New York Times* (24 November 1985).

"Eight Mediterranean States Vows [*sic*] to Fight Terrorism." *Reuters* (21 June 1999).

Elmagd, Nadia Abou. "Gadhafi Supports U.S. Right to Retaliate." *Ottawa Citizen* (24 October 2001).

Elton, Sarah. "U.S. Woman Had .357-Calibre Gun on Toronto Flight." *Toronto Star* (24 July 1999).

Emling, Shelley. "'Remote Frisk' Seen as a Naked Assault on Human Rights." *Edmonton Journal* (9 June 2001).

Ersoy, Ercan. "Turkish Court Sentences Ocalan to Death." *Reuters* (29 June 1999).

Evans, Dominic. "Britain Moves to Outlaw Tamil Tigers: Terrorist Organization, Group among 21 to Be Banned under New Legislation." *National Post* (1 March 2001).

Evans, Michael. "Former Bosnian General Arrested: Special British Unit Nabs Man Behind Sarajevo Siege." *Ottawa Citizen* (21 December 1999).

———. "IRA Trio on Mission to Test Weapons." *London Times* (15 August 2001).

———. "SAS Emerged from Swamp to Launch Deadly Attack." *London Times* (11 September 2000).

Evans-Pritchard, Ambrose. "Case Collapsing Against Oklahoma Bomb Suspect." *Calgary Herald* (2 February 1997).

Evenson, Brad. "Canada Poorly Prepared for Germ Warfare." *National Post* (1 February 2001).

"Experts: U.S. Not Ready for Germ Warfare." *USA Today* (3 October 1998).

"Ex-Soviet Leaders to Discuss Security at Summit." *Reuters* (1 December 2000).

"Facing up to the Agroterror Threat: How Biological Warfare Could Devastate Crops and Livestock." *Hamilton Spectator* (25 June 1999).

Farrell, Stephen, and Ian Cobain. "Security Staff Were Behind Hijacking: Gun Brought Aboard in Pilot's Forgotten Travel Bag." *Ottawa Citizen* (16 October 2000).

Farrell, Stephen, and Michael Evans. "Hostages Wait as Rebels Stick to Demands." *London Times* (10 August 1999).

"FBI Conduct a Terrorism Attack Simulation." *Reuters* (25 October 2000).

"FBI Puts Osama bin Laden on 10-Most-Wanted List." *Ottawa Citizen* (8 June 1999).

"FBI Working with U.S. Allies on bin Laden—Freeh." *Reuters* (6 November 1999).

"FBI's Inquiry in Cole Attack Nearing a Halt." *New York Times* (21 August 2001).

Fenton, Ben. "Wanted: Trainee Spies, Starting at $34,000 (U.S.): CIA Espionage Is Back in Vogue around Washington." *National Post* (30 July 1999).

Fialka, John, Marilyn Chase, Neil King and Ron Winslow. "Deadly Biological Attack Feared." *Ottawa Citizen* (24 September 2001).

Fife, Robert. "CSIS Insider Blasts Lax Security in Canada." *National Post* (10 May 1999).

———. "Terrorists, Spies Using Canada's Immigrant Communities, CSIS Says." *National Post* (11 June 1999).

"53 Names on List." *Jerusalem Post* (30 June 1976).

"Fighting the New Terrorism." *Vancouver Sun* (6 May 1980).

"Five Facing Secret Trial over Bid to Down Jet." *Globe and Mail* (7 July 1977).

Fletcher, Martin, Michael Evans, and Anthony Loyd. "CIA Licence to Kill Bin Laden." *London Times* (22 October 2001).

"Foreign Minister: Colombian Guerrillas Pose 'Threat.'" *El Peruano* (18 August 1999). Translated in FBIS.

"14 Years Later, No Charges Laid in Bombing of Air India Jetliner." *Globe and Mail* (10 May 1999).

Fox, Maggie. "Be Afraid, Be Very Afraid about Bioterrorism, Experts Tell U.S. Conference." *Reuters* (28 November 2000).

Francis, Diane. "Cyber Threats Are All Too Real: Governments Fail to Comprehend Information Warfare." *National Post* (20 February 1999).

———. "The Most Dangerous Nation on Earth." *National Post* (28 May 1999).

Freeman, Alan. "Car Bomb Explosion in London: Dissident Group Real IRA Blamed for Blast Outside BBC." *Globe and Mail* (5 March 2001).

"French Police Uncover Basque Bomb Factory." *Reuters* (11 March 1999).

French, Carey. "Talking a Tough Line on Terrorism." *Globe and Mail* (14 May 1988).

———. "Terrorist Threat Growing: Just When You Thought it Was Safe." *Globe and Mail* (11 February 1992).

"Frenchman Was al-Qaeda Member." *Ottawa Citizen* (16 December 2001).

"FRG Chancellor Cables Thanks to Somalia's Barre, Others." *FBIS* (18 October 1977).

"FRG Spokesman Reads Joint Statement on Hostages' Rescue Operation." *FBIS* (18 October 1977).

Friedman, Thomas L. "Diplomacy by Other Means." *New York Times* (3 November 2000).

"Future Terror Havens Target of Philippine Exercise." *Reuters* (12 March 2002).

Gabor, Thomas. "Fighting Fair: The Geneva Conventions Set Strict Rules on War and How it Is Conducted." *Ottawa Citizen* (7 January 2002).

Gannon, Kathy. "Bin Laden Manual Lists 'Rules of Destruction.'" *National Post* (1 October 2001).

Garrett, Laurie. "Bioterrorism Frightens the Experts." *Montreal Gazette* (22 February 1999).

Gearan, Anne. "Clinton Predicts Century of Technological Advances." *Globe and Mail* (28 December 1999).

Gee, Marcus. "I Know You Are, but What Am I?" *Globe and Mail* (24 November 2001).

"Germ Warfare Fears Grow." *Vancouver Province* (26 September 2001).

"German Experts to Establish Saudi CT Unit." *Defense and Foreign Affairs Daily* (12 May 1987).

"German Troops See Action in War on Terrorism." *National Post* (25 February 2002).

"Germany Synagogue Attack." *Associated Press* (6 October 2000).

Gershberg, Michele. "Israel Says Bin Laden Seeks Local Operatives." *Reuters* (25 June 2001).

Gershberg, Michele. "Ships Deadly Cargo Seized by Israel." *National Post* (5 January 2002).

Giacomo, Carol. "U.S. Still Has Much Work to Do on Securing Embassies." *Reuters* (4 August 1999).

Gilmore, Inigo. "Female Bomber Raises Israel's Security Fears." *National Post* (26 January 2002).

Glaberson, William. "Guerrilla Warfare over the Internet." *New York Times* (12 April 1997).

"Global Effort to Find Bin Laden's Millions Could Come up Short." *Canadian Press* (20 September 2001).

"Global Force Proposed to Fight Terrorist Threat." *Toronto Star* (27 April 1986).

Goldberg, Andy. "Israel Opens 'Rambo Academy' to Train Troops for Guerrilla War." *Sunday Times* (21 September 1997).

Goodman, Anthony. "UN Report Religious Extremism Is 'Ever-growing Scourge.'" *Reuters* (19 October 2000).

Gordon, Michael R. "When an Open Society Is Wielded as a Weapon Against Itself." *New York Times* (12 September 2001).

Gorman, Brian. "Doomsday Bugs." *Ottawa Sun* (26 November 1997).

Graham, Patrick. "Israel Calls its Assassination of Enemies 'Early Retirement.'" *National Post* (18 August 2001).

Graham, Stephen. "Berlin Fears Imminent Attack." *Ottawa Citizen* (16 December 2001).

"Greek Praise for Firm Bonn Stand." *New York Times* (19 October 1977).

Green, Leslie C. "An International SWAT Team to Control Terrorism." *Toronto Star* (20 January 1986).

Green, Robert. "U.S. Court Convicts Palestinian for 1985 Hijacking." *Reuters* (19 July 1996).

Green, Sara Jean, and Jill Mahoney. "Hijack Attempt Sparks Security Review." *Globe and Mail* (12 May 1998).

Greenaway, Norma. "Canada 'A Gateway for Terrorists, Thugs.'" *Ottawa Citizen* (28 February 2001).

———. "U.S. Offers Antiterror Assistance to Israel." *Ottawa Citizen* (15 March 1996).

Greenberg, Joel. "Israel Military Leader 65, Directed Entebbe Rescue." *Ottawa Citizen* (17 July 1995).

Grier, Peter. "A Terrorist Version of NATO?" *Christian Science Monitor* (19 February 2001).

Grossman, Dave. "Television's Virus of Violence." *Globe and Mail* (23 May 1998).

"Group Helped Ressam Get Canadian Passport for Terrorist Activities." *Canadian Press* (26 October 2000).

"The Guys—Israel's Anonymous Heroes." *Ottawa Journal* (5 July 1976).

Hacaoglu, Selcan. "'Baby Killer,' or Struggling Statesman." *Ottawa Citizen* (17 February 1999).

"Hackers Launched 'Major Attack' on Pentagon Computer System." *NSI Advisory* (1 April 1999).

Hall, Allan. "Neo-Nazi Threat 'Played Down.'" *London Times* (7 October 2000).

"Hamas Leader Threatens New Suicide Operations Against Israel." *Cairo Al-Ahram* (18 December 2000). Translated in FBIS.

Hamilton, Graeme. "Mafiaboy Pleads Guilty to Online Attacks." *National Post* (20 January 2001).

Hammer, Joshua. "Portrait of a Terrorist." *Ottawa Citizen* (18 January 1997).

Handelman, Stephen. "Security Chiefs Prepare for New Terrorist Tactics." *Toronto Star* (4 December 1994).

Hanley, Charles. "Experts Note Common Traits in Terrorists." *Ottawa Citizen* (19 April 1986).

———. "International Terrorism: Global Order Shaken by Wanton War." *Ottawa Citizen* (19 April 1986).

Harel, Amos. "Fear Sends Hamas Men Back to Jail." *Ha'aretz Daily* (19 December 2000).

———. "15 Fatah Men Held for Role in Shooting Barak: 'The IDF Will Strike at Anyone Who Harms Israelis.'" *Ha'aretz* (16 November 2000).

———. "Sharon Says Killing Terrorists Works." *Ha'aretz* (21 August 2001).

Harnden, Toby. "IRA Testing Missiles, Clues Indicate." *Ottawa Citizen* (13 April 1999).

Harrison, David and Daniel Foggo. "Terrorists Target Lab's Shareholders." *Telegraph* (13 December 2000).

Hastings, Chris and David Bamber. "Police Foil Terror Plot to Use Sarin Gas in London." *Telegraph* (18 February 2001).

Hays, Tom. "Bin Laden Sought Uranium, Trial Hears; Ex-Aide Testifies in Embassy-Blast Case." *Globe and Mail* (9 February 2001).

"Head of German Raid Is Linked to Entebbe." *New York Times* (22 October 1977).

Hepburn, Bob. "Mideast Peace Deal Still Far Off, Baker Says." *Toronto Star* (19 October 1991).

"Hezbollah Commander Killed by Bomb, Lebanese Guerrillas Blame Israel for

Attack on Abu Hassan, Vow It 'Will Not Go Unpunished.'" *Globe and Mail* (17 August 1999).

"Hijackers, Holding 92, Back Kidnappers in Schleyer Case." *International Herald Tribune* (15 October 1977).

"Hijackers Worked 'On Amazingly Little Money,' but Banking Hints Were Missed." *National Post* (3 October 2001).

"Hijacking of Egyptian Airliner to Malta; Subsequent Storming of Aircraft by Egyptian Commandos." *Keesing Record of World Events* 32 (April 1986).

"Hijacking of Jet With 91 to Dubai Linked With German Kidnapping." *New York Times* (15 October 1977).

"Hijacking Ordeal Ends in Baghdad." *Ottawa Citizen* (15 October 2000).

Hijazi, Ihsan A. "Hijackers Linked to Palestinian Faction." *New York Times* (26 November 1985).

Hindell, Jullet, and David Sapsted. "747 Pilot Killed as 500 Hijacked." *Weekly Telegraph* (28 July–3 August 1999).

Hoagland, Jim. "Americans must Confront a New Age of Terrorism." *Toronto Star* (25 July 1996).

Hockstader, Lee. "Firing Squads Execute Palestinians." *Ottawa Citizen* (14 January 2001).

———. "Fly in Mideast Cyber-War." *Washington Post* (27 October 2000).

Hodgson, Godfrey. "Terrorism Will Never Go Away." *Independent* (16 August 1996).

Hoffman, Bruce. "Keeping Mum: Terrorists Are Killing More, but Bragging Less." *Montreal Gazette* (22 August 1996).

Hosenball, Mark, and Nordland, Rod. "Pointing A Finger at bin Laden." *Newsweek* (30 October 2000).

Howe, Marvine. "Hijackers Leave Dubai." *New York Times* (17 October 1977).

Hume, Stephen. "Are We Open to Attack?" *Edmonton Journal* (17 February 2001).

Humphreys, Adrian. "U.S. Professor Accused of Financing Terror." *National Post* (21 March 2002).

Ibbitson, John. "Bush Signs Antiterror Legislation into Law." *Globe and Mail* (27 October 2001).

"If Pimps Don't Get You, the Crocs Will: Australia Scraps Scare Campaign." *Ottawa Citizen* (13 January 2001).

Ikramullah. "Usama bin Laden 'Letter' Calling for 'Global Islamic State.'" *Nawa-i-Waqt* (8 January 2001). Translated in FBIS.

"Interview with J. Lee and Richard Reynolds." *CBC Morning* (19 August 1999).

"Islamic Group Claims Bombing." *Toronto Star* (19 March 1992).

"Israel Hails Argentine Court Statement on Bombing." *Reuters* (11 May 1999).

"Israel Says Soviet Hijackers Are Criminals." *Ottawa Citizen* (3 December 1988).

"Israel to Distribute Anti-Terror Plan." *Toronto Star* (20 September 1986).

"Israeli Government Meeting to Assess Hijack Situation." *Agence France Presse* (1 July 1976).

"Israeli Hit Team Linked to Slaying of Top PLO Official." *Globe and Mail* (18 April 1988).

"Israelis Fall Foul of Hizbollah Trap." *Independent* (24 February 1999).

"Italy Arrests Four Moroccans with Cyanide, Maps." *Reuters* (20 February 2002).

Jamil, Salah. "2 February Set for the Lockerbie Trial." *Al-Sharq al-Awsat* (11 December 1999). Translated in FBIS.

"Japan Textbook Explosion." *Canadian Press* (12 August 2001).

"Jerusalem Reports FRG Antiterror Unit in Persian Gulf." *FBIS* (17 October 1977).

Jiwa, Salim. "Board Probes Fund-raising for Terrorists in Schools." *Vancouver Province* (18 December 2000).

———. "How I Became a Terrorist." *Vancouver Province* (30 November 2001).

———. "Osama bin Laden's Global Network." *Vancouver Province* (30 November 2001).

John, Mark. "German Neo-Nazis Flock to Internet-Security Chief." *Reuters* (25 July 1999).

Johnston, David. "1985 Arab Hijacker Faces Penalty Today." *New York Times* (7 October 1996).

"Joy at Rescue of Hostages." *Jerusalem Post* (5 July 1976).

Kahl, Werner. "Saudis Want Mogadishu Hero to Help Anti-Terror Effort." *German Tribune* (7 December 1986).

Kalman, Matthew. "Blast Kills Three Israelis, Suicide Bombers." *Globe and Mail* (5 March 2001).

———. "Convicted Palestinian Spy Sentenced to Death." *Globe and Mail* (8 December 2000).

———. "Israelis Kill Officer in Arafat Guard: Palestinian Led Double Life as Head of Terrorist Cell, Army Says of Target." *Globe and Mail* (14 February 2001).

———. "Palestinian Bomber Targets Bus Queue." *Globe and Mail* (23 April 2001).

Karpukhin, Sergei. "Commandos Storm Seized Russian Bus, Kill Hijacker." *Reuters* (31 July 2001).

Kehaulani, Goo. "Some Pilots to Receive Stun-gun Training." *Washington Post* (19 October 2001).

Keyser, Jason. "World Must Wake Up, Israeli Pilot Warns." *Ottawa Citizen* (30 September 2001).

Khalil, Tahir. "Afghan ForMin Promises 'Crushing Reply' If U.S. Attacks." *Rawalpindi Jang* (27 October 2000). Translated in FBIS.

Kiley, Sam. "'I Want to Die as a Martyr,' 12-year-old Says: Thousands of Youngsters Trained in Warfare at PLO Camps." *Ottawa Citizen* (25 October 2000).

———. "Israelis Kill Guerrilla Chief: Hezbollah Kingpin Had Links to Arafat." *Ottawa Citizen* (14 February 2001).

"Killer Jailed for Life." *Globe and Mail* (23 January 1981).

Knickerbocker, Brad. "U.S. Goes on Alert for New York's Terrorists; Security Is Widespread, Intense as Nation Readies for Trouble from Inside and Out." *Christian Science Monitor* (21 December 1999).

Knipe, Michael. "Broadcast 'Put Lives in Danger.'" *New York Times* (19 October 1977).

Knox, Paul. "Guerrilla Handed Fujimori Reason to Attack." *Globe and Mail* (24 April 1997).

———. "Ocalan's Capture a Blow to Hopes for Autonomy." *Globe and Mail* (17 February 1999).

———. "Probe Stirs Spectre of Bin Laden A-bomb." *Globe and Mail* (27 October 2001).

Koring, Paul. "Al-Qaeda Plots Foiled, U.S. Claims." *Globe and Mail* (15 January 2002).

————. "17 Feared Dead in Warship Blast." *Globe and Mail* (13 October 2000).

————. "Some Border Security Gaps Plugged, Many Remain." *Globe and Mail* (14 March 2001).

————. "Terrorism Jitters Lead Seattle to Cancel New Year's Plan: 'We Did Not Want to Take Chances with Public Safety,' Says Mayor as City Scrubs Celebration at Space Needle Landmark." *Globe and Mail* (29 December 1999).

————. "U.S. Faces a Growing Terror: the Military Has Lost More People to Terrorism than in Wars since 1975, a Trend Paul Koring Writes, Expected to Escalate." *Globe and Mail* (20 October 2000).

Krauss, Clifford. "In Visit to Colombia, Clinton Defends U.S. Outlay." *New York Times* (31 July 2000).

————. "U.S. Spies in Guatemala Never Came in from Cold War: Declassified Reports Show the CIA Kept Close Ties to the Central American Country's Death Squads for 40 Years." *Montreal Gazette* (9 March 1999).

Krauthammer, Charles. "The Moral High Ground is a Slippery Slope." *National Post* (28 January 2002).

Labaton, Stephen. "National Security Adviser Warns of Risk of Terrorism." *New York Times* (20 December 1999).

La Guardia, Anton. "Al-Qaeda Biological Lab Found in Caves." *Ottawa Citizen* (23 March 2002).

La Guardia, Anton. "Israel Asserts 'National Duty' to Assassinate." *Ottawa Citizen* (6 October 1997).

————. "Israeli Commandos Killed in Botched Raid on Lebanon." *Ottawa Citizen* (6 September 1997).

————. "A Nation Born in Terror." *Ottawa Citizen* (30 April 1998).

————. "Suicide Bombers Kill 7, Wound 192 in Jerusalem." *Ottawa Citizen* (5 September 1997).

————. "Three Dead as Saudis Storm Hijacked Jet." *Ottawa Citizen* (17 March 2001).

Lahoud, Lamia. "IDF Officer Confirms Tracking down and Killing Militants." *Jerusalem Post* (22 December 2000).

Lancaster, John, and Helen Dewar. "N.J. Mail Carrier, CBS Employee Have Anthrax." *Washington Post* (19 October 2001).

Landay, Jonathan S. "U.S. Military Outpaces its NATO Peers." *Christian Science Monitor* (29 September 1997).

————. "U.S. Takes Global Precautions to Stem Threat of Terrorism." *Christian Science Monitor* (23 July 1996).

Landers, "CIA Says Terror War Not for Faint-hearted." *Calgary Herald* (19 October 2001).

Landy, Keith M. "Martyrs or Murderers? *Ottawa Citizen* (25 June 2001).

Lardner, George, Jr. "Cold War Adversaries Discuss Cooperation; International Terrorism Said to Be Most Likely Target of Any CIA-KGB Joint Operation." *Washington Post* (13 November 1990).

"A Large Dose of Terror: An Inside Look at How the Soviet Union Developed

Lethal Germ Weapons, and Why the End of the Cold War Has Made the Threat of Biological Warfare Even Worse." *Toronto Star* (26 June 1999).

Lashmar, Paul, and Shraga Elam. "MI5 Was Feuding with Mossad While Known Terrorist Struck in London." *Independent* (19 June 1999).

Lauria, Joe. "Iraq Bought Anthrax from U.S." *Ottawa Citizen* (23 October 2001).

Lavie, Mark, and Alan Philps. "Israel Assassinates Palestinian Officer." *National Post* (14 February 2001).

Leblanc, Daniel. "Terrorist Fundraisers Will Face Jail." *Globe and Mail* (3 October 2001).

Lee, Stella. "Cyber-Criminals 'Now More Skillful.'" *South China Morning Post* (29 November 2001).

Leppard, David. "Spy Chiefs Hunt for 20 'Terror' Ships." *Ottawa Citizen* (23 December 2001).

Leppard, David, Paul Nuki and Gareth Walsh. "Britain's 'Murder Inc.' Plotted to Kill Rebel Leader." *Sunday Times* (22 August 1999).

"Lessons from USS Cole." *Washington Post* (27 October 2000).

"Lethal Tigers: No End Looks Likely in Sri Lanka's Long War." *London Times* (25 July 2001).

Levy, Adrian, and Cathy Scott-Clark. "Back with a Vengeance: Bin Laden Is Training Recruits to Unleash a Fresh Wave of Terror against the West." *Sunday Times* (20 December 1998).

Lewis, Ian. "Hostages Freed in Bloody Raid." *Ottawa Citizen* (23 April 1997).

"Libya Remains a Pariah State to U.S.: Suspension of Sanctions Unlikely to Affect Frozen Assets or Washington's Ban on Trade, Travel." *Globe and Mail* (7 April 1999).

"Libyan Arrested for '86 Bombing." *Toronto Star* (28 August 1997).

"Lockerbie Crash: Syria Linked to Bomb." *Ottawa Sun* (19 April 1992).

Loeb, Vernon. "Anthrax Vial Smuggled in to Make a Point at Hill Hearing." *Washington Post* (4 March 1999).

"Looking to Future, CIA Should Focus on Human Intelligence." *Christian Science Monitor* (6 August 1997).

Loyd, Anthony. "Al-Qaeda Tested Terror Weapons." *Ottawa Citizen* (29 December 2001).

Luttwak, Edward. "How to Win: Bombs Plus Brawn." *Globe and Mail* (8 January 2002).

MacCallum, Heather. "Infrastructure Protection Key Issue." *Fredericton Daily Gleaner* (20 November 2000).

Maceskill, Mark, and Nicolas Ruford. "Muslim Calls for Bio-Weapon Holy War." *Sunday Times* (5 September 1999).

MacFarquhar, Neil. "Portrait of a Suicide Bomber: Devout, Apolitical and Angry." *New York Times* (18 March 1996).

Macintyre, Ben. "CIA Ignored Warnings That Embassy Address Was Incorrect." *Ottawa Citizen* (25 June 1999).

Mackenzie, Hilary. "Terrorism Strategy Paying Off." *Ottawa Citizen* (1 May 2001).

MacKinnon, Mark. "Canada Blind to Bioterror, Critic Warns." *Ottawa Citizen* (28 April 2001).

Macko, Steve. "Peru Hostage Crisis Comes to a Violent End." *http://www.emergency.com/peruhos7.htm*.

Macleod, Ian. "Mounties Fear Y2K Terrorists' Cyber-Attacks: Computer Crisis Ties up Experts, Risks Security." *Ottawa Citizen* (15 June 1999).

Magnish, Scot. "After the War Toronto Gears up for NATO Meeting amid Concerns over Terrorism." *Toronto Sun* (15 August 1999).

Mahnaimi, Uzi. "Israel Plans to Assassinate Arafat Aides: Sharon Pledges to Strike 'Those Who Attack Us and Those Who Send Them.'" *Ottawa Citizen* (1 April 2001).

———. "Israelis Risk All in Undercover Missions: Elite Squad Goes Behind Enemy Lines Posing as Arabs." *Ottawa Citizen* (22 October 2000).

———. "Palestinians Draw up Israeli Hit List." *Ottawa Citizen* (2 September 2001).

———. "Terrorist's Trip to Oblivion." *Edmonton Journal* (10 December 2000).

"Malayan Guerrilla Lays Down His Arms after 41-year Fight." *Toronto Star* (3 December 1989).

Malik, Adran. "Three Killed as Saudis Storm Hijacked Russian Jet." *Toronto Star* (17 March 2001).

"The Man Who Protects America from Terrorism." *New York Times* (1 February 1998).

Marcus, Yoel. "Arafat Shoots down Hope: The Palestinian Leader Is Unable to Make the Switch from Guerrilla Warrior to Statesman." *Ottawa Citizen* (5 April 2001).

———. "Showing Arafat's True Colors." *Ha'artez* (5 June 2001).

Marenko, Qobi. "No Israeli Reaction to Assassination of Hizballah Senior." *Channel 2 Television Network: Jerusalem* (16 August 1999). Translated in FBIS.

"Mauritius: Alert over Possible Aircraft Hijacking by Hizbullah Supporters." *Port Louis L'Express* (21 December 2000). Translated in FBIS.

McCabe, Aileen. "Britain Learns to Live with Terrorism after Decades of Blasts." *Ottawa Citizen* (4 August 1996).

———. "Facing Terror with a Stiff Upper Lip." *Montreal Gazette* (3 August 1996).

McFadden, Robert D. "German Troops Free Hostages on Hijacked Plane in Somalia; 3 Terrorists Reported Killed." *New York Times* (18 October 1977).

McGonigle, Steve. "Florida College Grapples with Islamic Jihad Ties; Group's New Leader Taught at University; Professor Has Denied Running Terrorist Front." *Dallas Morning News* (4 June 1996).

McGregor, Glen. "Airport Security Redesign 'Work in Progress.'" *Kingston Whig Standard* (12 March 2002).

McGregor, Glen. "Police Probe Reports of Aerial Poison Plot." *Ottawa Citizen* (26 September 2001).

McGrory, Daniel. "Israel Fears Chemical Strike by Hamas." *Ottawa Citizen* (2 January 2002).

McKenna, Barrie. "Porous Canadian Border a Menace, U.S. Legislators Told." *Globe and Mail* (15 April 1999).

McKittrick, David. "The IRA's Grand Strategy." *Independent* (7 April 1997).

———. "The Irish Bombers: What Sort of People Are They?" *Independent* (26 September 1996).

"Media Terrorism." Editorial, *Ottawa Citizen* (30 July 1996).

Middleton, Drew. "British Raid: The Lessons." *New York Times* (7 May 1980).

———. "Key to Raid's Success: Analysts Cite Strategic and Tactical Surprise, Achieved Through Deception." *New York Times* (5 July 1976).

Miller, Judith. "U.S. Explores Other Options on Preventing Germ Warfare." *New York Times* (25 July 2001).

Miller, Judith, and William J. Broad. "Clinton Describes Terrorism Threat for 21st Century." *New York Times* (22 January 1999).

————. "Fire, Not Bullets, Reported to Kill Most Victims on Hijacked Plane." *New York Times* (28 November 1985).

————. "From Takeoff to Raid: the 24 Hours of Flight 648." *New York Times* (27 November 1985).

————. "New York City Developing Plans to Counter Chemical, Germ Attacks." *New York Times* (19 June 1998).

Miller, Judith, and Neil MacFarquhar. "American Intelligence Officials Said Yesterday That They Received Reports in Late May That a Militant Egyptian Islamic Group Was in the Final Stages of Preparing a Terror Attack." *New York Times* (20 October 2000).

Mitchell, Alanna. "How Stress and Illusion Breed Panic." *Globe and Mail* (17 October 2001).

Mitrovica, Andrew. "Terror Attacks Rare, U.S. Report Says, but Getting Deadlier." *Globe and Mail* (24 December 1999).

Mofina, Rick. "Military Ill-Prepared for Attack on Ottawa." *Ottawa Citizen* (11 January 2002).

Mofina, Rick, and Mike Blanchfield. "Utilities Most Likely Terrorism Targets." *Ottawa Citizen* (22 December 1999).

Monchuk, Judy. "Canada Not Ready for Bio Attacks." *Calgary Herald* (20 August 2001).

"More to Fear than Russian Germ Warfare: Brain Drain of Bio Weapon Scientists Threat to World Safety." *National Post* (17 February 2001).

Moritsugu, Ken, Nancy San Martin, and Sumana Chatterjee. "Anthrax Found in Second Capital Hill Office." *Ottawa Citizen* (21 October 2001).

"Mother of All Hijackers." *Independent* (19 March 1996).

Mullin, John. "Real IRA Re-Emerges with New Name, New Threats." *Globe and Mail* (26 June 1999).

Munro, Margaret. "Lasting Impression." *National Post* (27 October 2001).

————. "Prepare for Bioterrorism Attack, Military Doctor Warns." *National Post* (19 February 2001).

Nacheman, Allen. "Terrorist Takes Stand in Pan Am Bomb Trial." *National Post* (11 November 2000).

"National Intelligence Agency Head Warns Indonesia 'Vulnerable' to Terrorism." *Jakarta Post* (24 August 2001) in FBIS.

Neergaard, Lauran. "How Bioterrorism Nearly Wiped out the U.S." *Ottawa Citizen* (22 February 1999).

Netanyahu, Benjamin. "Operation Jonathan: The Rescue At Entebbe." *Military Review* (July 1982), 2–23.

————. "Through Common Resolve, Terror Can Be Defeated." *International Herald Tribune* (17 May 1985).

"New Style Terrorist Is a Lone Fanatic." *London Times* (4 May 1999).

Newton, Christopher. "U.S. Talib Defends Terrorists in Interview." *Ottawa Citizen* (20 December 2001).

Nickerson, Colin. "Bio-Terror Threats as Scary as Real Thing." *Kitchener Waterloo Record* (5 February 2001).

Nolen, Stephanie. "What Motivates Suicide Bombers?" *Vancouver Sun* (17 August 1997).

"Notebook Contains Plan for Bombing London." *Ottawa Citizen* (16 December 2001).

O'Neill, Julie. "100 More U.S. Guards Sent to Border with Canada." *National Post* (27 October 2001).

O'Neill, Juliet. "PM Offers Canadian Training for Colombian Peacekeepers." *Ottawa Citizen* (1 June 1999).

O'Sullivan, Arieh. "Defense Officials Rethinking Terror Responses." *Jerusalem Post* (11 September 2001).

———."IDF Strikes Back at Hizbullah." *Jerusalem Post* (25 February 1999).

———. "Israel Captures Members of Palestinian Lynch Mob." *Jerusalem Post* (19 October 2000).

Ottaway, David B., and Don Oberdorfer. "Administration Alters Assassination Ban: In Interview, Webster Reveals Interpretation." *Washington Post* (4 November 1989).

Ousten, Rick. "Seized Explosives Ignite Major Hunt for Militia Group." *Ottawa Citizen* (29 October 1997).

"Outsmarting Suicide Terrorists." *Christian Science Monitor* (24 October 2000).

Owen, Richard. "Italian Cardinal Attacks Muslim Immigration." *London Times* (15 September 2000).

"Palestinians Are Not Afraid of Death." *Ottawa Citizen* (14 August 2001).

"Peru: Shining Path." *Canadian Press* (16 August 2001).

Petrou, Michael. "Discovery of Deadly Virus Raises Fears of Biological Weapons." *Ottawa Citizen* (12 January 2001).

———. "How Canada Is Boosting Cyber Security." *Ottawa Citizen* (14 March 2002).

———. "Rebels Without a Cause." *Ottawa Citizen* (18 August 2001).

Philipp, Peter. "Israelis in Nairobi Hospital." *Jerusalem Post* (5 July 1976).

"Philippine Military Rescues Three Hostages Held by Muslim Rebels." *Associated Press* (25 October 2000).

Philps, Alan. "'Happy' Man with a Bomb Strapped to His Waist." *Telegraph* (16 August 2001).

———. "Israel Warns of Revenge for Suicide Bombing." *National Post* (5 March 2001).

———. "Palestinian Militant Leader Assassinated." *National Post* (15 January 2002).

Phillips, Don, and Ellen Nakashima. "FBI to Check More Airport Workers." *Washington Post* (18 October 2001).

Picard, André. "Disease Fit for a Stephen King Thriller." *Globe and Mail* (7 February 2001).

Piller, Charles. "Hackers Could Worm Way into Power." *Calgary Herald* (14 August 2001).

Pincus, Walter. "CIA Had Hit List of 58 Guatemalans in the 1950s: Agency Reveals Details of Covert Action against President Arbenz, Overthrown but Not Killed." *Washington Post* (24 May 1997).

————. "Top Spy Retiring from CIA: Downing Led Revamp of Clandestine Service." *Washington Post* (29 July 1999).

Pipes, Daniel. "Behind the Will of Islam: Once a Religion of Worldly Success, Islam Has Endured Two Centuries of Trauma. Solutions Have Presented Themselves in the Forms of Secularism and Reformism, but It Is the New Option of Fundamentalist Islam That Presents a Threat to the West." *National Post* (7 August 1999).

"Polish Border Guards Arrest 3 Chechens With Explosives, Ammunition." *Berlin DDP* (10 August 2000). Translated in FBIS.

"Politics Trumping Security: Ex-Spy: Former CSIS Chief Accuses Liberals of Being Timid on Terror for Fear of Losing Ethnic Votes." *National Post* (9 March 2001).

"Potent Virus Travelled the World for a Decade: Pan-Asia Strain 'Unstoppable.'" *Ottawa Citizen* (6 March 2001).

Potter, Mitch. "Settlers Live under the Gun in Besieged Israeli Outpost; 'There Is No Defence Against Someone Who Will Kill Himself to Kill You,' Soldier Says in the Wake of Suicide Attack." *Toronto Star* (27 October 2000).

Powell, Michael. "4 Bombers Get Life Sentences." *Washington Post* (19 October 2001).

"Protecting Diplomats Increasingly Complex." *USA Today* (20 December 1996).

Pugliese, David. "Only 11 Nuclear Bombs to 'Take Out' Canada." *Ottawa Citizen* (2 January 2002).

Rachid, Ahmed. "U.S. Seeks Alliance with Moscow for Raid on bin Laden." *Telegraph* (22 November 2000).

"Racist Groups Hard to Penetrate—U.K.'s Straw." *Reuters* (26 April 1999).

"Raid Reconstructed: Israelis Knew Airport." *New York Times* (5 July 1976).

Rajghatta, Chidanand. "Israeli Teams Training Forces in Kashmir." *Times of India* (17 August 2001).

"RCMP Probe Terrorist Link." *Montreal Gazette* (19 August 2001).

"Rebel Suicide Boats Attack Sri Lanka Troop Ship." *Reuters* (15 September 2001).

"Red Army Faction Terrorist Group Disbands." *Globe and Mail* (21 April 1998).

"Red Brigades Announce Plan to 'Strike at the Heart of Imperialism.'" *La Spezia* (20 October 2000). In FBIS.

Regan, Tom. "Cyber Wars—Wars of the Future . . . Today." *Christian Science Monitor* (29 June 1999).

"Remains of 2 in U.K. Siege Flown to Iran." *Globe and Mail* (14 May 1980).

"Report Catalogues Dangers of Anthrax as Weapon." *Reuters* (11 May 1999).

"Report Says U.S. May Drop Libya from Terrorist List." *Reuters* (17 August 1999).

"Report: U.S. Unprepared for Bioterrorism." *USA Today* (18 June 1998).

"The Rescue of Hostages Held in Uganda by Israeli Commandos." *CBC Sunday Magazine,* hosted by Bob Oxley and George Rich (4 July 1976). Transcript.

Robinson, Albert. "Four Die in Suicide Bombing in Northern Israel." *Reuters* (29 November 2001).

Roddam, "Croatian Arms Haul Linked to Irish Guerrillas." *Reuters* (28 July 2000).

Roman, Karina. "Threat of Germ Warfare 'A Reality.'" *Ottawa Citizen* (1 February 2001).

Rosato, Bill. "Overnight Attacks Increase N. Ireland Tensions." *Reuters* (30 July 2000).

Rose, Alexander. "Terror Has a New Name: The Internet: 'The First Web War.'" *National Post* (3 July 1999).

———. "A Time and a Place for Political Assassination" *National Post* (19 February 2001).

———. "The Trouble with Biological Weapons." *National Post* (28 July 2001).

Rosenblum, Jonathan. "Think Again: This is War." *Jerusalem Post* (17 August 2001).

Rosin, Hanna. "Robertson Espouses Assassin Solution." *Washington Post* (10 August 1999).

Roslin, Alex. "When the State Turns Assassin." *Montreal Gazette* (20 October 2001).

Rudge, David. "Assassination Also Carries Risks to the Assassin." *Jerusalem Post* (14 February 2001).

"Rumsfeld Seeks Help in Caucasus." *Ottawa Citizen* (16 December 2001).

Sage, Adam. "French al-Qaeda Fighter Was 'Brainwashed,' Father Says." *Ottawa Citizen* (27 December 2001).

Sakurai, Fusako. "Japanese Police Arrest Defiant Female Terrorist Leader: Red Army Group Killed 24 People in 1972 Israeli Attack." *Ottawa Citizen* (9 November 2000).

Sallot, Jeff. "Guarding Canada's E-frontier: New Federal Agency Aims to Protect Critical Infrastructure from Hack Attacks." *Globe and Mail* (20 February 2001).

———. "Hackers Targeting Spy Computers: Sensitive Networks under Constant Attack Officials Tell Electronic Security Conference." *Ottawa Citizen* (22 February 2001).

Sankey, Derek. "Terrorists Target Oilpatch: Security Specialist Gives Warning." *Calgary Herald* (19 November 1999).

Saunders, Doug. "Bin Laden at Heart of Ressam Trial." *Globe and Mail* (3 March 2001).

———. "Suburban Guerrillas Fight Sprawl with Fires: Arsonists of the Earth Liberation Front Target Giant Homes and SUV Dealerships." *Globe and Mail* (24 April 2001).

———. "Witness Implicates Ressam." *Globe and Mail* (9 March 2001).

Scarborough, Rowan. "U.S. Special Forces Troops Calling the Shots in Afghanistan." *National Post* (24 November 2001).

Scherer, Ron. "New Antiterrorist Weapon: Lassie vs. 'Carlos the Jackal.'" *Christian Science Monitor* (8 August 1996).

Schiff, Ze'ev. "A Lack of Purpose in the Choice of Targets." *Ha'aretz* (15 August 2001).

Schmetzer, Uli. "Spawning a New Breed of Terrorist: Religious Zealots Believe Their Deaths Will Be Rewarded, Experts on Islam Say." *Ottawa Citizen* (15 October 2000).

Schmidt, Sarah. "Canada to Give U.S. More Details on Travelers." *National Post* (29 December 2001).

"Schroeder Says Not Enough Done to Fight Extremism." *Reuters* (29 August 2000).

Schuler, Corinna. "Inside the Mind of a Suicide Bomber." *National Post* (10 November 2001).

"The Scourge of Terror." *Jerusalem Post* (27 August 1997).

"Security at Germ Banks Is Often Lax." *Ottawa Citizen* (21 October 2001).

Seidman, Karen. "Tougher Stance Needed to Beat Terrorism: Expert." *Montreal Gazette* (16 December 1985).

"Seizure Claimed by Arabistan Iranians." *Reuters* (30 April 1980), 1411 GMT.

Shahin, Mike. "FBI Builds Case Against Shoe Bomber." *Ottawa Citizen* (29 December 2001).

Shala-Esa, Andrea. "U.S. Vows Reassessment of Spy Operations after Attacks." *Reuters* (17 September 2001).

Sharrock, David. "Victim Turns on Police over Omagh 'Cover Ups'; Widower Demands Answers." *Telegraph* (16 August 2001).

Shenon, Philip. "Military at Compound Earlier than Thought: Declassified Papers— 'The Department of Defense Played No Operational Role,' FBI Says." *National Post* (6 September 1999).

Sheridan, Mary Beth. "U.S. Moves to Tighten Security on Borders." *Washington Post* (18 October 2001).

"Shoring Up Security against Cyberterrorists." *Christian Science Monitor* (10 October 1997).

"Sikh, in Punjab, Vows Fight for New Nation." *New York Times* (28 June 2001).

Simpson, Daniel. "Germans Suspend Soldier over Racist Web Site: Investigation Launched." *National Post* (11 August 2000).

"Small British Firm Spearheads Production of Smallpox Vaccine." *National Post* (20 October 2001).

Smith, Kevin. "Irish Security Sources Say Bomb Attack Thwarted." *Reuters* (11 July 2000).

Smith, Michael. "French Military Accused of Blocking Karadzic's Arrest: British SAS Feels it Could Easily 'Snatch' Accused War Criminal." *Ottawa Citizen* (14 August 2000).

Smith, R. Jeffrey. "CIA Drops Over 1,000 Informants." *Washington Post* (2 March 1997).

———. "Secret Meetings Killed Karadzic Capture Plan: U.S. Blames French in Foiled Mission." *Washington Post* (23 April 1998).

Smith, Terence. "Hijackers' Orders Challenge Israel." *New York Times* (30 June 1976).

———. "Israelis Say Extension of Deadline by the Hijackers Was Crucial to Raid's Success." *New York Times* (6 July 1976).

"Soviet-Israeli Ties Warm up after Return of Hijackers." *Ottawa Citizen* (5 December 1988).

"Soviet Police Take Custody of Hijackers from Israelis." *Toronto Star* (4 December 1988).

Spears, Tom. "Anthrax Difficult to Harness as a Weapon." *Toronto Star* (1 February 2001).

Spears, Tom. "Smallpox Is the Most Dangerous Virus Ever." *Ottawa Citizen* (11 January 2002).

"Special Branch Is Set to Join War on Organized Crime." *Telegraph* (30 August 1999).

"Spies, Damned Lies and Information." *Independent* (6 May 1999).

Spinner, Jackie. "Life Insurers Want Study of Future Terrorism's Cost." *Washington Post* (19 October 2001).

"Spy Agency Urges Watch on Refugees, Immigrants." *Kitchener Waterloo Record* (11 June 1999).

"Sri Lankan Rebels Step up Attacks Suicide Bomber Strikes in Capital." *Globe and Mail* (20 October 2000).

Stackhouse, John. "Bin Laden Evidence Satisfies NATO Allies." *Globe and Mail* (3 October 2001).

———. "U.S. Bombs Terrorist Training Camps." *Globe and Mail* (21 August 1998).

"State Department Drops Iran as Terrorist." *New York Times* (1 May 1999).

Stephen, Chris. "NATO Plans Karadzic Swoop." *Sunday Times* (17 August 1997).

Stern, Jessica. "Taking the Terror out of Bioterrorism." *New York Times* (8 April 1998).

Stern, Leonard. "Canada Faces 'Real' Terrorism Threat." *Ottawa Citizen* (8 March 2002).

Stewart, Phil. "Colombia Rebels Kidnap Senator's Family, 12 Others." *Reuters* (27 July 2001).

Stock, Jon. "Commandos Set to Storm Hijacked Jet." *Weekly Telegraph* (29 December 1999–4 January 2000).

Stonehouse, David. "Biological Agents 'Quintessential' Terror Weapons." *Ottawa Citizen* (24 October 2001).

Strauss, Julius. "British Arrest Ex-Commander of Bosnian Camp." *Ottawa Citizen* (26 June 2000).

Sudam, Mohammed. "English, Trickery Help Pilots Foil Yemeni Hijacker." *National Post* (24 January 2001).

"Suicide Bomber Left Video Confession." *Ottawa Citizen* (29 March 2001).

Swain, John. "Armed Troops in Training for Seoul Olympics." *Sunday Times* (29 May 1988).

Syal, Rajeev, Olga Craig and David Bamber. "Neo-Nazis' Tactics Inspired by IRA.'" *Ottawa Citizen* (2 May 1999).

"Taleban Oppression Justified Hijacking of Plane." *National Post* (3 October 2001).

Taqui, Jassim. "MI-6, CIA Accused of Planning to Assassinate bin Ladin." *Frontier Post* (14 February 1999).

Taylor, Kenneth D. "Options for Dealing with State-Sponsored Terrorism." *Chronicle Herald* (23 March 1987).

Taylor, Scott. "Bin Laden's Balkan Connections." *Ottawa Citizen* (15 December 2001).

Tendler, Stewart. "Cleric Recruits Terrorists, Say MI5 Officers." *London Times* (17 August 1999).

———. "Verdicts of Justifiable Homicide on Terrorists." *London Times* (5 February 1981).

"Terrorism Took Record Toll in 1998, U.S. Report Says." *Kitchener Waterloo Record* (1 May 1999).

"Terrorist Security Company." *Canadian Press* (19 October 2001).

"13 Nations Training Commandoes to Save Air-Hijacking Hostages." *New York Times* (22 October 1977).

Thomas, Jo. "New Face of Terror Crimes: 'Lone Wolf' Weaned on Hate." *New York Times* (16 August 1999).

Thomas, John Ungoed and Rosie Waterhouse. "Britain Battles 'Ultimate Adversary.'" *Ottawa Citizen* (5 March 2001).

Thompson, Allan. "Is It Terrorism to Attack Terrorists?" *Toronto Star* (22 August 1998).

Thompson, Elizabeth. "Food Supply Vulnerable to Bioterrorism, Agency Head Says." *Ottawa Citizen* (24 October 2001).

Thorne, Stephen. "Consultations on Strategy Against Biological Threats Continue." *Canadian Press* (31 January 2001).

Tibbetts, Janice. "PM Considers Security Perimeter." *Ottawa Citizen* (21 October 2001).

"Time Interview: Bin Laden Says He Instigated Terrorist Attack." *American Press* (AP) (3 January 1999).

Trainor, Bernard E. "Assault on Terror Camps? The Risks." *New York Times* (4 February 1987).

Travers, James. "Covert Action Will Be Nasty." *Kitchener-Waterloo Record* (25 September 2001).

———. "Israel: Even Good Anti-Terrorist Operations Must Expect Costly Failures." *Ottawa Citizen* (22 March 1986).

———. "Past Time to Curb Terrorists." *Kitchener Waterloo Record* (19 December 2000).

Trickey, Mike. "'The World Is Not Ready for a UN Army,' Ambassador Laments: Fowler Says Global Fear of 'World Government' Makes UN Unable to Stop Genocide Before it Starts." *Ottawa Citizen* (28 December 1999).

Turgut, Pelin. "Ocalan Calls on Kurd Rebels to End Struggle." *Reuters* (3 August 1999).

"Turkish Prosecutors Seek Death Penalty for Ocalan." *Reuters* (20 April 1999).

"20 Iraqis Die During Weapons Training." *Ottawa Citizen* (2 September 2001).

"Uganda Radar Operators Executed, Sources Say." *Toronto Star* (8 July 1976).

"U.N. Considers its Own Army to Intervene Early in World Crises." *Toronto Star* (2 February 1992).

Unal, Elif. "Russia and Turkey Co-operate on 'Terrorism.'" *Reuters* (23 October 2000).

"Understanding Anthrax." *Washington Post* (18 October 2001).

"U.S. Army Linked to Waco Assault: Military Says it Merely Sent Observers, Advisers." *Globe and Mail* (26 August 1999).

"U.S. Army Seeks OK to Kill Terrorists." *Montreal Gazette* (11 April 1989).

"U.S. Clandestine Service Steps in When All Else Fails, Says CIA Deputy Director." *Reuters* (12 December 2000).

"U.S. Commandos Enter Afghanistan to Arrest Bin-Ladin." *Voice of the Islamic Republic of Iran First Program Network* (26 May 1999). Translated in FBIS.

"U.S. Gets Low Grade for Computer Security." *Reuters* (11 October 2000).

"U.S. House Votes CIA Funding for More Spies." *Reuters* (13 May 1999).

"U.S. Navy Revises Story of Ship's Bombing: New Version of Events Contradicts Report That Bombs Struck While Vessel Mooring." *Globe and Mail* (21 October 2000).

"U.S. on Alert after Threats of Terrorism: Mideast, Jakarta Embassy Warned of Possible Attacks." *Ottawa Citizen* (25 October 2000).

"U.S. Said Blaming Pakistan for U.S. Commando Disappearance." *Pakistan Observer* (12 May 1999). In FBIS.

"U.S. Targeting Terrorism with More Funds." *Washington Post* (2 February 1999).

"U.S. Trains Sri Lanka in Counter-Terrorism." *Reuters* (12 October 1997).

"U.S. Tries New Tack in Hunt for bin Laden." *Reuters* (7 November 1998).

"U.S., W. Germany Trained Egypt's Anti-Hijack Team." *Montreal Gazette* (26 November 1985).

Vaidya, Abhay. "Defence Forces Focus on Threats of NBC Warfare." *Times of India* (20 January 2001).

Vanpraet, Nicolas. "New Breed of Terrorism Has Investigators Guessing: Is Montreal Man Tied to Terrorist bin Laden? Proof Is Elusive." *Ottawa Citizen* (9 January 2000).

Vedantam, Shanakar. "Bioterrorism's Relentless, Stealthy March." *Washington Post* (18 October 2001).

Vick, Karl. "Man in Kenya Gets U.S. Letter Containing Anthrax." *Washington Post* (19 October 2001).

Vincent, Isabel. "Bin Laden's Greatest Asset Is Ability to Handle Money." *National Post* (14 September 2001).

———. "Fighting Censorship in the 'New War.'" *National Post* (20 October 2001).

———. "Terrorist Plans Seized in Bosnia." *National Post* (21 March 2002).

Walker, Robert. "Canada Unprepared for Attacks by Biological Terrorists, Experts Say: Poor Co-Ordination, Limited Resources Hinder Effective Response to Anthrax, Ebola Attacks." *Ottawa Citizen* (9 August 1999).

Wallace, Charles. "Bomb Downed Jet, Officials Says." *Toronto Star* (28 May 1991).

Walters, Joan. "Mounties Use Secret Cameras at Pearson: System Looks for Criminals but Raises Privacy Worry." *Toronto Star* (19 January 2001).

Walton, Dawn. "Virus Last Came to Canada with Migrant." *Globe and Mail* (15 March 2001).

Wapshott, Nicholas. "Telltale Signs Failed to Stop Shoe Bomber." *Ottawa Citizen* (24 December 2001).

Warren, Marcus. "German Army Plagued by Right-Wing Extremists." *Calgary Herald* (21 September 1997).

"Washington Foils Seven bin Laden Bomb Attempts." *Ottawa Citizen* (25 February 1999).

Watson, Paul. "Angry Military Defends Bungled Attack." *Toronto Star* (31 August 1993).

———. "U.S. Troops Bungle Raid, Arrest Aideed's Enemies." *Toronto Star* (16 September 1993).

Watson, Roland and Michael Evans. "U.S. Targets Bin Laden's Fortress," *London Times* (29 November 2001).

Watts, David. "Tension Rises in Conflict 'That Surpasses All Boundaries': Virtual Warriors Fire Opening Shots in Cyber Battle." *London Times* (18 August 1999).

Wayne, E. A. "U.S., Soviets to Tackle Terrorism." *Christian Science Monitor* (10 May 1989).

Weiner, Tim. "C.I.A. Teaching Palestinian Police the Tricks of the Trade." *New York Times* (5 March 1998).

———. "Commandos Hope to Pounce on bin Laden: They're Counting on His Afghan Protectors Betraying Him, American Officials Say." *Globe and Mail* (17 April 1999).

Weisbrot, Mark. "Complicit in Terror." *Montreal Gazette* (10 March 1999).

Weiser, Benjamin. "Embassy Suspect Warned U.S. of Yemen Attack, Papers Show." *New York Times* (18 January 2001).

———. "Word for Word: Tips for Terrorists: Lose the Toothpick, Don't Talk to Cabbies, and Watch Where You Park." *New York Times* (3 April 2001).

Weiss, Rick, and Justin Blum. "The Man Who the FBI Believes Flew an American Airlines Plane into the World Trade Center Sept. 11 Apparently Walked into a U.S. Department of Agriculture Office in Florida Last Year and Asked about a Loan to Buy a Crop-duster Plane." *Washington Post* (25 September 2001).

West, Julian. "Bin Laden's Fingerprints All over These Attacks." *Telegraph* (15 October 2000).

———. "Diplomats Fear 'Massacre of Foreigners': Attack on bin Laden Will Lead to Reprisals, Clerics Warn." *Ottawa Citizen* (22 October 2000).

———. "'Fingerprints of bin Laden Are All over These Attacks': Terrorist Strikes in Yemen Start of New Campaign by Saudi Millionaire, Western Experts Believe." *Ottawa Citizen* (15 October 2000).

"What Will Make the Terrorist Go Away?" *Globe and Mail* (16 March 1996).

"When the Commandos Arrived." *Jerusalem Post* (5 July 1976).

Whitelaw, Kevin. "The Ball Goes Up, but What Comes Down? Assessing Terrorists' Plans for the Millennium." *U.S. News Online* (27 December 1999).

Whittell, Giles. "Chechen Leader Snared by Russia: Undercover Operation Surprises Rebel Surrounded by Bodyguards." *Ottawa Citizen* (14 March 2000).

Wilkinson, Isambard. "Police Claim Destruction of ETA Cell with Help of Cubans." *Telegraph* (8 November 2000).

Williams, Brian. "Police Warn of Racist Campaign after Second London Bomb Blast." *Globe and Mail* (26 April 1999).

Willmer, Tanya. "Arafat Blamed for Gaza Suicide Bomb: More Terrorism Feared." *Jerusalem Post* (27 October 2000).

Winkhaus, Uta. "Munich: The Massacre That Changed the World: Fallout from Olympics Terror Still Swirls 25 Years Later." *Toronto Star* (30 August 1997).

"Witness Tells How bin Laden Group Works: Embassy Bombing Trial Hears from Defector." *Washington Post* (7 February 2001).

Wolf, Jim. "U.S. Government Computer Security Said Lax." *Reuters* (11 September 2000).

Woodhead, Michael. "Stasi Spy Files Reveal Secret Hit Squad." *Ottawa Citizen* (9 May 1999).

Woodward, Bob. "Bush to CIA: Do 'Whatever Necessary' to Kill Bin Laden." *Ottawa Citizen* (21 October 2001).

———. "CIA After bin Laden for 4 Years, Report Says." *Ottawa Citizen* (23 December 2001).

Wordsworth, Arminta. "Low Pay Drove Laden Aide into Arms of U.S. Law." *National Post* (9 February 2001).

———. "Ocalan Capture Sparks Global Kurd Protests." *National Post* (17 February 1999).

Worsnip, Patrick. "Shortage of Spies in Lebanon Hampers Efforts to Find Hostages." *Globe and Mail* (5 August 1989).

Wright, Oliver, and Daniel McGrory. "Kidnapper's Release a 'Disgrace.'" *Ottawa Citizen* (3 January 2000).

York, Geoffrey. "Hijackers down Russian Plane." *Globe and Mail* (16 March 2001).

———. "World's Rebels Chilled by bin Laden Effect." *Globe and Mail* (29 December 2001).

Zakaria, Tabassum. "U.S. Intelligence Analyst Quits over Cole Attack." *Reuters* (25 October 2000).

———. "U.S. Trying to Pry bin Laden out of Afghanistan." *Reuters* (30 November 2000).

GOVERNMENT REPORTS

"Uganda Hostage Situation: Israeli Reaction." Report. Canadian Embassy Tel Aviv to Department of External Affairs, Ottawa, Canada. (30 June 1976).

"Israeli Rescue Operation: Kampala." Report. Canadian High Commission, Nairobi, Kenya to Department of External Affairs, Ottawa, Canada (4 July 1976).

"Uganda Hostages: Israeli Reaction." Report. Canadian Embassy Tel Aviv to Department of External Affairs, Ottawa, Canada (5 July 1976).

"Crisis Management in Schleyer Kidnapping/Lufthansa Hijacking Case Summary." Report. Canadian High Commission, London, to Department of External Affairs, Ottawa, Canada (14 November 1977).

"Hijacking of Lufthansa Aircraft—13 October 1977." Canadian Government Memorandum. Canadian Embassy Bonn, to Ottawa, Canada (23 November 1977).

"Israeli Reaction to American Bid to Rescue Hostages." Report. Canadian Embassy Tel Aviv to Department of External Affairs, Ottawa, Canada (28 April 1980).

INTERVIEWS

Discussion with a British government official, Ottawa, Canada (31 March 1982).

Interview with a senior Canadian intelligence officer, Ottawa, Canada (13 December 1984).

Interview with a Canadian intelligence officer, Ottawa, Canada (8 February 1986).

Interview with a senior British Parachute Regiment officer, London, England (4 October 1997).

Interview with a senior counterterrorist operator, Ottawa, Canada (4 May 1998).

Discussion with a senior intelligence officer, Ottawa, Canada (22 June 1998).

Discussion with a senior British Special Air Service officer, London, England (4 October 1998).

Interview with a senior British Special Air Service officer, London, England (5 October 1998).

Interview with an army officer of the Sultan's Armed Forces, Muscat, Oman (17 October 1998).

Interview with a senior British officer, seconded to the Sultan's Armed Forces, Muscat, Oman (18 October 1998).

Interview with a senior British Special Air Service officer, London, England (26 October 1998).

Interview with a former British Special Air Service operative, Ottawa, Canada (24 February 1999).

Interview with a Canadian intelligence officer, Ottawa, Canada (26 February 1999).

Discussion with a Canadian intelligence officer, Ottawa, Canada (1 March 1999).

Discussion with General Ulrich K. Wegener, Ottawa, Canada (3 October 2000).

Discussion with General Ulrich K. Wegener, Royal Military College, Kingston, Canada (4 October 2000).

Discussion with General Ulrich K. Wegener, Royal Military College, Kingston, Canada (5 October 2000).

Discussion with General Ulrich K. Wegener, Kingston, Ontario (7 March 2002).

Interview with a former British Special Air Service operative, Ottawa, Canada (30 October 2001).

Index

About the Author

J. PAUL DE B. TAILLON is Adjunct Professor at the Royal Military College of Canada. He is the author of *The Evolution of Special Forces in Counter-Terrorism: The British and American Experiences* (Praeger, 2001).